REVELATION

Worthy is the Lamb!

ISBN-13:
978-1724344861

ISBN-10:
1724344862

All Scripture citations taken from: Crossway Bibles. *ESV: Study Bible: English Standard Version.* Wheaton, Ill: Crossway Bibles, 2007.

ACKNOWLEDGMENTS

REVELATION in Grace Church's Teleios Academy was developed by Wes D. Van Fleet, a covenant member and pastor of Kaleo Church, El Cajon, CA.

"For God is not unjust so as to forget your work and the love which you have shown toward His name, in having ministered and in still ministering to the saints" (Hebrews 6:10).

DEDICATION

Dedicated to Kaleo Church. May you read the words of this book and be blessed (Rev. 1:3). May Jesus continue to walk among our faithful little church as we seek to glorify Him until that great Day when he wipes all our tears away and we see Him face to face (cf. Rev. 21:1-4; 22:4). Also, to Dave Swart: Thank you for modeling Christ's love for His bride as you faithfully loved Lora until the end. She is now truly a child who made it to the home for which she so deeply longed.

A large host of people played a part in this Teleios study coming to fruition. To list them all would take pages. But the list below represents those who had major roles in this work. About seven years ago I began praying for the Lord to allow me time and space to write a book on Revelation that would help the people of Kaleo Church grasp the main message of the beauty of Christ. That opportunity came in late 2017 when Jordan Thomas and Nathan Sawyer asked if I wanted to contribute to Grace Church's *Teleios Academy* series of inductive Bible studies. As I heard their vision, I knew this was the opportunity God has put on my heart years earlier. I actually cried with gratitude after Jordan's first call. Thank you for allowing me to contribute to such a great series of Bible studies. Also, to all of the editors that helped in this process, an abundant thank you for being so patient with all my errors and lack of formatting capabilities. You all are the real heroes behind this volume.

To Tim and Abbey Cain, for being kind enough to spur me on to do this project and to pray for me. Thank you! To all of my friends at Kaleo Church who asked questions along the way and were longsuffering as I talked about Revelation in *every* ministry setting. Maybe one day I will preach through Revelation?

A special thank you to my sweet bride Jenn, and my two littles, Olivia and Hadley. Thank you for being the loving, supportive, and fun family. Your "interruptions" made this project more life-giving during this writing process. You ladies are God's greatest gift to me.

This work would never had been possible if it were not for Dr. Dennis Johnson. While in seminary, you challenged me to take a fresh look at Revelation. I had no idea that would lead to nearly a decade of studying this rich book. I am more eager for the triumph of the Lamb because of your investment. Thank you for the many times you exalted Christ in the pages of Revelation with your eyes full of tears.

Ultimately, my deepest gratitude is to the Lord Jesus Christ, the Lion and the Lamb. Through the book of Revelation, I have tasted the promised blessings (cf. Rev. 1:3) as my eyes have been opened to the multi-faceted glory that is enjoyed by beholding You. May this volume bring glory to You and You alone. Soli Deo Gloria!

TABLE OF CONTENTS

WHY "TELEIOS ACADEMY"?

The Greek word *Teleios* (τέλειος; pronounced: tell-eye-os) means, "mature" or "complete." The New Testament uses this word many times to describe *the ultimate goal of the Christian life*. For example:

Colossians 1:28 – "We proclaim [Jesus], admonishing every man and teaching every man with all wisdom, so that we may present every man **complete** (*teleios*) in Christ." (NASB)

Ephesians 4:13 – "...until we all attain to the unity of the faith, and of the knowledge of the Son of God, to a **mature** (*teleios*) man, to the measure of the stature which belongs to the fullness of Christ." (NASB)

Hebrews 5:14 – "But solid food is for the **mature** (*teleios*), who because of practice have their senses trained to discern good and evil" (NASB)

Matthew 5:48 – "Therefore you are to be **perfect** (*teleios*), as your heavenly Father is **perfect** (*teleios*)" (NASB)

By God's wise design, His people will mature in Christ through prayer-saturated immersion in His Word. Doing so in concert with God's Spirit-filled people amplifies our opportunity for maximum profit. While Grace Church's *Teleios Academy* studies may be used profitably by individuals, they are designed to guide God's people through His Word *together*. The ideal use is for individuals to complete a week's worth of the study, then meet as a group for discussion, application, and prayer.

The ultimate aim of these Bible study tools is to aid users to be more and more *Teleios* in Christ until we see His lovely face. May it be so!

HOW TO SEEK GOD

Before we dive into the details of the book of Revelation, consider what the Bible has to say about seeking God in His Word.

1. LOOK TO JESUS AND BE SAVED

Looking to Jesus by faith has always been God's way for us profit from the truth of Scripture. Until you have believed upon The Lord Jesus Christ for salvation, you cannot rightly understand the Bible. 2 Corinthians 3:14-16 explains this clearly: "But their minds were hardened; for until this very day at the reading of the old covenant the same veil remains unlifted, because it is removed in Christ…but whenever a person turns to the Lord, the veil is taken away" (cf. Romans 10:17).

In God's love, Jesus, the eternal Son of God, came to earth through the womb of the virgin Mary. Truly God and truly Man, Jesus of Nazareth lived a sinless life, perfectly glorifying God. Then, He was sacrificed for sinners on the cross, suffering the wrath of God for His people's sins. Three days later, He was raised to life forevermore, and is now seated on heaven's throne at His Father's right hand. He will come again to judge the world in righteousness and establish His eternal kingdom. All who confess and turn from their sins, and trust in Christ for forgiveness, submitting to Him as Lord, will be saved. Turn from your sin, believe on Jesus, and be saved.

2. LOOK TO JESUS AND BE SANCTIFIED

A sure fruit that one has believed upon Christ for salvation is an insatiable appetite to love, know and honor Him. When Christ is embraced as Lord, His glory will be desired and delighted in (2 Corinthians 3:18). As a babe longs for milk, so also Christians *want* to behold our Savior in His Word (cf. Hebrews 5:11ff).

That's why Christians love the Bible. God's Word is a Spirit-inspired window through which we most clearly see the greatness and glory of our Savior, the Lord Jesus. Our greatest need is to know God according to His Word (cf. John 17:3, 17).

HOW TO USE THIS STUDY

Grace's *Revelation* Teleios study exists to encourage careful attention to God's Word, *not* replace it. Our prayer is that this workbook *will not* end with these pages, or even the words of Scripture, but with our great God, Who reveals Himself to us in His Word.

There is no replacement for walking with God by looking to Jesus in the Scriptures, under the illumination of the Spirit's light. And, there is no greater joy on this side of heaven for His people than communion with God. May the Lord "open your eyes to behold wonderful things from His Law" (Psalm 119:18). Even if you can't complete all of the daily study questions, *read the Bible!*

1. PRAYER

God's intends for us to approach His Word with a heart full of prayer, asking continually for His help for proper understanding and application. Talk with God about *everything* as you read in Scripture. Pray before, during, and after your encounter with His Word. Ask the Holy Spirit to illumine your understanding, and to apply His truth to your mind, heart, and actions. Keep Jesus' explanation of the Bible at the forefront of your petitions for God's help as you read: That the whole Bible points to Him (cf. Jn. 1:45; 5:39-47; Lk 24:23-25, 44).

2. FAITH

Ask the Lord for the gift of faith, to believe and obey all He reveals in His Word. Similarly, ask for grace to believe that God's Word "is living and active and sharper than any two-edged sword, and piercing as far as the division of soul and spirit, of both joints and marrow, and able to judge the thoughts and intentions of the heart" (Hebrews 4:12). Trust the Lord to deal with you personally through His Word, and to minister to your deepest needs right where you are in life.

3. PATIENCE

Real patience is not achieved by will-power but is a fruit of the Holy Spirit (cf. Galatians 5:22). Such patience is especially needed when reading Scripture. While it is beneficial to intake large portions of the Bible at once, it is also profoundly life-giving to soak *deeply* in a few verses, or less, in one sitting. This Teleios study is broken down into twelve weeks, covering the twenty-one chapters of Revelation. Some days will direct you to give serious attention to just a few lines of Scripture. Ask God for patience as you seek Him in His Word. Pray especially for grace to meditate on *the specific words* of God's Word. The goal is not to rush through the reading of the verses in order to supply answers to the questions. The goal is to fellowship with the Lamb of God. A faithful translation of the Bible is essential for careful meditation on each word (Grace Church recommends: The New American Standard; The English Standard Version, Christian Standard Version, or The New King James Version).

4. PEOPLE

Saturate your life in Scripture because you need God (cf. John 15:5). Trust the Lord to deal with *you*. That said, even as you study God's Word, consider others as more important than yourself (Philippians 2:3). Immersion in Scripture is part of God's way of conforming Christians more into the image of His Son (Romans 8:29). Yet, Bible study ought never end with you. Thinking deeply *with God* in His Word and jotting down notes from your Bible study will help you share God's Truth with your small group, and with others God puts in your life. As God uses you to point others to Christ in His Word, your own joy in God will be elevated (cf. Philippians 2:1-2).

REVELATION

Worthy is the Lamb!

INTRODUCTION TO JOHN'S APOCALYPSE

In the mega-motion picture "The Matrix," the viewers watch as Neo, played by Keanu Reeves, is presented with an option to take a red or blue pill. Morpheus, the sage-like character, presenting Neo with the two different pills warned him, "*You take the blue pill, the story ends. You wake up in your bed and believe whatever you want to believe. You take the red pill, you stay in Wonderland, and I show you how deep the rabbit hole goes.*" Reading the book of Revelation, the way it was meant to be read is a lot like taking the red pill. I mean this in two ways. First, the book of Revelation is one of the few books in the Bible where God pulls back the curtain of our sense of reality, giving us an unadulterated glimpse into His perspective of what is actually real. Second, the popular modern interpretation of Revelation will be challenged if you read it the way the book intends.

Let me tell you a bit of my own story and the reason I am so honored to write this study on Revelation. In 2005, the Spirit of God made me new after the Lord called me to Himself. The first book I was told to read, other than the Bible, was the first in a popular Christian fiction book series entitled *Left Behind*. If you have not heard of this series, you might be the only person on the planet. These books take the popular viewpoint of pre-tribulational dispensationalism (that's a mouth full, huh?) and put them in story form. The books sold millions and millions of copies. I was still in the Army at the time and remember being in the middle of the desert devouring these books, not knowing how quickly they would shape a sort of theological foundation for *everything I believed*.

Fast-forward three years. I began going to the Bible College that one of the authors of the Left Behind series founded. The statement of faith of the school and the church it was attached to was orthodox, but the end times section was about ten times as long as any other section. I thought this was the norm and entrusted myself fully to the faculty. The men were godly in their example and loved me and all their students well. However, the more I was taught the end times doctrines of the rapture, a seven-year tribulation, a millennial kingdom, etc., I found myself becoming more and more confused. It actually resulted in a type of fearful waiting for Jesus to secretly return. I could relate to the more current words of Grammy award-winning country artist, Chris Stapleton when he sings,

There's a scarecrow in the garden
That looks like Lucifer
And I've been reading Revelations
With my bare feet in the river.

I've been sitting here all morning
I was sitting here all night
There's a Bible in my left hand
And a pistol in my right.[1]

---

[1] Chris Stapleton, *Scarecrow in the Garden, 2017.*

After graduating Bible College, I enrolled in a Reformed seminary near me in San Diego. The more I listened to the professors teach about the book of Revelation and the end times, I felt as if I was confronted with a blue and red pill. One professor specifically, to whom this volume is dedicated, sat me down one day. After raising concerns about the book of Revelation, he looked me in the eyes and gently challenged me to forget everything I was taught. He challenged me to start reading the book while reading all the cross-references in my Bible. As I did so, the red pill digested into my system and the book of Revelation unfolded to me like a newly-blossomed rose in the springtime. All the Old Testament allusions! All the songs throughout the book! And above all, the simple message lined throughout every passage declaring the triumph of Christ and His comfort to suffering saints! The book became a gem. It became a book that I read devotionally and prayerfully.

Over the last 7-8 years, I have given the majority of my private study time to learning this beautiful closing book of the Bible. The more and more I have studied, the deeper my longing has become to create something that would guide the modern church in understanding, loving, and applying this deep treasure that promises blessing to its readers (Rev. 1:3). When Jordan Thomas and the Teleios Academy began talking with me about this project, my heart leapt with excitement at the opportunity of creating an inductive Bible study and commentary that could help guide people into loving this book. With that said, thank you for reading this work. I cannot express the depth of riches the book of Revelation holds. May the Spirit deeply bless you and comfort you as you get a glimpse behind the curtain as you behold the Lamb of God, who takes away the sin of the world (John 1:29).

In Christ,
Wes D. Van Fleet
June, 2018

REVELATION
12-Week Study Outline | Teleios Academy

WEEK 1 — Introduction
DAY 1 — Taking Jesus at His Word (Luke 24)
DAY 2 — Understanding the New Testament Use of the Old Testament
DAY 3 — Revelation's Genre: Prophetic, Apocalyptic, Epistle
DAY 4 — Layout: Seven Angles of the Same Story
DAY 5 — Different Perspectives on the Millennium

WEEK 2 — Greetings from The Eternal One (Rev. 1:1-8)
DAY 1 — The Revelation/Apocalypse of Christ (1:1-3)
DAY 2 — The Sovereign Ruler of the Churches (1:4-5a)
DAY 3 — A Letter from the Beloved (1:5b-6)
DAY 4 — The Hope of Salvation (1:7)
DAY 5 — The Alpha and the Omega (1:8)

WEEK 3 — The Glorious Chief Shepherd of the Flock (1:9-20)
DAY 1 — Pastor and Partner in the Tribulation (1:9-11)
DAY 2 — The Glorified Prophet, Priest, and King (1:12-15)
DAY 3 — He Who Hold His Church (1:16)
DAY 4 — The Gospel of Love (1:17-18)
DAY 5 — Lord of the Lampstands (1:19-20)

WEEK 4 — Jesus Walks Among His Church: Part 1 (Rev. 2)
DAY 1 — Remembering Your First Love: Part 1 (2:1-7)
DAY 2 — Remembering Your First Love: Part 2 (2:1-7)
DAY 3 — The Glory of Death (2:8-11)
DAY 4 — Faithfulness in Enemy Territory (2:12-17)
DAY 5 — Hold Fast, Beloved (2:18-29)

WEEK 5 — Jesus Walks Among His Church: Part 2 (Rev. 3)
DAY 1 — Reviving the Dead (3:1-6)
DAY 2 — My Grace is Sufficient (3:7-10)
DAY 3 — A New Name (3:11-13)
DAY 4 — Come to the Fountain (3:14-18)
DAY 5 — Repent and Conquer (3:19-22)

WEEK 12 — Conclusion (Rev. 22)

DAY 1 — Access Granted: The New Eden (22:1-5)
DAY 2 — The Word is Trustworthy and True (22:6-9)
DAY 3 — For the Churches (22:10-16)
DAY 4 — Feast on His Word (22:17-19)
DAY 5 — Eager Expectation (22:20-21)[2]

---

[2] This outline is original to the author, with a little influence from the Richard Phillips' outline in *The Reformed Expository Commentary: Revelation*, vii-ix.

TELEIOS

ACADEMY

WEEK 1
STUDY

REVELATION
Overview

Note: It may be helpful to read the commentary notes for Week One (p. 29) before working through today's questions.

MEDITATION: Read Luke 24:13-35, 44-45 asking God to open your mind to understand the Scriptures (cf. v. 45).

1. After Jesus patiently walked alongside the two saddened disciples, why did He rebuke them (v. 24-27)?

2. What is the proper response to seeing Christ's glory and gospel labors in Scripture (v. 32)?

3. When you think of the book of Revelation, do you tend to expect your heart to burn within you at the sight of Christ or do you think of something else? If you think of something else, what is it?

4. What does Jesus teach us in Luke 24 about the aim we should have as we encounter Old Testament passages/allusions in Revelation?

APPLICATION: Do you read the Old Testament Scriptures with a prayerful longing that the Spirit would open your eyes to see Jesus? When was the last time your heart burned within you as you saw Christ in the Old Testament Scriptures? Pray to the Spirit who loves to glorify Christ (John 16:14) and ask Him to do so.

MEDIATION: Behold the Lamb of God as you read Acts 2:22-41.

1. What Old Testament texts does Peter preach from immediately after he receives the Holy Spirit?

2. Read the Old Testament passages you listed above. What point does Peter make about Jesus from these passages? Why do you think he used these Old Testament passages?

3. Read John 1:29. As a new reader of the Bible who only had the book of John, what significance would the phrase "Lamb of God" have?

4. Look at Exodus 12 for Old Testament background about "the lamb." How does this background inform your understanding that Jesus bears the beloved title, "The Lamb of God?"

APPLICATION: Take time to confess to the Lord any way you may have neglected the Old Testament, and therefore missed the fullness of the New Testament. Ask for the Spirit's help to devote yourself to saturating in the Bible as God intends. Write out a verse to memorize on page 305.

MEDITATION: As you read James 1:5-8 ask the Lord for wisdom to better understand His Word, how it fits together, and to use Scripture to unite you heart to fear His Name (Psalm 86:11).

1. Revelation is as patchwork of three different genres (prophecy, apocalyptic, and propositional epistle). What part(s) of this book intimidate you and why?

2. Which prophetic book of Scripture have you enjoyed the most? Why?

3. Which epistle in Scripture have you enjoyed the most? Why?

4. What apocalyptic book in Scripture have you enjoyed the most? Why?

APPLICATION: Ask God *now* to use the next 12-weeks of this study of various genres—prophecy, epistle and apocalypse—to help *you and your small group* better grasp His glory. See the footnote below for a link to watch the two-part introduction to *The Book of Revelation* by The Gospel Project.[3]

---

[3] Introduction videos to Revelation by the Gospel Project: https://www.youtube.com/watch?v=5nvVVcYD-0w and https://www.youtube.com/watch?v=QpnIrbq2bKo

MEDITATION: Glance through Psalm 119 and observe how it is structured in eight-verse stanzas according to the Hebrew alphabet. Praise God for His well-designed Word as you read Psalm 119:9-16.

1. If the book of Revelation is really seven different perspectives/angles of the time period between Jesus' crucifixion and His Second Coming, would this make the book easier or harder to understand (Feel free to consult the commentary notes on page 29-36). Why?

2. Imagine how suffering for your faith in Christ would cause you to eagerly await His Second Coming (cf. Heb. 9:28). How would the announcements of Christ's return from the seven angles in the book of Revelation help you in such suffering?

3. If the number seven seems to have a repetitive use throughout Revelation, and the Bible as a whole, are you comfortable with entertaining the proposed structure (Again, feel free to consult the commentary on page 29-36 to see why this study suggests such a structure to Revelation)? Why or why not?

APPLICATION: Read the Seven Beatitudes in Revelation (1:3; 14:13; 16:15; 19:9; 20:6; 22:7; 22:14) and give God glory by prayerfully singing one of these hymns/prayers in worship to Him.

MEDITATION: Today's study requires careful and humble consideration of various millennial views. Ask the Lord for His help and a teachable spirit as you prayerfully read Revelation 19:17-21 and then 20:1-15.

1. Does it appear that Revelation 20:7-15 is retelling Revelation 19:11-21 from a different angle? Why would be this connection be important to consider?

2. What is your current view of the millennium and where did you learn it? How does this motivate you live in view of eternity? Or, have you tried to avoid thinking about this issue for some reason? If so, why?

3. What is on the line if we interpret the thousand years in Revelation 20:1-6 literally or symbolically? Try to list some different consequences of these two views.

APPLICATION: Read John 17:20-21 and discuss with your group why unity in Christ among believers is necessary even if we differ on our interpretations of the millennium.

TELEIOS
ACADEMY

WEEK 1
COMMENTARY

REVELATION
Overview

OVERVIEW OF REVELATION

GENRE

The Apocalypse of John (Revelation) is unlike any other book in the Bible because it has three genres patched together to make a beautiful interpretive quilt. Understanding how these genres mesh together is absolutely imperative if we are going to rightly understand the book and God's ultimate purposes in giving it to us. The three genres in Revelation are prophecy, epistle, and apocalyptic. Let's look at each genre individually to better define and grasp what God has breathed out to us (2 Tim. 3:15-17) in the book of Revelation.

PROPHECY:

The book of Revelation is a prophecy in a couple of different ways. When many of us think of prophecy we tend to think of a foretelling of future events. This is very true with the book of Revelation, but you might be surprised to find out that it is prophetic in a far different way as well. First, in Revelation 1:10 John says he was *"in the Spirit."* For the 21st century reader, this phrase might seem vague and mysterious. But for the 1st century reader, especially a Jew, images of Old Testament prophets would come to mind. For example, when Ezekiel was about to receive a vision from the Lord, just like John in Revelation, he says, *"Then the Spirit lifted me up…"* (Ezekiel 3:12, 14).

Second, the role of the prophet who communicated the prophecy from God was a sort of lawyer that would bring a covenant lawsuit against God's covenant people. They brought a message of judgment for covenant-breakers as well as a message of hope and salvation for God's faithful remnant. As Michael Horton writes, "The Prophets are more than anything else covenant attorneys, representing the claims of God to the people and vice versa."[4] We especially see this type of prophetic work from the Lord Jesus — *The* Prophet (cf. Deut. 18:15; Heb. 1:2) — as He walks among His churches in Revelation 2-3 correcting and encouraging them.

EPISTLE:

The genre of epistle is the most familiar for most since it is primarily a letter. Most of Paul's epistles have a greeting, a prayer, and a benediction. That is not necessarily the format of this epistle, but it still functions as an epistle because it is written to seven churches with necessary information regarding who God is, what He has done, and what He will do.

---

[4] Michael Horton, *Introducing Covenant Theology* (Grand Rapids, MI: Baker Books, 2006) 52.

APOCALYPTIC:

This is a genre that is extremely foreign to most modern minds. In fact, I would argue that because most people do not approach Revelation with this in mind, it leads to various misinterpretations leading to fear and a hermeneutic wrongly bound to current events. What is Apocalyptic literature? In short, it is a form of writing meant to form pictures in our head. These pictures are meant to relay truths about God and His redemptive work, though not always meant to be taken literally. Dennis Johnson says, "[*The title*] *'Revelation' represents the Greek word Apocalypsis, and hence some English scholars speak of this book as the Apocalypse; this noun is cognate to a verb (ἀποκαλύπτω) that speaks of the removal of a veil or other covering to disclose what lies behind it (see Matt. 10:26)."*[5] For example, Revelation 1:13-15 gives us a picture of the glorified Jesus Christ. John continues to use the term "like" to make clear the nature of the writing. To help wrap our minds around this, look again at the questions from Week 1 | Day 1 regarding Revelation 1:13-15 (cf. p. 23).

For our sake, understanding Apocalyptic literature is understanding that God is, in a real sense, pulling back the curtains of history to show us reality from His perspective. As William Hendriksen notes, Revelation is an *"unveiling of the plan of God for the history of the world, especially the Church."*[6] The truth is, this is not a genre that is limited to the book of Revelation. It is a genre ribboned through many biblical books such as Daniel, Ezekiel, and Zechariah. Blessed reader, the following line demands close attention: To have a high view of God's inerrant Word does not necessitate a literal-only reading of the Bible (cf. 1 Cor. 4:6). Some books are Apocalyptic in nature, and as separated as we are from this ancient genre we must submit to God's forms of revealing Himself if we want to be led into greater knowledge and worship. As James K.A. Smith writes, *"The point of apocalyptic literature is not prediction, but unmasking—unveiling the realities around us for what they really* are."[7] My encouragement is to let the reader understand and be blessed (Rev. 1:3).

OLD TESTAMENT ALLUSIONS

The author of this inductive Bible Study and Commentary believes this to be the most important piece in the interpretive puzzle that Revelation often seems to be to many of us. Throughout the book of Revelation, John uses *400+* allusions to the Old Testament. Unlike most New Testament books that quote the Old Testament, John most often alludes to the Old Testament in ways that demand the reader to know the Old Testament well to understand the picture he is trying to paint.

For example, to read about Jesus coming again on the clouds in Revelation 1:7 without understanding the allusion to Daniel 7:13-14 and its original context, is to make a grave interpretive mistake that has massive implications in how we understand the person of Christ and how He has revealed Himself to His people. This is no small matter. ***The following study and commentary will spend a lot of time on these allusions to better help you understand John's purpose in the book of Revelation****. As an added bonus, the careful reader will set sail into the vast seas of the Old Testament in a way that will bless you ten-fold...I promise. As prominent Revelation scholar G.K.

---

[5] Dennis Johnson, *Triumph of the Lamb* (Phillipsburg, NJ: P&R Publishing, 2001), 7.
[6] William Hendriksen, *More Than Conquerors* (Grand Rapids, MI: Baker Books, 1998), 51.
[7] James K.A. Smith, *You Are What You Love* (Grand Rapids, MI: Brazos Press, 2016), 39.

Beale writes, "*There is a general acknowledgement that the Apocalypse contains more OT references than any other NT book.*"[8]

STRUCTURE

In addition to our culture's distance from apocalyptic literature, we are equally removed from forms of biblical structure. We must avoid trying to read our American teachings of chronological order and five basic parts of a paragraph into the biblical structures of books written over 2,000 years ago. This is difficult, but nonetheless, we ought to labor to let the Bible speak for itself and teach us its own structures, genres, etc. With that being said, Revelation has a unique structure unlike any other book in the Bible. What is written might be new to you, or maybe you have heard it before, but remember that patience is a fruit of the Spirit (let the reader understand). **The structure of the book of Revelation is primarily this:** *Seven angles of the same time period: The Cross to the Second Coming.* Again, if this is new to you, patience will serve you well. Even if you disagree, after completing this study on Revelation, you will better grasp and understand an interpretive approach to Revelation that was prominent for the first 1,850 years of the Church.

Think about having all your friends over for the Super Bowl and your team is playing. Late in the fourth quarter, your favorite wide-receiver catches what appears to be a touchdown pass from the quarterback. The referees immediately call the touchdown back believing the receivers feet were out of bounds. If that were the end of it, you would be disappointed, right? But then the coach throws out the red challenge flag. Then, the next 5 minutes you see the play from every angle possible, confirming in your mind that the catch was indeed a touchdown. Finally, the referee reverses the call and your team wins the Super Bowl. That is like the structure of the book of Revelation. These 7 different angles from God's perspective are meant to help us see the multi-faceted victory of Christ in a world where Satan seems to be winning. But, the final call is that Jesus wins, and because of His victory, His people win and are comforted while they await the full fruition of His victory at His Second Coming. Most commentators agree on a repeated order of themes in order of importance, such as: judgment, persecution, and salvation reward. Regarding the repeated themes, Beale argues that these themes also progress in intensity.[9] Not only is the author persuaded to this view due to a simple reading of Revelation, but the amount of times the number "seven" is used in the book only adds weight to this seven-structure outline. With all of this in mind, here are the seven parallel sections of Revelation:

1) *Christ in the midst of the lampstands (1:1-3:22)*

2) *The vision of heaven and the seals (4:1-7:17)*

3) *The seven trumpets (8:1-11:19)*

4) *The persecuting dragon (12:1-14:20)*

5) *The seven bowls (15:1-16:21)*

---

[8] G.K. Beale, *The New International Greek Testament Commentary: The Book of Revelation* (Grand Rapids, MI: Wm. B. Eerdmans Publishing Co., 1999), 77.
[9] Ibid., 144.

6) The fall of Babylon (17:1-19:21)

7) The great consummation (20:1-22:21)[10]

The amount of "sevens" in the structure of the book are inescapable, but also a technique meant to be a blessing.

SYMBOLISM

Much of John's Apocalypse is to be interpreted symbolically. That does not mean that you should not also read it literally. Throughout the book you have clear examples of symbolism with beasts, trumpets, olive trees, etc. Main reasons for differences of opinion with the book of Revelation come from fairly modern interpretations of the Bible that attempt to interpret everything literally. The Bible clearly has a vast majority of books that should be interpreted literally, but when you have an apocalyptic book meant to be read in pictures, then symbolism naturally becomes a counterpart. While this might seem removed from our modern culture, one of the biggest critiques I hear from refugees in my city that are trying to learn English is the insurmountable idioms and metaphors we use. For example, if I told you that my life has been a rollercoaster as of late, how would you interpret that? Would you look inside my house for rollercoaster tracks, a cart with four wheels, etc.? Or would you know that I am explaining that my life has been a series of ups and downs?

Symbols are not literal but enforce an actual meaning. In fact, if you were to read the book of Revelation as only literal, it would not only be confusing, it would not match the other 65 books of the canon of Scripture. In your daily study of week one, you are asked to work on a few of these examples to get into the habit of recognizing symbolism and interpreting these passages the way the Spirit of God intended. To get you started, take a look at Revelation 1:16; 2:16; 19:15 and determine whether or not Jesus will actually have a literal sword fashioned between His teeth. Then read Hebrews 4:12-13 to better understand what the symbol might be referring to.

MILLENNIAL VIEWS

There is a famous saying, "Don't miss the forest for the trees." My hesitancy in discussing different millennial views plays into what often happens with the book of Revelation. Where Christ as the Triumphant Victor as a means of comfort to His people is the main point of the book, many have become paralyzed by using it to defend their view of the millennium. Yet, the way you interpret the millennium greatly affects the way you will look to the future with or without eager expectation (Heb. 9:28).

In general, there are four major interpretive positions on the millennium found in Revelation 20:1-6. Unfortunately, these views have been the cause of division, and worse still, have drowned out the clear beauty and glorious message of the book of Revelation. As you read through Revelation and study this comforting book for Christ's suffering people, be generous to others who hold a different perspective and be slow to speak. First and foremost, the purpose of this study and commentary is to get you to a place of understanding the message of Revelation. Try not to be a people divisive over

---

[10] William Hendriksen, *More Than Conquerors,* 16-18.

what is not abundantly clear. Move toward being united over the person and work of Christ in Revelation. With that said, the ESV Study Bible has some helpful charts posted below representing the four major views. But for the sake of the author's goal in making clear the primary things of Revelation, little more will be said apart from the commentary portions on the passages concerning the millennium. This helpful series of charts from the ESV Study Bible will give a basic overview of the prominent views:[11]

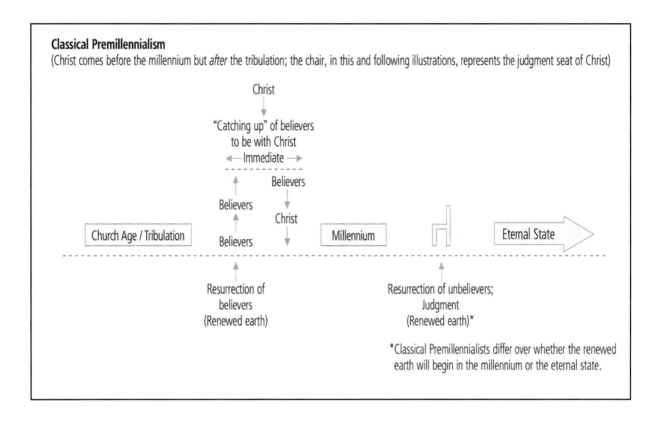

Classical Premillennialism
(Christ comes before the millennium but *after* the tribulation; the chair, in this and following illustrations, represents the judgment seat of Christ)

Christ

"Catching up" of believers
to be with Christ
←— Immediate —→

Believers

Believers

Christ

Church Age / Tribulation

Believers

Millennium

Eternal State

Resurrection of
believers
(Renewed earth)

Resurrection of unbelievers;
Judgment
(Renewed earth)*

*Classical Premillennialists differ over whether the renewed earth will begin in the millennium or the eternal state.

---

[11] ESV Study Bible, Revelation Notes (Wheaton, IL: Crossway, 2008), 2459-60.

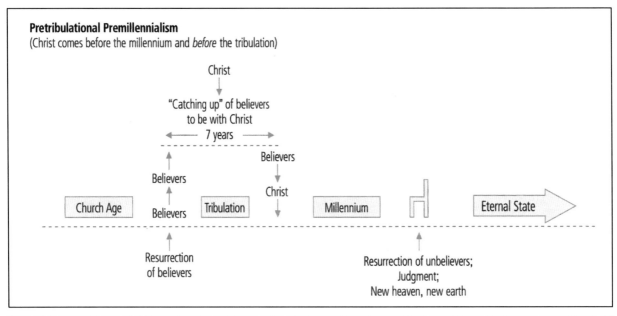

Pretribulational Premillennialism
(Christ comes before the millennium and *before* the tribulation)

Christ

"Catching up" of believers
to be with Christ

◀——— 7 years ———▶

Believers

Believers

Christ

Believers

Believers

| Church Age | | Tribulation | | Millennium | | Eternal State |

Resurrection
of believers

Resurrection of unbelievers;
Judgment;
New heaven, new earth

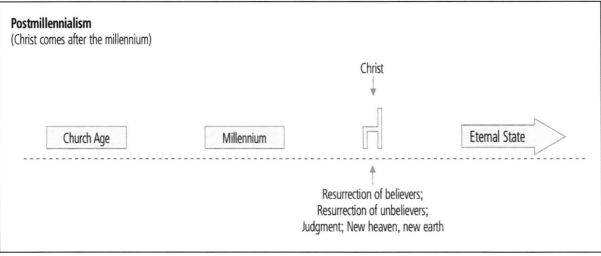

Postmillennialism
(Christ comes after the millennium)

Christ

| Church Age | | Millennium | | | Eternal State |

Resurrection of believers;
Resurrection of unbelievers;
Judgment; New heaven, new earth

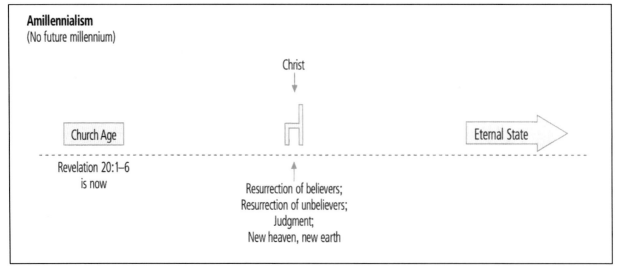

Amillennialism
(No future millennium)

Christ

| Church Age | | | Eternal State |

Revelation 20:1–6
is now

Resurrection of believers;
Resurrection of unbelievers;
Judgment;
New heaven, new earth

TELEIOS

ACADEMY

WEEK 2
STUDY

REVELATION 1:1-8

Greetings from the Eternal One

TELEIOS
ACADEMY

MEDITATION: Open to Revelation 1:1-3, ask God to reveal Himself as you read.

1. Where is Jesus physically located as He gives this apocalypse/revelation to the Apostle John?

2. How trustworthy is the One giving this revelation, especially considering His location?

3. The Apostle John is imprisoned on the little island of Patmos at the time he wrote. Read Revelation 1:1b-2 along with 1 John 1:1-4 and list how John "*bore witness to the word of God and the testimony of Jesus Christ.*"

4. John is primarily a witness here, so whose message is this?

5. Read Revelation 1:3. This is a divine blessing from Christ Himself. If you were to be blessed by reading Revelation aloud, what other means follow in 1:3 that also lead to divine blessing? Is there a sense of urgency in this verse?

APPLICATION: If this book is a message from Jesus and about Jesus, then what is the proper response to this book? Has this typically been your response in the past when reading Revelation?

MEDITATION: Be mindful when you turn to Revelation 1:4-5 that you are learning from the Faithful Witness. Beseech His help as you read these short verses three times.

1. As John begins penning this letter to the seven churches in Asia (1:4), *from* whom does he offer grace and peace?

2. Read Exodus 3:13-16 and John 8:58. Why is it important that God is the One *"who is and who was and who is to come"*?

3. As the overview notes stated, *seven* is a biblical number for completeness or perfection. With this in mind, who is John describing when he says, *"from the seven spirits"*?

4. In Isaiah 11:2 there are seven aspects listed of the Spirit. In Zechariah 4:2-6 we read of the imagery of a lamp stand with seven bowls shining light into the darkness. Read these verses, then describe how you see the Triune God at work in Revelation 1:4-5a.

5. Revelation 1:5a contains three titles of Jesus Christ. Using the parallel passages below describe why it is significant that these realities are true of Him.

    a. What does it mean that Jesus is the faithful witness (Heb. 1:2)?

    b. What does it mean that Jesus is the firstborn from the dead (Rom. 8:29-34; Col. 1:15)?

    c. What does it mean that Jesus is the ruler of the kings on earth (Ps. 89:27; 1 Tim. 6:15)?

6. When John gives the title "the ruler of kings on earth" to Jesus, this is meant to be a great comfort to the seven churches. Spend a couple minutes researching (a.k.a. Google) the Emperor Domitian from first century Rome. How did he treat Christians?

APPLICATION: Knowing that Jesus walks among His church, what are some things you think Jesus would celebrate and some things He would rebuke as He walks among your own church (Be gracious, you are a part of His body which He loves and for whom He shed His own blood!).

MEDITATION: In the broader context of Revelation 1, Jesus is presented as the all-glorious eternal Prophet, Priest, and King. Worship Jesus as the One Who released you from your sins as you read Revelation 1:5b-6 three times, emphasizing different phrases each time.

1. Write down your response *to the Lord* in light of the description of Jesus as the One "*who loves us and has freed us from our sins by His blood.*"

2. How would declarations of Christ's eternal love and forgiveness minister to suffering Christians facing persecution? (Read the prayer in Daniel 9:1-23 and pay special attention to Daniel 9:23 to get a glimpse of what the Apostle John probably had in mind).

3. The wondrous gospel of Jesus' life, death, and resurrection (1:5), not only saves us but also makes us a kingdom of priests. Read Revelation 1:6 and Exodus 19:1-6 and make some observations on what it means to be a kingdom of priests.

APPLICATION: Exodus 19:6 is predictive in its words, "*You will be a kingdom of priests,*" but Revelation 1:6 is present in its words, "*and made us a kingdom, priests…*" How can we imitate Christ's priestly work of being faithful unto death in the midst of a world that does not know Jesus?

MEDITATION: Behold the One who was pierced as you meditate upon Revelation 1:7.

1. Where Revelation 1:5 told of Christ's life, death, and resurrection (First Coming), Revelation 1:7 tells of His Second Coming. Read Daniel 7, paying close attention to 7:13-14, and list some similarities between God's people who were in exile with Daniel with those suffering in the first century with the Apostle John.

2. With Daniel 7:13-14 in mind, why would John write to the suffering seven churches about Jesus' Second Coming? What will take place on that Day?

3. In Revelation 1:7, John alludes to another Old Testament passage. Read Zechariah 12:1-13:1, paying close attention to 12:10. When you consider these passages, do you eagerly await Christ's Second Coming (Heb. 9:28)? Why/why not?

4. According to Revelation 1:7, how wide-scale will the second coming be observed? As one who is loved by God and freed by Him (1:5b), ought you have any fear about that great Day?

APPLICATION: How would a focus on the future coming of Christ practically change your affections, desires, and goals? Write out a verse to memorize on page 305.

MEDITATION: Revelation 1:8 includes one of the many names of God. Read and worship Him according to this particular description of who He is.

1. The title God uses for Himself in v. 8, "The Alpha and the Omega" is a way of saying that He is the eternal God, not bound by time. But it is also an interpretive key to understanding the whole book of Revelation. If this is a book about God's perspective of the church and the world what comfort might this particular truth bring to suffering believers?

2. Read Isaiah 41:1-4, paying close attention to v. 4. With Isaiah 41 in mind, what is the primary message is John trying to communicate to the seven churches in Revelation?

3. Fast-forward to Revelation 11:17. What words are dropped from the phrase used in Revelation 1:8 and what significance does that have?

APPLICATION: Revelation 1:8 closes with God declaration that He is "the Almighty." What are some areas in your life where you feel weak and incompetent? How does this description motivate you to run to Him in your weakness?

WEEK 2
COMMENTARY

REVELATION 1:1-8
Greetings from the Eternal One

REVELATION 1:1-8

GREETINGS FROM THE ETERNAL ONE

REVELATION 1:1-3

John's opening words in the book of Revelation are *"The revelation of Jesus Christ."* Often this final book of the Bible is rightly called "The Apocalypse." This comes from the use of a Greek word in the opening line (*Apocalupsis*), which means 'the Apocalypse.' Eyes reading in English might not pick up on the connection in John's mind, but there is an Old Testament scene in view here. In the Greek version of the Old Testament (Septuagint; LXX), this same word for apocalypse is used five separate times in Daniel 2:28-30, 45-47. If you read the context of Daniel 2, God is "revealing" mysteries to Daniel while he is in exile amongst a wicked people. Likewise, the suffering churches of John's day are also a people in a type of exile between the crucifixion of the Lord Jesus Christ and His Second Coming. Likewise, as Daniel interpreted King Nebuchadnezzar's dream to have an end result of God's victorious kingdom reigning over all other oppressive kingdoms, so John is laying forth that Christ the King is the same rock from Daniel 2:35 that will defeat the present-day kings in Revelation. As G.K. Beale writes, "John was anticipating God's victory over evil and the inauguration of the kingdom, made clear from Daniel 2 (and 7) context, as well as from what follows in Revelation 1."[12]

This book is clearly to a suffering people, but what exactly is the content of this book? According to Revelation 1:1 it is the "revelation of Jesus Christ." As we follow the transmission process of this message, it occurs in 4 steps:

1) God "gave" the revelation to Jesus Christ (to show His bondservants)
2) Jesus revealed the revelation through an angel
3) The angel communicated the revelation to John
4) John bears witness to all he saw, writing to the seven churches (1:2, 4).[13]

We can clearly see it is a revelation **from** Jesus Christ, but the book as a whole is also a revelation **about** Jesus Christ. As Daniel Wallace writes regarding the language of 1:1, *"the revelation is*

---

[12] Beale, *Revelation*, 182.
[13] Johnson, *Triumph of the Lamb*, 29-30.

supremely and ultimately about Christ."[14] God in His grace is revealing to His beloved disciple a message from and about Christ. Revelation 1:2, in describing the Apostle John, takes us back to similar witness and apostolic authority language found in 1 John 1:1-3. Remember, this same beloved disciple is suffering in a prison cell for his association with Jesus. Not only that, but the seven churches that will hear this letter are being persecuted for their association with Jesus. Does John sneak in a "therefore, be careful of talking about Jesus too loudly?" No! Verse 3 is the first of Seven Beatitudes in Revelation. This one declaring that the person who reads, hears, and keeps what is written will be blessed. The human heart that has been renewed by the Spirit of God cannot contain the delight found in the revelation from and about Jesus Christ. James Hamilton Jr. says, *"How good must John's experience of Christianity be for him to declare this blessing! In spite of persecution, in spite of the ways Christianity will not advance people in Roman culture, in spite of the fact that Christianity could cost you your life, you're blessed if you hear and keep the faith revealed in this book. John must think it's better to stand right before God by faith in Christ, forgiven and free of all sin, then it is to have all Rome bow before you."*[15]

If John was writing about things that **"must soon take place" (1:1)**, how much more today ought we understand the richness and blessing found in gazing upon Christ while hearing and keeping what is written in this book? When we look at the blessings of our American culture, one ought to remember we are first and foremost citizens of heaven (Phil. 3:20). In the same way the revelation of Jesus Christ was pulling back the curtains of reality to show how small and insignificant Rome was in comparison to the kingdom of God, so we would be greatly comforted to apply this same reality in the present. As James K.A. Smith encourages us, *"The point of apocalyptic literature is not prediction but unmasking—unveiling the realities around us for what they really are. While the Roman Empire pretends to be a gift to civilization and the zenith of human accomplishment, John's apocalyptic perspective from a heavenly angle shows us the reality: Rome is a monster."*[16]

REVELATION 1:4-5a

What good news to a suffering network of churches to hear "**grace and peace.**" Jesus is preparing to begin this apocalyptic and prophetic epistle by reminding these enduring believers who He is and what He has done. In fact, I would argue the whole book of Revelation must be grounded on Jesus' self-description in chapter 1. One must not miss though that anything Jesus does is not a rogue mission apart from the rest of the Triune Godhead. If you look closely, the Father is the eternal one **"who was and is and is to come,"** the Spirit is characterized as the **"seven spirits,"** and Jesus Christ is clearly named following the Spirit. Due to the importance of numbers in Revelation, seven is a consistently used to emphasize God's perfection or complete action in history. Hendriksen notes regarding the seven spirits, *"The expression of the 'seven spirits' refers to the Holy Spirit in the fullness of His operations and influences in the world and in the Church."*[17] John begins his greeting by writing, "**Grace and peace from Him who is and who was and who is to come.**" For Christians suffering under the torturous rule of Domitian, wondering about their seemingly uncertain future, imagine what a comfort this would have been to them—to know that their resurrected Lord was not bound by present circumstances but rules over time and space. This would have spurred on a more concrete trust in

---

[14] Daniel B. Wallace, *Greek Grammar: Beyond the Basics* (Grand Rapids, MI: Zondervan, 1996), 121.

[15] James M. Hamilton Jr., *Preaching the Word: Revelation* (Wheaton, IL: Crossway, 2012), 33.

[16] James K.A. Smith, *You Are What You Love*, 39.

[17] William Hendriksen, *More Than Conquerors*, 53.

Him. As David Chilton writes, *"as the early Christians faced what seemed to them an uncertain future, they had to keep before them an absolute certainty of God's eternal rule."*[18]

When John writes of God's eternality in 1:4, he is alluding back to God's Self-revelation in Exodus 3:14. Moses, out on his daily walk, sees a bush burning and hears the voice of God. The Voice then reveals that it is *YHWH* speaking. He reveals to Moses His covenant name: *"I AM WHO I AM."* The self-sufficient and sovereign God is declaring to Moses that He is outside of time and the ruler of all creation. Likewise, John is reminding the churches of Revelation and us today that the God who was faithful to Moses has been faithful to His people throughout redemptive history.

JESUS: PROPHET, PRIEST & KING

The three-fold titles of Jesus in Revelation 1:5a emphasize His threefold office of Prophet, Priest, and King. First, as ***"the faithful witness,"*** Jesus is the True and Greater Prophet (Deut. 18:15; Heb. 1:2). Christ not only reveals the *Word of God* to His people, but He *is the Word of God Himself*. Second, Jesus is ***"the firstborn from the dead,"*** which makes Him our Great High Priest (Lev. 16; Heb. 5-10) who is alive and interceding for His blood-bought people (Rom. 8:34). Third, Jesus is ***"the ruler of kings on earth,"*** making Him the King we so desperately need.

An Old Testament allusion is found in John's reference to Jesus as ***"the ruler of kings of the earth"*** (1:5). If we look back at Psalm 89:27 we read, *"I will make Him the firstborn, the highest of the kings of earth."* This royal and Messianic Psalm was a signpost looking forward to the King of kings that would rise from the dead and ascend to His rightful throne as ruler of the cosmos. Again, for a suffering Christian facing the threats of death under the tyranny of Domitian, God's people were to find comfort in knowing that Christ alone is the victor over death and all earthly rulers. As Andrew Maclaren writes: *"His dominion rests upon love and sacrifice. And so, His Kingdom is a kingdom of blessing and gentleness; and He is crowned with the crowns of the universe, because He was first crowned with the crown of thorns. His first regal title was written upon His Cross, and from the Cross His Royalty ever flows."*[19]

The Old Testament allusions in Revelation 1:4-5 have great meaning. Of major importance is that God wants his suffering people to know He is not absent. He wants His beloved bride to know that His Son entered into this world to suffer and defeat the evil in this world. The Lord Jesus was resurrected in victory and has taken His throne as a loud declaration to His people that all will be made right. Whether it is tribulation, persecution, or death, all suffering has become a stream of grace leading to the ocean of everlasting grace. He suffered first so our suffering isn't meaningless. He was raised first as a promise that we shall follow. As Paul exuberantly declares, *"Who is to condemn? Christ Jesus is the one who died—more than that, who was raised—who is at the right hand of God, who indeed is interceding for us. [35] Who shall separate us from the love of Christ?"* (Rom. 8:34-35a). So, let us declare the glory the resurrection brings by singing,

> *He breathes in, His living lungs expand*
> *The heavy air surrounding death turns to breath again*
> *He breathes out, He is word and flesh once more*
> *The Lamb of God slain for us is a Lion ready to roar*
> *And His heart beats."*[20]

---

[18] Richard Phillips, *Reformed Expository Commentary: Revelation* (Phillipsburg, NJ: P&R Publishing, 2017), 21.

[19] Andrew Maclaren, *Expositions of Holy Scripture,* 17 vols. (Grand Rapids, MI: Baker Books, 1982), 17:124.

[20] Andrew Peterson, *His Heart Beats* from Resurrection Letters vol. 1, 2018.

REVELATION 1:5b-6

When Christ is seen as the One this revelation is from and about, the only proper response is doxology. As our hearts are comforted by God's eternal care for His sheep we erupt with a sort of bursting out in praise and gratitude. And so, it is with John in Revelation 1:5b-6. Due to the person and work of the Triune God, especially revealed in Christ, John breaks forth by declaring, **"To Him who loves us and has freed us from our sins by His blood and made us a kingdom, priests to His God and Father, to Him be glory and dominion forever and ever."** This verse is the heartbeat of the book of Revelation. Remove this verse and you move the lifeblood that causes the whole body to function.

The reality that this eternal Prophet, Priest, and King loves His people and has freed us from our sins weds together the motive in God's heart for sending His Son with what the gospel work the Son came to accomplish. I imagine that as John was writing, his grasp of God's love was fuller than what this little phrase appears to describe at first glance. Think of 1 John 4:7-21, where John describes God's love from numerous angles—an astonishing twenty-three times. The love of God is meant to have a heart-changing effect that can turn the worst of suffering into a springboard of delight and doxology. As Dane Ortlund writes, *"A Christian is one who has been welcomed into the great dance of mutual delight within the triune Godhead, having had the very love of this Godhead implanted in his own soul."*[21]

Both of my daughters delight to sing, "Jesus Loves Me, this I know, for the Bible tells me so" for the same reason we all long to hear that our God loves us: Plainly because it is worth our marvel. Really, can you believe such a thing? Imagine being a suffering Christian in the first century, probably bearing the wounds of family and friends who lost their lives at the hands of persecution. Then imagine the authoritative voice of God coming down to you and declaring, *"I love you."* Is anything more important in this world? Not only does He love us, but that love was most clearly expressed on the cross when Christ Jesus voluntarily laid down His life for ours. His unchanging and covenantal love freed us from our sins. As Phillips so winsomely describes, *"To say that Jesus 'freed' us from sins, John uses the Greek verb 'luo,' which normally has the meaning of 'loosen' or 'unfasten.' It is used for the taking off of clothes or the unbuckling of armor. When used of persons, 'luo' speaks of setting a prisoner free. For this reason, a noun form, 'lutron,' came to mean 'a ransom that is paid.' From this comes the main words for redemption (apolutrosis), which speaks of the freeing of a slave by payment of a price."*[22] And if the effect of this redemption were to come into question in the midst of suffering, Donald Barnhouse writes, *"Ours were the sins; His was the blood. Let no man wonder hereafter if salvation is sufficient."*[23]

The close of John's doxology is declared with an awe of who we are in Christ due to His loving sacrifice for us. He calls us a **"kingdom, priests to His God and Father."** The first century Jew or Christian would have picked up the allusion here, especially with verse 5 in mind. In verse 5 we have the mention of Jesus loving and freeing His people, which leads to a kingdom of priests in verse 6. The book of Exodus contains the greatest redemptive event prior to Jesus' death and resurrection. In the Exodus account, the blood of an innocent lamb sets free the people of Israel. The Apostle John, like other New Testament writers, is showing that Christ's sacrifice as the Lamb of God was that which freed God's people from slavery to sin and into the loving care of the Triune God.

---

[21] Dane C. Ortlund, *Edwards on the Christian Life: Alive to the Beauty of God* (Wheaton, IL: Crossway, 2014), 59.

[22] Phillips, *Revelation,* 31.

[23] Donald Grey Barnhouse, *Revelation: An Expositional Commentary* (Grand Rapids, MI: Zondervan, 1971), 24.

Take a look at Exodus 19:6a to help understand Revelation 1:6. Moses writes just after the redemption of Israel from slavery, *"and you shall be to Me a kingdom of priests and a holy nation."* Israel and the church today are both a kingdom under the rule of the King that is sovereign over the kings of earth (Rev. 1:5). The Word that became flesh is the One who rules this kingdom by His living and active word (Hebrews 4:12). Also, priests of this nature are to bear witness to the glory of God in the world. Israel was meant to go out into the world declaring the grace of their God and His redemption. Likewise, we are called to proclaim the same message to those around us. The first century suffering saints were not only loved and freed but given a purpose to be priests that give glory to the Father. We too are a kingdom of priests who are just as loved, just as free, and given a purpose to glorify our Father.

REVELATION 1:7

In the doxology of Revelation 1:5b-6, John was comforting the seven churches with the great news of the Gospel; the reality that God loves His people and has sent His own precious Son to free them from their sins. He was reminding them of their foundation in Christ, the Rock upon which they stand. But where are they going? How are God's people to look to the future? When I was in the Army a lot of my job depended on good land navigation. The compass and a map became dear friends that often got me to my desired destination. Yet, many times I would be halfway to that destination and have to look back to where I started, as well as to where I was going, to get a right understanding of my location. Similarly, John is giving the seven churches two necessary coordinates. First, Christ loves and freed His from their sins. Second, Christ will return to judge the wicked and save His people.

We see this in verse 7 when John writes, **"Behold, He is coming with the clouds, and every eye will see Him, even those who pierced Him, and all tribes of the earth will wail on account of Him."** This verse is jam-packed with two Old Testament allusions that John expects his readers and hearers to understand. In Daniel chapter 7, there is a vision of these horrific beasts rising out of the sea, which symbolize succession of world governments from Babylon to Rome. At the pinnacle of this terrifying vision that shows the power of world governments comes a vision that shows God's sovereign power over all nations (7:9-11). Despite the good news that God rules over evil nations, which would be a comfort in John's day as well, Daniel is given another vision of a Messiah-type figure that would rule and reign over all things. This is where we see our first Old Testament allusion. Daniel 7:13-14 says, *"I saw in the night visions, and behold, with the clouds of heaven there came one like a Son of Man, and He came to the Ancient of Days and was presented before Him. 14 And to Him was given dominion and glory and a kingdom, that all peoples, nations, and languages should serve Him; His dominion is an everlasting dominion, which shall not pass away, and His kingdom one that shall not be destroyed."*

John sees the circumstances of the suffering churches as very similar to Daniel and the suffering exiles. Both audiences are enduring suffering. Both audiences are to see this world as a bridge leading to their true home in heaven. Both audiences are being called to trust their God in the midst of a seemingly powerful world government. The same applies to us today. As Iain Duguid writes, "Our challenge is to live our lives with our eyes firmly fixed on the heavenly throne room.

Instead of being terrified by the beasts we must daily live remembering the one who will deliver the final and decisive judgment."[24]

If one looks at the context of Daniel 7, it seems abundantly clear that the kingdom and dominion of the world is handed to this "Son of Man" who will also come visibly on the clouds (See also Ex. 19:16-19; 1 Kin. 8:10-11; Ps. 104:3). This is meant to show the churches in Asia that despite their suffering, the Almighty Messiah will one day come on the clouds to exercise judgment on all evil and rescue His people. The question for Daniel's generation, Revelation's generation, and our generation is, "Are we eagerly awaiting the coming of Jesus on the clouds in a way that changes the way we live in the present?"

The second part of Revelation is an allusion to Zechariah 12:10, with a little change in the language. Revelation 1:7 says, "even those who pierced Him, and all tribes of the earth will wail on account of Him." G.K. Beale notes that John adds the two phrases "every eye" (*pas ophthalmos*) and "of the earth" (*tes ges*), signifying that what was once seen as not merely for Israel but for all nations.[25] The way that John is using Zechariah though is not meant only to show that there will be worldwide judgment, but that the Judge is none other than the One crucified, or pierced, for those whom He came to save. This idea of judgment and salvation is the context for Zechariah's listeners as well as the churches in Revelation. The same Messiah whose side was pierced as a fountain of mercy to cleanse people from their sins (Zech. 13:1) is the same Messiah that will come to demand the blood of all not found in Him (Rev. 19:13). As those who are in this already-not-yet station, we are to look back often to Christ's loving sacrifice for us. But let us not forget to often long for and eagerly await His Second Coming. As Charles H. Spurgeon once preached, "*Brethren, no truth ought to be more frequently proclaimed, next to the first coming of the Lord, than His Second Coming.*"[26]

REVELATION 1:8

Revelation 1:7 was surrounding our lives as priests to God the Father between the crucifixion of Jesus and His Second Coming. After John's praiseworthy description of Jesus' being pierced on the cross and details of His Second Coming (1:7), John zooms-out from the church-age and gives us God's own summary statement of His viewpoint from Heaven. God says in Revelation 1:8, "**'I am the Alpha and the Omega,' says the Lord God, 'who is and who was and who is to come, the Almighty.'**" The emphasis here is to help the churches in Asia see that their God, who was gracious enough to enter into time and space to die, resurrect, and ascend, is still the Almighty and eternal One that stands outside of time. While these believers suffer under the hand of Domitian, and others suffer still today, God is more powerful and not bound to the limitations of time and space.

The well-versed Jewish reader would hear this declaration of God and be quickly transported back to the Prophet Isaiah's time. In chapter 41 of Isaiah there is a beautiful assurance to Israel where God promises to act on behalf of His people. He will come swooping in on the coastlands to deal with the nations (41:1) and with fatherly care He tells His people, "*Fear not, for I am with you*" (41:10; 13). In the midst of these beautiful promises, God tells Israel in Isaiah 41:4, "*Who has performed and done this, calling the generations from the beginning? I, the LORD, the first, and with the last; I am He.*" What we have here is God telling the people of Israel that despite the powerful nations around them moving in and out

---

[24] Iain Duguid, *Reformed Expository Commentary: Daniel* (Phillipsburg, NJ: P&R Publishing, 2008), 119.

[25] Beale, *Revelation,* 196-197.

[26] Phillips, *Revelation,* 39.

like swift horses, what seems to have no end in sight, God was before and after and is with His people. What a comfort to the Seven Churches in Asia, right? To know that God is showing up and declaring these same words almost eight-hundred years later, yet with such a similar meaning! Whether it is Domitian's violent persecution, the mockery from loved ones, or the lack of acceptance in society, John is taking the same eternal truth about the unchanging eternal God of glory and comforting the seven suffering churches. On one hand, evil cultures and men may rise but they all end up six-feet under. On the other hand, the God of creation and redemption is not shaken by the changing tide of culture, nor is He moved by evil men, but instead He laughs and holds them in derision (Ps. 2:4).

To hear the words of God here is to be blessed (Rev. 1:3). It is a true and eternal blessing because God is before and after all things. By saying He is the Alpha and Omega, "*John intends us to understand that all that lies between…comes from him. It is an affirmation of his sovereignty. He is 'the Almighty', an expression which will be repeated eight more times (4:8; 11:17; 15:3; 16:7; 19:6, 15; 21:22).*"[27] The call for suffering believers is not to cast our hope upon a change of circumstances but upon the unchanging God who is outside of time and space, while in absolute control of all of time and space. Mark Jones comments, "*He inhabits billions of years in one moment, and each moment is to him billions of years, in a manner of speaking. Jesus possesses this attribute of eternity. He is the Ancient of Days (Dan. 7:9, 13, 22).*"[28] And this great God, unfathomable in so many ways, came to us in the flesh to identify with fellow sufferers. John Calvin once wrote, "*Here is something marvelous: the Son of God descended from heaven in such a way that, without leaving heaven, he willed to be born in the Virgin's womb, to go about the earth, and to hang upon a cross; yet he continuously filled the world even as he had done from the beginning.*"[29] Our call as redeemed men and women is to not be anxious about today (Matt. 6:25-34), but to trust the Lamb who entered into our world–the same One who controls every atom and deeply cares for His people (Matt. 6:26).

---

[27] Derek Thomas, *Let's Study Revelation* (East Peoria, IL: The Banner of Truth Trust, 2011), 9.

[28] Mark Jones, *Knowing Christ* (East Peoria, IL: The Banner of Truth Trust, 2016), 37.

[29] John Calvin, *Institutes of the Christian Religion.* ed. Henry Beveridge. (Peabody, MA: Hendrickson Publishing, 2008), 2.13.4.

WEEK 3
STUDY

REVELATION 1:9-20

The Glorious Chief Shepherd of the Flock

MEDITATION: Incline your ear to listen to God's voice as you read Revelation 1:9-11 twice.

1. Does John use the word "tribulation" to refer to the past, present, or future? When considering this in light of the original audience, how does it shape your view of "the tribulation?"

2. What three things are found "in Jesus" in Revelation 1:9? Do you find yourself looking to your union with Christ for these three things as well? Where are we tempted to look for these things instead of Christ?

3. According to verse 9, why is John isolated to Patmos? Does the Word of God have this type of life and death weight in your life?

4. What does "in the Spirit" mean in Revelation 1:10-11 (Read 1 Kings 18:12 and Ezekiel 3:12 for help)?

5. To whom is John functioning as a prophet and pastor in this passage?

APPLICATION: List the names of those the Spirit of God is urging you to share the "word of God and the testimony of Jesus" with. Share this with your small group and pray together for them.

MEDITATION: Ask the Lord to open your eyes to see and your heart to believe as He reveals Himself to you in Revelation 1:12-15.

1. Who or what are the seven golden lampstands in Revelation 1:12 (cf. 1:20)?

2. Who is in the midst of the lampstands (cf. 1:13)?

3. Read the following word pictures (and their Old Testament cross-references) in Revelation 1:13-15. Jot a few notes on John's descriptions of the Person and work of Jesus.

   a. One like a son of man (Dan. 7:13)

   b. Clothed with a long robe and with a golden sash (Ex. 28:4; Lev. 16:4)

   c. The hairs of his head were white, like white wool, like snow (Dan. 7:9)

   d. His eyes were like a flame of fire, his feet were like burnished bronze, refined in a furnace, and his voice was like the roar of many waters (Dan. 10:5-6)

4. Note some ways these images help us understand Christ's offices as Prophet, Priest, and King. Why do we need Jesus to fulfill all three offices?

APPLICATION: This week, have your longings and affections been aimed at the glorious Christ revealed in Revelation 1? If not, where has your heart focused? Write out a verse to memorize on page 305.

MEDITATION: Ask God to rest your heart in Christ as He is revealed to you in Revelation 1:16.

1. Read Ephesians 3:10. What is God presently using to make His wisdom known to the rulers and authorities in the heavenly places? Does your view of the local church match this verse?

2. What is the resurrected, ascended, and glorified Christ holding in His right hand? What two images does John use in Revelation 1:20 to describe the church?

3. Read Daniel 10. Who is bringing a message of hope to Daniel? Also, if John has Daniel 10 in mind here, is there a chance that the "angels of the seven churches" are actual angels?

4. What is the significance of the "sharp two-edged sword" coming out of Jesus' mouth? Read Isaiah 49:2 and its surrounding context, as well as Ephesians 6:17 and Hebrews 4:12 to get a better picture.

5. Read Daniel 10:6 and 12:3. What picture is John trying to create in the heads and hearts of his readers as he uses these passages from Daniel as Old Testament background? Try to describe a time you set your hope on your future resurrection where you will shine in the presence and glory of Christ.

APPLICATION: If Jesus is ruling his church with His Word, and walking among her in His glory, how ought this inform how we think about, and relate to, the church?

MEDITATION: Ask the Father to grant you His own understanding of Christ as He is revealed in Revelation 1:17-18.

1. What is John's response to seeing the glorified Christ? Is this a proper response for someone who is already forgiven by Jesus? Why/why not?

2. Read Daniel 10:9-12. What similarities and differences are there when you compare that passage to Revelation 1:17-18?

3. When you consider John's words and the usage of Daniel 10:9-12, what is Christ's disposition towards His people?

4. What specific work of Jesus is all of John's love and care based upon (Read Rev. 1:18)?

5. The Gospel is fundamentally about the historic death and resurrection of Christ (Rev. 1:18; 1 Cor. 15:1-6). If Jesus rose victoriously from the dead and has the keys of Death and Hades, what does this do to the power of sin over His people?

APPLICATION: If you are loved by God, commanded not to fear, and accepted because of the Gospel, what is there to fear? Confess and repent of unhealthy anxieties you are currently carrying. Ask God to assure your heart that you are of more worth to Him than other creatures who receive His daily care (i.e., birds of the air and the flowers of the field; Matthew 6:25-34).

MEDITATION: Thank God for what has been written in Revelation 1:19-20 as you prayerfully ask Him to help you to understand and believe it's message.

1. Chapters 2-3 of Revelation are the messages of Jesus as He walks among His churches. Read Revelation 1:20 and write down some observations that connect chapter one to Christ's messages to these seven churches.

2. Returning to the picture of the lampstands again, read Zechariah 4, and then go back and zoom in on 4:6-7. With this passage in mind, who builds the church? How is that a comfort to God's people?

3. Imagine John as he is exiled to prison on the island of Patmos. How might Revelation 1:12-20 be a comfort to John during this experience?

APPLICATION: Take some time to thank God for faithful pastors you have/know. If one of them were to be exiled tomorrow, what are some encouraging things you would want to share with him/them tonight that you have never shared before? Write some of these on notecards and place them on the pulpit or drop them in the mail soon.

TELEIOS

ACADEMY

WEEK 3
COMMENTARY

REVELATION 1:9-20
The Glorious Chief Shepherd of the Flock

THE GLORIOUS CHIEF SHEPHERD OF THE FLOCK

REVELATION 1:9-11

As John continues the introductory portion of Revelation, we quickly realize he is suffering on the island of Patmos. In the first century, individuals in opposition to the Roman government were often sent to the island of Patmos to help keep the peace (Pax Romana). This beloved disciple of Jesus was more than likely the elder and pastor of the seven churches/lampstands in Revelation 2-3. With this letter most likely being written around 95 A.D., John would have been an old man by now. As a faithful shepherd of the seven churches, no doubt his heart was longing to be with and pastor the flock from which he was separated. It is safe to conclude that the book of Revelation is not just a letter declaring Jesus' victory as a comfort to the seven churches but is also the glorious Chief Shepherd comforting His beloved disciple, John.

Notice how John identifies Himself as **"your brother and partner in the tribulation."** There are some that see the book of Revelation as containing a literal seven-year tribulation that comes after Jesus' secret rapture. And no doubt, the Scriptures do tell of a Great Tribulation that comes at the end of time (Matt. 24:21; Rev. 7:14). The "tribulation" here though, is one that all Christians experience between the cross and Second Coming. As Dennis Johnson states, "*John's focus here is on the fact that his experience of tribulation, far from being extraordinary, was one that he shared with all the churches: to follow Jesus faithfully is to suffer affliction (2 Tim. 2:12).*"[30] Not only are Christians partners in this tribulation, but we also share in the kingdom (1:9). This makes more sense as we consider what we already studied in Revelation 1:5-6, revealing that we serve the ruler of the kings of earth and have been made a kingdom of priests to God. As Maclaren writes, "*We are His kingdom in so far as our wills joyfully and lovingly submit to His authority; and then, in so far as we are His kingdom, we are kings.*"[31] As verse 9 closes, we get a glimpse into the arrest records of John as we read that he is on the island of Patmos **"on account of the word of God and the testimony of Jesus."** As the faithful shepherd of the seven churches, John was merely living out his calling by being faithful to Gospel ministry, which led him to a prison cell. Are your affections for Christ deep enough to make you content with the possibility of prison for your faith?

---

[30] Dennis Johnson, *Triumph of the Lamb*, 55.
[31] Alexander Maclaren, *Expositions of Holy Scripture*, 17.153.

The next question becomes, "Will John abandon his faith due to his current circumstances?" Well, I think we get the answer in verse 10 when we see he is still keeping the Lord's Day. Picture this old man, beloved and faithful disciple, holding a service in his prison cell. Preaching boldly to all in ear's reach. On one hand, John is enduring tribulation. On the other hand, he is experiencing the grace of God on the Lord's Day. What happens next demands we understand the weight of the phrase, *"in the Spirit."* For the untrained eye, one might simply conclude that John was enjoying fellowship with the third person of the Trinity. But if one seeks to have ears to hear and eyes to see with the whole of Scripture in view, the reason John used this particular phrase will be understood. While there are many Old Testament accounts of this phrase, it is primarily used of God's prophets who would be brought up into God's presence to see a vision that would be relayed to the people of God. One example of this is Ezekiel 3:12, which says, *"Then the Spirit lifted me up, and I heard behind me the voice of a great earthquake: 'Blessed be the glory of God from its place!'"* Again, in Ezekiel 3:14, *"The Spirit lifted me up and took me away…"* (See also Ezek. 2:2; 11:1; 43:5). And what the Spirit will show John in Revelation 1:9-20 is the powerful revelation of the glorified Christ that sets the stage for the rest of the book (hence, why the author of this book spends so much time on these matters in chapter 1). As Richard Phillips delights, *"This opening vision is representative of God's intention for the entire book. This first vision sets before John the sovereign glory of Christ, complete with emblems of his triumphant, saving work, so that John will be encouraged to endure in worship of and service to his Lord."*[32]

While *"in the Spirit"* on that Lord's Day, John heard a voice behind him *"like a trumpet"* commanding to write what he sees in this vision and send it to the seven lampstands. Take a step back for a second and try to wrap your mind around this: What you are reading was given from the mouth of Christ Himself, to a suffering disciple 2,000 years ago, for the sake of comforting a suffering people. What you have in your hand are the very words of your Great and Chief Shepherd. Blessed are you to hear and read (Rev. 1:3). Before we move on to the vision itself, understanding the nature of trumpets is integral to our understanding of end times. Due to the popular acceptance in Americanized theology, the idea of a secret rapture where Jesus comes for His people before a seven-year tribulation is often synonymous with a trumpet blasting from the sky. For many who hold that position, the trumpet is a future promise to rescue them from suffering. But what we have already seen, and will continue to see in Revelation, is that John is a fellow partner in the tribulation. Likewise, Paul argues that if we do not suffer, we are not children of Abba (Rom. 8:15-18). So, can I propose a different view of the trumpet? In short, I believe these trumpets were a signal of judgment and salvation, judgment for the unrighteous, and salvation for the righteous.

Johnson gives a biblical theology of trumpets by writing, *"The trumpet blast signaled the Lord's descent to meet Moses at Sinai (Ex. 19:16, 19; 20:18), and it was later associated with the Lord's entering His temple (Ps. 47:5). Trumpets called the troops to battle and the congregation to worship. The sound of the shofar, the ram's-horn trumpet, on the Day of Atonement every fiftieth year signaled liberation of God's people and land (Lev. 25:8-10). Poet composer Michael Card captures this dimension of the trumpet voice heard by John: Jesus is our Jubilee. In his voice we hear the trumpet sound that tells us we are free. He is the incarnation of the year of Jubilee."*[33] This means, for John and for us, that the trumpet we so eagerly await is not a trumpet that merely marks an escape from suffering but will be the final trumpet when the Lord comes in glory to separate the wheat from the chaff (2 Thess. 1:5-10). And yet, the trumpet John heard is the voice of Christ speaking both words of judgment and salvation to the seven churches (Rev. 2-3).

---

[32] Richard Phillips, *Revelation*, 58.
[33] Dennis Johnson, *Triumph of the Lamb*, 57.

66

REVELATION 1:12-15

The Old Testament allusions we come across in this great and glorious vision of our exalted Savior are rooted in Daniel 7, which we will come back to *a lot*. John says in 1:13-16,

> **"...and in the midst of the lampstands one like a son of man, clothed with a long robe and with a golden sash around His chest. The hairs of His head were white, like white wool, like snow. His eyes were like a flame of fire, His feet were like burnished bronze, refined in a furnace, and His voice was like the roar of many waters. In His right hand He held seven stars, from His mouth came a sharp two-edged sword, and His face was like a sun shining in full strength."**

This little section is so packed with allusions. With the point of this book being to help the average person grasp these allusions in a way that helps them understand Revelation, I will not belabor each one but try to ignite a spark for your own further looking. The one thing that is most helpful and encouraging is the absolute certainty that John is using Daniel 7 for most of this vision, as well as Daniel 10. Before I list a visually easier way to connect these visions, let me remind you of two things: First, John's goal is to comfort a suffering group of churches with the reality that Jesus is the Sovereign Ruler and has won the victory over all evil. Second, Daniel 7 is an amazing narrative and vision where God the Father (The Ancient of Days) is handing over the Kingdom to His victorious Son (the Son of Man). Here is my attempt to help see the connections between Daniel 7 and Revelation 1:

DANIEL 7	REVELATION 1
"one like a son of man" (7:13)	*"one like a son of man"* (1:13)
"and the hair of His head like pure wool" (7:9)	*"The hairs of His head were white, like white wool."* (1:14)
"I lifted up my eyes and looked, and behold, a man clothed in linen, with a belt of fine gold from Uphaz around His waist. (10:5-6)	*"clothed with a long robe and with a golden sash around His chest"* (1:13; cf. Ex. 28:4; Lev. 16:4)
His body was like beryl, His face like the appearance of lightning, His eyes like flaming torches, His arms and legs like the gleam of burnished bronze, and the sound of His words like the sound of a multitude." (10:5-6)	*"His eyes were like a flame of fire, 15 His feet were like burnished bronze, refined in a furnace, and His voice was like the roar of many waters. 16 In His right hand He held seven stars, from His mouth came a sharp two-edged sword, and His face was like the sun shining in full strength."* (1:14b-16)

As you can see, John is taking liberally from the Old Testament and applying these texts to the exalted God and Savior, Jesus Christ. We also ought to be very aware that reading these texts about Jesus apart from the Old Testament allusions puts us in a very dire situation in which we risk interpreting this vision of God without the full and proper meaning.

The meaning behind John's vision matters because suffering and struggle can present itself as far more tremendous than it really is. I don't mean that to minimize our suffering, but to show us something, or *Someone*, bigger. John's use of these OT allusions is to comfort suffering Christians with the comfort of their Savior. As Richard Phillips shows in his tremendous work on Revelation, John is highlighting Jesus as The Savior as Priest, King, and Prophet.[34]

JESUS, OUR PRIEST

Jesus is the High Priest who was the atoning sacrifice for our sin, and now prays for us and grants us access into His presence (cf. Hebrews 5-10). This two-fold work of Christ cleansing us and interceding for us are meant to comfort us in a way that gives us confidence before God (Heb. 4:15-16). What a comfort to those who feel like they have nowhere to go when they suffer because everything around them seems grim? As Maclaren wrote, *"The heart that beats beneath the golden sash is the same that melted pity and overflowed with love at the cross."*[35] Have you come to a place of believing and resting in the grand reality that Christ is not angry with you? If you are His by faith, you cannot out-sin His fountain of mercy. Where we often have limited amounts of grace and mercy, Christ the Creator is the maker and dispenser of all grace and mercy. He never gets tired of lavishing these upon His people (Heb. 4:16). He can intercede for each one of His sheep because He died to cleanse them. And, in a real but mysterious way, we died with Him (Galatians 2:20). Mark Jones writes, *"The high priest, when he entered, had the names of the twelve tribes upon His shoulders. Christ also took the names of His sheep upon the shoulders as His Father struck His breast. In this way, we died with Him (2 Tim. 2:11)."*[36] Let this drive the way we read Revelation and the High Priestly Prayer of John 17. When one rightly grasps onto Christ as Priest, any veil that seems to separate us from His presence comes down in a haste and we boldly approach the Father.

JESUS, OUR KING

Jesus is the King whose face shines in splendor through the darkness of the evil kingdoms of this world. He is the King of kings that judges all nations with His double-edged sword. What a great encouragement to those oppressed by evil rulers and wanting nothing more than to see their Savior? Again, imagine with me the brutal onslaught of Roman Emperor Domitian as he wields his authority and destroys followers of Jesus one-by-one. Now think of this glory-vision of Christ the King ruling over all the rulers of earth. Domitian is but a small pebble in the shoe of the believer who rightly recognizes the King of kings. As Philippians 2:6-11 traces the low-stooping King who again is exalted to His proper place of glory, Christians can know for certain that every knee will bow to Him and every tongue will confess Jesus as Lord. And while we long for the physical kingdom to come, Christ truly is now reigning spiritually. After His resurrection and ascension, Jesus took His rightful seat at the right hand of His Father. As Mark Jones expands on this, we see what a King we have: *"Upon ascending, He led a military triumph (Psa. 68:18; Eph. 4:8). This triumph displayed the fact that His death on the cross had in fact been a victory leading to further victories (e.g. resurrection, ascension). Those with Him in Paradise, like the criminal, are with Him as part of the church triumphant, a victorious kingdom. There is no question that being seated at the right hand of the Father in glory brings to completion the exaltation of Christ that began with His*

---

[34] Phillips, *Reformed Expository Commentary: Revelation,* 64-65.

[35] Maclaren, *Expositions of Holy Scripture,* 17:147.

[36] Mark Jones, *Knowing Christ,* 223.

resurrection. The majesty, power, and glory of the God-man are realized. He is exalted, forever exalted, and we will praise Him as the exalted king.”[37]

JESUS, OUR PROPHET

Jesus is the Prophet who is the full and final Word from God (cf. Hebrews 1:1-3). In a world where words spew out liberally, often without depth or purpose, Jesus is the Word that speaks blessing and triumph to His people, while promising perfect justice towards evil. What great news for those surrounded by words of evil and oppression? The same Prophet of Revelation 1, ascended and glorified, is the same Prophet that the Apostle John got a glimpse of in Matthew 17. There on that mountain top, Jesus revealed His glory to Peter, James, and John. After the great Old Testament prophets disappeared into the shadows of His glory, only Jesus remained. And as the disciples fell on their faces, the voice of the Father thundered from the heavens demanding that all ears pay attention to the Voice of the Word. Many of us would sacrifice anything to be present at such a scene, but Peter declares that we have something more certain than that amazing experience: We have the Word of God itself, which is surer than that glorious day on that mountain (Pause now and read 2 Peter 1:16-21 in a spirit of Godward worship).

To know Christ fully, is to know Him as Prophet, Priest, and King. That is what John is teasing out in Revelation 1:12-15 (1:5) as a means of showing Christ's humiliation and exaltation as a pattern for what God's people must follow as well. We should all rejoice and herald with the 1689 London Baptist Confession of Faith:

"It pleased God, in His eternal purpose, to choose and ordain the Lord Jesus, His only begotten Son, according to the covenant made between them both, to be the mediator between God and man; the prophet, priest, and king; head and Savior of the church, the heir of all things, and judge of the world; unto whom he did from all eternity give a people to be His seed and to be by Him in time redeemed, called, justified, sanctified, and glorified (Isaiah 42:1; 1 Peter 1:19, 20; Acts 3:22; Hebrews 5:5, 6; Psalm 2:6; Luke 1:33; Ephesians 1:22, 23; Hebrews 1:2; Acts 17:31; Isaiah 53:10; John 17:6; Romans 8:30).”[38]

REVELATION 1:16

When my youngest daughter was two, she loved singing the song, *"He's Got the Whole World in His Hands”*[39] after family worship. We would do well to have childlike faith and rest in the reality of that song, especially the verse that will connect us to Revelation 1:16. Sue Thomas sings,

He's got the sun and the rain in His hands,
He's got the moon and the stars in His hands,
He's got the wind and the clouds in His hands,
He's got the whole world in His hands.

---

[37] Ibid., 227.
[38] The London Baptist Confession of Faith of 1689, 8.1.
[39] Sue Thomas, *Spirituals Triumphant: Old and New.*

God indeed has the whole world in His hand and He holds it together, in Christ (Col. 1:16). Whereas my daughter would loudly and joyfully sing about the stars being held in His hand, the Apostles John and Paul join together in saying He also holds some other "**stars**" in His hand. These stars are the church of Christ Jesus whom He loves and has freed (cf. Colossians 1:18 and Revelation 1:16). Imagine John being exiled to Patmos and being concerned for the well-being of the churches. Now imagine the churches worried about their own well-being as they endure suffering. Now, imagine the glorified Christ sovereignly revealing to John and the seven churches that, "**in His right hand He held the seven stars**" (Rev. 1:16). Is there any safer place to be than in the hand of King Jesus? James Hamilton writes, "*That Jesus holds the seven stars in His right hand means that He is in control of the churches, and that He is among the lampstands means that He is present with the churches. The incomparable glory of the risen Christ motivates John's audience to heed what John has been commissioned to write. The matchless splendor of Heaven's King attracts the attention and compels the obedience of the churches John addresses. The risen Christ in glory summons forth obedience from His churches.*"[40]

In Revelation 1:16 there is another picture meant to make known a reality about the ascended and glorified Christ. This picture is of a two-edged sword coming from the mouth of Christ. Not only is this a reminder of His Prophetic office, but more so a picture of His precise and devastating judgment. Grab your Bible and look at Isaiah 11:4 and 49:2. Look also at the surrounding context. Who was Isaiah looking forward to and what was the function of this sword? As G.K. Beale argues, "*The Christians in Asia are to understand that Jesus will do battle in this manner and not only against the evil nations (19:15) but also against all those among the churches who compromise their faith (2:16).*"[41] In the same way, Hebrews 4:12 picks up the same imagery in showing that the Divine Word of God destroys enemies but also cuts God's people at times to keep them on the path of righteousness.

The same One who holds the church in His hand and dispenses judgment through His two-edged Word-sword, is the exalted King whose "**face shines like the sun**" (Rev. 1:16). When Jesus prayed His high-priestly prayer in John 17, He asked that the Father glorify Him with His eternal glory that He did not cling to in His humanity (cf. John 17:5; Phil. 2:6-8). After ascending to His Father, the shekinah glory was fixed upon Christ forever, and here in Revelation 1:16 the church that seems to walk in suffering and darkness is lit up and highlighted by this glory. Not only does He hold the church in His hands, but the glorified Christ shines amongst His suffering people. In Daniel 10:6, we read of this Christlike figure that has a face "like the appearance of lightning," which leads to the people of God reflecting such brightness as they are promised that they will shine like stars (Dan. 12:3). The good news of the gospel entails that the Son of God suffered and was shamed, and so will His people. But, as He rose from the dead to glory, we will also reflect this glory (Col. 1:27). In my estimation, there is no greater truth than this: "*Beloved, we are God's children now, and what we will be has not yet appeared; but we know that when He appears we shall be like Him, because we shall see Him as He is*" (1 John 3:2).

Our great Savior had hidden His glory in the flesh in His first coming but speaks now to His churches in His unfiltered glory. This is the great and glorious God who loves us and has freed us. Derek Thomas words this beautifully when he writes, "*We cannot look directly at the sun without risking permanent blindness; its rays are too strong for the naked eye. Similarly, the resplendent majesty of Christ is a thing too dazzling to see. This majesty was hidden, or veiled, in Christ's incarnation, only to be glimpsed in His works (John 2:11), and, once, in the transfiguration (Matt. 17:2; Mark 9:3). God accommodates His majesty to us by clothing*

---

[40] James M. Hamilton Jr., *Revelation*, 51.
[41] Beale, *Revelation*, 212.

Himself in human flesh (John 1:14)."[42] In His first coming we behold Him in the flesh, but He is preparing us to see Him in His grand holiness as He makes us more and more like Himself (cf. Rom. 12:2; 2 Cor. 3:18).

REVELATION 1:17-18

In the context of all the imagery of the glorified Christ in Revelation 1 so far, how would you respond in His presence? Envision with me the Apostle John spending three years at the side of Jesus during His earthly ministry. I am sure there were very ordinary moments walking from city to city, interacting with people, etc. However, despite one occasion (Matt. 17:6), the disciples didn't typically bow before Jesus day in and day out. But what we have here, in Revelation 1:17, is the proper response of every created person before their Creator. John is lifted up into the presence of Christ, and unlike the three years of ministry where they walked and talked together, John **"fell at His feet as though dead."**

The glory of Christ is nothing to be trifled with, but responded to with absolute reverence and awe (cf. Heb. 12:28-29). Once again, to really behold the brevity of what is in front of us, we must retrace John's steps to the Old Testament allusions he has in mind. In Daniel 8:17-18, Daniel also bowed as though dead in the presence of a Christlike heavenly being. Again, in Daniel 10:9-15, a heavenly Christlike figure stands before Daniel as he immediately hits the deck with his face to the floor. Do we have a reverence and awe that responds in such a way? The danger of our comfortable Christianity often holds the truth of Christ's imputed righteousness in one hand while forgetting to equally balance His holiness and majesty in the other hand.

To be strengthened by Christ is to first understand our weakness when left to ourselves. Beale writes, *"John's response to the vision in v.17a follows the fourfold pattern found in Daniel 8 and 10: the prophet observes a vision, falls on his face in fear, is strengthened by a heavenly being, and then receives further revelation from that being."*[43] Now, this fourfold pattern is not necessarily to be repeated by all of us today, but the heart of God in the fourfold pattern should be believed and held on to with an open heart and open hands. As John trembles with fear before his beloved Messiah, which is a right response, we are given a picture of the Messiah's response to that fear. The Glorified and Exalted King of kings reaches His hand down and places it on His beloved disciple's shoulder and comforts him by saying, **"Fear not, I am the first and the last…"** Fear not, weary saint. When one fears the majesty of Christ, we must not forget these faithful words to "Fear not!" Yet, it gets better. When one traces John's picture here back to Daniel, we get almost the same exact response from Daniel and the heavenly being in chapters 8 and 10, with one major difference: *"And behold, a hand touched me and set me trembling on my hands and knees. And He said to me, "O Daniel, greatly loved…"* (Dan. 10:10-11) and again, *"Again one having the appearance of a man touched me and strengthened me. And He said, 'O man greatly loved…"* (Dan. 10:18).

Be strengthened by two things here: First, in the rightful reverence and awe of our God, He descends to our level while commanding us not to fear but also reassuring us with His love. Second, the same beloved disciple that wrote of God's love twenty-three times in fourteen verses (1 John 4:7-21), needed to be reminded *again* of God's love. Oh, brothers and sisters, how often we need to be assured of His love! Not only does John hear of God's great love for him, but he is reminded that the God-man is **"the first and the last, and the living one" (1:17-18)**. James Hamilton comments by

---

[42] Derek Thomas, *Let's Study Revelation*, 14.
[43] Beale, *Revelation*, 213.

saying, *"The reason that John shouldn't be afraid is not because Jesus isn't scary. The glory of the risen Christ is terrifying! Jesus tells John that he shouldn't be afraid because 'I am the first and the last" (1:17). This is a declaration from Jesus that He is what God is—before all things and after all things."*[44] Not only does this quench the fear of John, but it is a title and reality that ties the eternality of Christ to the eternality of God the Father (Rev. 1:8).

In the throng of imminent death in first century Rome, it is Christ Himself who holds the keys of Death and Hades (1:18), not Emperor Domitian. Jesus walked through death and is alive forevermore, reminding first century believers and us as well that we ought not be afraid of the rulers and authorities, nor put our hope in the promises of politicians, but place all of our trust in the one in whom all the promises of God find their declarative and absolute, "Yes" (2 Cor. 1:20). There is nothing for John to be afraid of, and we are to follow suit. Graeme Goldsworthy pulls this together and shepherds us to Christ by writing, *"But live in the present we must. John writes for the present in the light of the past victory of Christ, the present reigning of Christ, and the future consummation of Christ's rule. And if Christ rules now, then He has overcome His enemies decisively in the past events of His life, death, and resurrection."*[45] Oh, what a freedom this gives the people of God to walk in and rest in the love and freedom we have in Christ. Not only should this spark our affections, but it should give us an absolute hatred of our sin, and bolster faith that allows us to joyfully obey our eternal King.

REVELATION 1:19-20

Revelation, as was said earlier, is a book of unveiling. It pulls back the curtains of our reality to show us things from God's perspective. In the closing of Revelation chapter 1, we become the honored guests at an unveiling of mystery. John writes, **"As for the mystery of the seven stars that you saw in my right hand, and the seven golden lampstands, the seven stars are the angels of the seven churches, and the seven lampstands are the seven churches"** (Rev. 1:19-20). The mystery made known is somewhat straightforward in the sense that the seven stars are the angels of the seven churches, while the seven lampstands are the seven churches. But this unveiled mystery is also much thicker and packed with meaning. In G.K Beale and Benjamin Gladd's book, *Hidden But Now Revealed: A Biblical Theology of Mystery*, they note that the full biblical picture of mystery shines more light on Revelation 1:19-20. They write, *"The revealed mystery in Revelation 1:20 weaves together two thematic threads: the church as the end-time temple and participation in the latter-day kingdom as prophesied in Daniel."*[46] In the same way that God was keeping His remnant faithful and the kingdom of God thriving in the midst of opposing kingdoms in Daniel, so Christ is amongst His bride upholding her as His kingdom flourishes. The question is, when suffering weighs heavy upon your shoulders, will you trust Him or your own understanding? As Hamilton notes, *"Your response to Jesus as He is revealed in this passage determines whether you will rule with him or be slain by the sword that comes from His mouth. He is risen. He is indestructible. He is unconquerable. He is Lord."*[47]

Regarding Old Testament allusions, John moves slightly away from Daniel (although the language of Rev. 1:19 is similar to Daniel 2:28-29) and sets before us the prophet Zechariah. In the

---

[44] Hamilton, *Revelation*, 50.

[45] Graeme Goldsworthy, *The Goldsworthy Trilogy: The Gospel in Revelation* (Colorado Springs, CO: Paternoster, 2012), 263-264.

[46] G.K. Beale and Benjamin L. Gladd, *Hidden But Now Revealed: A Biblical Theology of Mystery* (Downers Grove, IL: InterVarsity Press, 2014), 263.

[47] Hamilton, *Revelation*, 52.

book of Zechariah, the people of God have returned from exile and the glory of the temple just isn't the same as it once was. In a time when all seemed dim, Zechariah 3 foretells of a Righteous Branch that would forgive our sins and impute His own righteousness to us. As the narrative turns to chapter 4, we are presented with a vision of golden lampstands (like Revelation 1). After an angelic being shows him these lampstands, Zechariah responds, *"What are these, my lord?" (Zech. 4:4)*. Let the prophet's confusion comfort us all as we realize we are not alone in the confusion. As the angel continues to guide the prophet along, we come to the key verse. In Zechariah 4:6-7, he tells the prophet regarding the lampstands, *"This is the word of the LORD to Zerubbabel: Not by might, nor by power, but by my Spirit, says the Lord of hosts. Who are you, O great mountain? Before Zerubbabel you shall become a plain. And he shall bring forward the top stone amid shouts of 'Grace, grace to it!'"* Say what? The vision of the lampstands is somewhat confusing but what we can take away is this: In the small and weak things that appear to have little to no power, the Spirit of God *is* the power that builds these things up. And if we understand that John is using this in reference to the church (lampstands), then we can know that the original audience would have been encouraged that despite all the persecution and seemingly small influence they were having, the Spirit of God was building His church. As Jesus said to Peter, *"And I tell you, you are Peter, and on this rock I will build my church, and the gates of hell shall not prevail against it"* (Matt. 16:18).

The mystery revealed here in Revelation 1 is the necessary picture of Christ and His bride that sets the stage for Christ's examination of His churches in Revelation 2-3. No matter the difficulties of this world, especially as we strive to be faithful to His bride, the call is to not define our successes by visible fruit. There will be times where all looks grim, but the Spirit of Christ is weaving together a beautiful tapestry that we are not yet aware of. Richard Phillips reminds us all, *"We will always encounter opposition in ministry; worldly and spiritual powers are intent on thwarting the advance of God's kingdom. However, God tells us to press on in the face of such obstacles. Notice that Zerubbabel is to leave the leveling of the mountain to God, while he gets on with the work God has given him. Likewise, God will make level paths for the ministry He wants us to do."*[48] What might seem like the little faith of a mustard seed today, could become a grand picture of the kingdom of God in heaven (Matt. 13:31-33). Let us be a people who are drawn into the glory and supremacy of Christ, while letting all our kingdom work flow from His beauty.

---

[48] Richard Phillips, *Reformed Expository Commentary: Zechariah* (Phillipsburg, NJ: P&R Publishing, 2007), 102.

TELEIOS
ACADEMY

WEEK 4
STUDY

REVELATION 2:1-29
Jesus Walks Among His Church: Part I

MEDITATION: Understand as you open to Revelation 2:1-7 you are meeting with the God who knows you. Ask Him for ears to hear what He is saying.

1. Looking at verse 1, describe the one walking in the midst of the church in Ephesus. How does this inform your understanding of Jesus' current ministry among His churches?

2. Going back to Genesis 3, how did Adam and Eve respond when God walked among them? If you were aware that Jesus were walking among your church today, what would He confront or affirm?

3. What does Revelation 2:2 tell us about the Christian life? What does it tell us about Jesus' knowledge of each church's actions?

4. Ephesus was a city with a temple dedicated to a pagan god named Artemis that led most of the population to widespread immorality. With this as the backdrop to verses 2-3, how does it highlight the faithfulness of the church in Ephesus?

APPLICATION: What is one way that you can be a faithful witness to Christ today in a hostile world?

MEDITATION: For the second consecutive day, meditate prayerfully on Revelation 2:1-7.

1. What does Jesus have against the Ephesian church? Knowing that He is the one who *loved* them and freed them from their sins by His blood (1:5), how does this inform your view of the seriousness of their offense?

2. How is it that the church could be so faithful to Jesus but not love Him the way they once did? Read verse 5 and describe the remedy Christ places before them. What will happen if God's people in Ephesus do not apply Christ's prescribed remedy?

3. Jesus follows the remedy to their sickness with another encouragement. Read verse 6 and describe what Jesus says about the works of the Nicolaitans. What does Jesus have in mind when He says, "which I also hate"? What is meant by the word "also"?

4. What did the Ephesians gain by following Christ's prescribed remedy (verse 7; read Revelation 22:1-5)? What does this teach us regarding how costly it is to walk in rebellion and not repent?

APPLICATION: Be transparent with someone this week and share how you may have lost your first love. What will your repentance consist of? How can the body of Christ walk with you in rekindling that first love?

MEDITATION: As you open to Revelation 2:8-11 you are seeing the words of the God who knows everything about you. Ask Him for ears to hear what He is saying.

1. As Jesus walks among the church in Smyrna, He only offers encouragements. Write some of them below.

2. As we think of the "successful" churches of our day, what is the biggest contrast between the church in Smyrna and our own ideas of a successful church?

3. In verse 10, what declaration did Jesus make about what would soon happen to some of the members of the church? How could He tell them something so awful while commanding them not to fear?

4. What does Jesus mean by the "second death" in verse 11 (See Revelation 20:5-6 for help).

APPLICATION: Can we trust Jesus even when He leads us into severe trials? Why, or why not?

MEDITATION: As you read Revelation 2:12-17, ask the Lord for ears to hear what He is saying.

1. How does Jesus reveal Himself to the church in Pergamum? Where else have we seen this in Revelation?

2. From verse 13, describe how Jesus encourages the church in Pergamum. What are God's people in this church clinging to in the midst of their spiritual battle?

3. The sword coming from Christ's mouth divides. As He slices through Pergamum, what is He aiming to cut off (2:14-15)? Take a moment to read Numbers 22-24, as well as Numbers 25:1-9 to better grasp John's Old Testament allusion and references to Balaam and Balak.

4. What is Christ's remedy for continued faithfulness? What do you think the three different rewards in verse 17 are describing?

APPLICATION: How is Christ's sword piercing you? Do you embrace *everything* God says? Write out a verse to memorize below. For reinforcement, write it again on page 305.

MEDITATION: As you read Revelation 2:18-29, meditate on the reality that God also knows everything about you.

1. How does Jesus reveal Himself to the church in Thyatira? Do you see any patterns in the way He addresses the churches?

2. What encouragement does Jesus give the church in Thyatira? Are these the things *you* are striving for in your life and church?

3. What grievous errors did Jesus, with his all-seeing eyes of fire, notice in this church (2:20-23)? What does He see in you?

4. Why does false teaching so easily and quickly distract people from God's truth? Are you vigilant to hold to what is true?

5. What will those receive who conqueror in Christ, who persevere in Christ's until the end? Read Psalm 2 and Daniel 12 to understand the Old Testament pictures that give insight into these rewards.

APPLICATION: Sexual immorality was a direct result of false teaching in Thyatira. What is the root cause of sexual immorality and the pornography epidemic in churches today? By God's grace, will you crucify this sin in your life (Colossians 3:5ff)? Will you bring others into this fight with you for prayer and genuine biblical accountability?

WEEK 4
COMMENTARY

REVELATION 2:1-29
Jesus Walks Among His Church: Part I

REVELATION 2:1-29

JESUS WALKS AMONG HIS CHURCH: PART I

The vision and description of Christ in chapter one of Revelation is entirely inseparable from the rest of the book. More so, the impact of chapter one is seen in the first verse of each letter to the churches in chapters two and three. As Jesus walks among His church, the Spirit of God emphasizes a specific part of the vision of the glorified Christ in Revelation one as His introduction to each local church. Each church is also addressed in a similar pattern. With a couple exceptions, the letters generally unfold as follows:

1) Praise for faithfulness
2) The need for repentance
3) Warning of judgement
4) Promised blessings for overcoming.

Also, a quick note of importance: There are some who find the seven churches symbolizing seven chronological eras representing the whole church-age between the ascension and return of Jesus. For example, John Walvoord writes, *"It would seem almost incredible that such a progression should be a pure accident, and the order of the messages to the churches seems to be divinely selected to give prophetically the main movement of church history."*[49] While this would somewhat fit the symbolic nature of the book, the specific historical context used in each church sways me to believe that John was writing to specific churches in the first century, rather than summarizing all of church history. Do these letters have implications for us today? Absolutely. But we ought to understand these messages to the lampstands as specifically addressed to the first century churches, and applied to all churches throughout history.

REVELATION 2:1-7

The first of the seven letters—each of which comprise one letter that would have been read to all seven lampstands—is to the church in Ephesus. As Jesus walks among this church, He is doing so as the one **"holds the seven stars in His right hand, who walks among the seven golden lampstands."** This is a reminder to all seven churches, especially Ephesus, that Jesus is the head of

---

[49] John Walvoord, *The Revelation of Jesus Christ* (Chicago, IL.: Moody Press, 1973), 52.

the church and holds them all together (cf. Col. 1:17-18). Not only this, but Jesus walking among His churches should harken our minds back to Genesis 3 when God walked among the Garden to confront Adam and Eve in their sin. When the pre-incarnate Christ approached our first parents "in the cool of the day" (Hebrew; *ruach*; literally rendered, "spirit") (3:8), we are to understand this word as synonymous with "the Spirit" bringing God's judgment. Likewise, Christ is walking in judgment and salvation among His bride in Revelation chapter two to encourage and correct. As we will see in this letter and the others, Jesus' walking among His church carries the dual aspects of judgment and salvation. He experienced judgment and accomplished salvation on the cross when purchasing each of these churches (cf. Acts 20:28). When Christ sets His gaze upon Ephesus, He will remind them of His sovereign care for His bride. Richard Phillips writes, "*Thus, when He says, 'I know' (2:2), we see that He is present with His people even though He is unseen. In this way, Christ, the Chief Shepherd of His flock, sets a good example for His undershepherds. Jesus is present with His churches, and He is interested in and involved with them.*"[50]

As Jesus begins walking through the church of Ephesus, He praises them for their **"works, toil, and patient endurance, and how you cannot bear with those who are evil but have tested those who call themselves apostles and are not and found them to be false."** What a sweet encouragement to hear from the Lord of Glory who patiently endured the shame of the cross! It appears from a cursory read of this text that they were facing something difficult. History tells us that the Temple of Artemis (Acts 19:8-9, 23-40) was the centerpiece of the famous harbor town of Ephesus. In fact, the Temple of Artemis was one of the seven wonders of the ancient world.[51] The toil mentioned is actually best defined as "hard labor" (κόπον), probably referring to the amount of labor it would have taken to stay pure in such a sexually immoral culture. The odds of walking by the Temple of Artemis and seeing sexual misconduct publicly was more than likely *a daily occurrence*. Richard Phillips quotes the ancient philosopher Heraclitus, who lived in Ephesus, who explained the city as a place "*no one could live in…without weeping at its immorality.*"[52] With this historical background, we see why Jesus praised this church for remaining pure.

However, in verse 4, Jesus gives a stern rebuke to this toiling church. The One who loves them and has freed them from their sins with His own blood (1:5), confronts them with the saddening reality that they have "***abandoned the love***" they had at first. Some commentators say that this lost love is either lovelessness toward other people masked by a zeal for correct doctrine (cf. 2:2), or lovelessness for Jesus Himself. I believe that both are in view here because—according to the greatest two commandments—Jesus taught that these loves are inseparable. 1 John 4:20 says, "*If anyone says, 'I love God,' and hates his brother, he is a liar; for he who does not love his brother whom he has seen cannot love God whom he has not seen.*" More than likely, John wrote 1 John from Ephesus, which gives more weight to the view that love was lacking in both areas in the Ephesians church. Maybe this is a rebuke to you as well? Maybe you have grown theologically astute at the cost of forsaking love for your brother or sister in Christ? Allow the sword of Christ's Word to pierce you, bringing you back to your first love.

What is the remedy for loveless coldness towards Christ and/or His bride? In verse 5, Jesus says, **"Remember therefore from where you have fallen; repent, and do the works you did at first. If not, I will come to you and remove your lamp stand from its place, unless you repent."** Repentance is the great gift of God as we turn away from our sin, and turn to Him in a way that leads to salvation without regret (cf. 2 Cor. 7:10). This repentance is driven by *remembering their first love, the Lord Jesus Christ*. What is interesting, though, is that this is not a command driven by feeling. Rather,

---

[50] Phillips, *Revelation*, 90.
[51] Phillips, *Revelation*, 91.
[52] Ibid., 91.

this is a love that is ferociously tied to actions—to good works (2:5). This command is best summarized by what John wrote in 1 John 4:19, *"We love because He first loved us."* The good work of neighbor-love is always a result of remembering God's agape love toward us. Churches today would be wise to pay better attention to these letters when assessing the "success" of our ministry. Instead of a contrived mountaintop experience or assessing and critiquing what is and is not working at our respective churches based on numbers, we should comb through these letters and fall on our knees as we seek to find what Jesus would encourage and rebuke. As Derek Thomas summarizes Christ's address to the church in Ephesus, *"This letter is a warning to those who can detect false doctrine a mile away, but whose hearts do not beat in tune with the love shown in the gospel."*[53]

REVELATION 2:8-11

We live in a world that is often at war against the God of heaven and earth. Yet, when the Spirit of God makes us new, we often find that living according to His kingdom values seems paradoxical. For example, we must die if we want to live (Luke 9:23-25). The most blessed are those that are poor in spirit (Matt. 5:3). Throughout Scripture we see these seeming paradoxes that are known by all born-again Christians. But if we are honest, we often feel more at home in this world than faithfully believing and applying these paradoxes. This is somewhat the case in Revelation 2:8-11 when Jesus walks among His church in Smyrna. Similarly, in 1:17-18, Jesus reveals Himself as the One who is the **"first and the last, who died and came to life."** With a direct connection to His own death and resurrection, Jesus tells Smyrna to **"not fear what you are about to suffer. Behold, the devil is about to throw some of you into prison, that you may be tested, and for ten days you will have tribulation."** This alarming and sure prophecy of the Prophet is terrifying on its own, but what exactly makes this a paradox (cf. Deut. 18:15; Heb. 1:3)? The shocking aspect of Jesus' letter to Smyrna—which should strike us as seemingly paradoxical—is that, unlike Ephesus, Jesus has only encouragements for them. No rebuke. No correction. Herein lies the great paradox: Despite absolute faithfulness to Christ, Smyrna will be thrown into the severe temptations and trial of being imprisoned by the Dragon. Sobering, indeed!

Not only does that paradox show itself in this passage, but another paradox about the Jews of the first century is exposed as well. In verse 9 Jesus exposes those that **"say they are Jews and are not but are a synagogue of Satan."** This shows that things are not always what they seem. A cursory read of this passage makes it clear that being a Christian in Smyrna was severely costly. Derek Thomas writes, *"Christians in this city would have a difficult time, particularly since the Jewish community was largely and on good terms with Rome—hence the reference to Jews in verse 9. It was in the interest of the Jews to be dissociated from Christians. Later, in the second century, the godly Polycarp, after following Christ for eighty-six years, was cruelly put to death, aided by the antagonism of the Jews in Smyrna."*[54] This reality exposes that our God is purposeful in using trials to conform us more and more into the image of His Son. The question is, why are we still surprised when the trials come (cf. 1 Pet. 4:12)? We can be tempted to look around our own church and see many brothers and sisters enduring suffering and conclude that God must be frustrated with them or us. Or, we can be tempted to look at the church down the street, or the church that is growing numerically through a host of programs, and conclude that God is blessing them. But the

---

[53] Derek Thomas, *Let's Study Revelation,* 21.
[54] Ibid., 22.

reality of the New Covenant church is that we are intimately blessed in our union with Christ…even though we experience great suffering (cf. Rom. 8:17).

The soothing news of the Gospel is the only balm that can make such sorrowful trials seem purposeful and our pain become mendable. Despite the trials coming Smyrna's way, we find the command to not fear (2:10). This command is founded on the good news that they are rich despite suffering (2:9). In a city that had its own temple dedicated to the goddess Roma,[55] the Christians in Smyrna would have suffered greatly for worshipping Jesus. This would have impacted them financially as they would have been prohibited from certain forms of trade due to their allegiance to Jesus. So, in another paradoxical way, they were poor (physically) but extremely rich (spiritually). The same word John uses for "poor" here, Paul uses for Christ's poverty in 2 Corinthians 8:9, which says, "*For you know the grace of our Lord Jesus Christ, that though He was rich, yet for your sake He became poor, so that you by His poverty might become rich.*" In a city where Christians would have more than likely been physically poor, it is not too far of a stretch to imagine they were walking around smiling, rejoicing in all their spiritual blessings in the heavenly places (cf. Eph. 1:3-14). They could smile because the ten days in prison, which is most likely a symbolic allusion to Daniel chapter one, would result in these believers in Christ having their faith strengthened rather than the weakened. Though Satan intended to harm them through suffering, God was using these very sufferings for their good and His glory (cf. Genesis 50:20). Even if they were to die at the hands of the evil one, it would merely usher into eternity with Christ who died for them. Douglas Kelly beautifully imagines Jesus' words to His suffering and imprisoned people: "*I have passed through the territory of death already. I have taken all of its terror away for believers. Now, the only thing that awaits you on the other side of death is holding my hand as we walk together into the new beauties of resurrection joy.*"[56]

Jesus concludes this meandering walk of love among His bride in Smyrna with an eternal comfort by the Spirit: ***"The one who conquers will not be hurt by the second death"*** (2:11). The second death is a phrase we will come back to later in chapter 20 but can be understood as the judgment to hell for those who are not found in Christ when they die the first death. Jesus is giving a benediction of sorts to comfort those that will soon be bound to prison and be forced under the weight of persecution. Jesus' words are the assurance that evil may have its day *now* by stopping our heartbeat temporarily, but one blink *later* we will see Jesus face to face. What might be the most terrifying moment of persecution and death, is followed by the far weightier glory of eternal joy (cf. Rom. 8:18). Polycarp famously said right before his death at the hands of his persecutors, "*Eighty and six years have I served Christ, and He never did me any injury: how then can I blaspheme my King and Savior?*[57] Richard Phillips expands, "*With that refusal, Polycarp was executed by public burning, having been faithful to the end and being certain of the promised crown from his Lord.*[58] This all brings weight to Jesus' command in verse 10 for Smyrna to ***"be faithful unto death, and I will give you the crown of life."*** The city of Smyrna was a beautiful harbor city that had a hill full of grand estates, giving this hill the nickname of "The Crown of Smyrna."[59] This lets us in on what was at cost for the Smyrnian church, and for us as well. Will we settle for earthly crowns found in the treasures of this world, or will we pursue the crown that comes with eternal access to the King of kings, who will crown all who overcome by faith?

---

[55] Phillips, *Revelation,* 100.
[56] Douglas F. Kelly, *Mentor Expository Commentary: Revelation* (Ross-shire, Scotland: Mentor, 2012), 41.
[57] Phillips, *Revelation,* 100.
[58] Ibid., 100.
[59] Ibid., 100.

REVELATION 2:12-17

In Revelation 1:16, we were confronted with the reality that the glorified Christ is the Prophet foretold in Deuteronomy 18:15. We were given the image of a **"sharp two-edged sword"** coming from His mouth. When He walks among the church in Pergamum, He is introduced as the One having **"The words of Him who has the sharp two-edged sword"** (2:12). The Great Physician will lovingly remove all unhealthy and cancerous growths as He continues to beautify His bride. We will see what He slices off in a bit, but let's begin with what Jesus commends as He walks among the church in Pergamum.

Verse 13 is a commendation which reads, **"I know where you dwell, where Satan's throne is. Yet you hold fast my name, and you did not deny my faith even in the days of Antipas my faithful witness, who was killed among you, where Satan dwells."** Pergamum was a city where Satan seemed to be initiating a brutal onslaught to condemn Christ's followers. G.K. Beale, speaking of the historical situation, says, *"'The throne of Satan' in Pergamum is a way of referring to that city as a center of Roman government and pagan religion in the Asia Minor region. It was the first city in Asia Minor to build a temple to a Roman ruler (Augustus) and the capital of the whole area for the cult of the emperor. The city proudly referred to itself as the 'temple warden' of a temple dedicated to Caesar worship. Life in such a politico-religious center put all the more pressure on the church to pay public homage to Caesar as a deity, refusal of which meant high treason of the state. Furthermore, Pergamum was also a center of pagan cults of various deities."*[60] To get to the heart of the matter, Jesus was commending believers in Pergamum for their outward and public faith in an arena that was clearly a very costly place to display such faith. The steep price is also remembered as Christ reminds them of the costly death of one of their own church members, Antipas, the faithful witness of Christ. We can be tempted to read a text like this and quickly move on but imagine for a second that you lost a dear member of your church due to a violent outworking of the evil one. As your city increases in its hatred for your church, would you remain faithful unto death?

Jesus follows the commendations by standing as the Prophet and Judge over the church in Pergamum. He clearly lays out His covenant lawsuit against His bride and their errors. The root of their sin against God was a commitment to false teaching. The great danger of false teaching is that if we believe it, our hearts will love it and our actions will follow. The Pergamum Church had been infiltrated with erroneous teaching that led to idolatry and sexual immorality (2:14-15).

To fully grasp what John is trying to get his readers to picture, we must turn back to the book of Numbers. In Numbers 22-24 (as well as 25:1-9), we are told of the prophet Balaam who sneakily advised Balak to *"send Moabite women to seduce Israelite men into sexual immorality and idolatry."*[61] Jesus is connecting the evil works that followed the false teaching of Balaam directly to the Nicolaitans and their influence upon the believers in Pergamum. Richard Phillips shows the grammatical similarities as well when he writes, *"Nicolaitans and Balaam have the same meaning, the first a Greek word and the second a Hebrew word meaning 'conqueror of the people.'"*[62] As Dennis Johnson so clearly puts it, *"Dabbling with idolatry or immorality denies that we belong to Jesus, our jealous husband who tolerates no rivals."*[63] Modern readers might shake their head in judgment as they read of this grievous error, but what would Jesus find among your life and your church today? If we are honest, the idols that we often bed with are not much

---

[60] Beale, *Revelation*, 246.
[61] Dennis Johnson, *Triumph of the Lamb*, 76.
[62] Phillips, *Revelation*, 113.
[63] Dennis Johnson, 77.

different than those in Pergamum. How many times have you entertained sexual images in a popular movie that led to sinful lust and idolatry? How many of us have closets full of name brand clothing that we don't wear but will not part with while hundreds in your city sleep on cold sidewalks? Maybe some of you don't like to ruffle any feathers and so you get along with everyone, slowly condoning and even believing some of their lifestyle choices that are in clear contradiction to the revelation of Jesus Christ in Scripture. While we are called to love everyone, might it be dangerous if we are loved by everyone? Jesus says in Luke 6:26, "*Woe to you, when all people speak well of you, for so their fathers did to the false prophets.*" Whatever our idols tend to be, let us not be too quick to read through a passage like this without asking the Spirit to slice the cancerous idolatries from us.

As in the letter to Ephesus (2:1-7), Christ has the perfect prescription for the sickness of false teaching and sexual immorality in Pergamum: **Repent!** If they do not repent, Jesus will personally cut them off with the sword of His mouth (2:16). Where Ephesus cared so deeply for doctrinal precision at the cost of loving their neighbor, Pergamum cared little about doctrinal truth as they have accepted false teaching. The blade is sharpened and those who turn to Jesus as the way, the truth, and the life (John 14:6), will experience His surgical removal of false teaching, and escape His sword that leads to the second death. Those who repent and receive the slice of the sword that saves, will also be the ones who enjoy the harvest of rewards.

In Revelation 2:17b, John writes, **"To the one who conquers I will give some of the hidden manna, and I will give him a white stone, with a new name written on the stone that no one knows except the one who receives it."** This verse is another example of the vital necessity of needing Old Testament proficiency to understand the meaning. If we try to read it without the Old Testament allusions in view, we might think that Jesus is offering us some bread, a rock, and entrance into some secret club that no one knows about but you. So, let us do diligence and mine the depths to get past the first layer of words and see what the Rock of Ages has in mind. Manna is the bread that God provided for Israel in the wilderness as they were *wholly dependent* on Him for life (cf. Ex. 16; Num. 11). Jesus picks up this picture in the Gospel of John and calls Himself the Bread of Life (cf. John 6:31-35). The white stones, as Dennis Johnson quotes from Colin Hemer, were typically used as "*tokens signifying a juror's vote to acquit, admission to entertainment events, honorable discharge from gladiatorial combat, initiation into the worship of Asclepios, and magical amulets bearing divine names.*"[64] We also see the "new name" theme in Isaiah 62:2 and 65:15. When we put this picture together with its Old Testament allusion, it no longer seems vague or odd. We can confidently see Jesus pointing forward to the climax of the church's overcoming pilgrimage between the cross and the Second Coming of her Lord. The desires and longings that led Pergamum—and often lead us—to idolatry, are being quieted and hushed as Jesus offers the Bread that satisfies, and a new name that He alone can give. Hamilton so sweetly and soothingly ministers this passage to us:

> "*I think these promises are meant to meet the needs that people seek to meet through idolatry and sexual immorality. Jesus promises to meet those needs. Jesus offers the provision of 'hidden manna,' which is a better provision than any idol offers. He tells us we don't need to go to other gods. Similarly, I suggested that sexual immorality arises from a longing for intimacy. The promise of 'a white stone, with a new name written on the stone that no one knows except the one who receives it' is a promise of intimacy. Whatever else it means, this promises that there will be a private communication between God and the one who overcomes. Surely God knows the name on the stone, and the one who receives*

---

[64] Ibid., 78.

the stone knows the name. And that exclusive knowledge, that private interaction that no one else shares, is the essence of intimacy. Jesus is arming us with weapons for the war on lust."[65]

REVELATION 2:18-29

As we get a front row seat to Jesus walking in the midst of the seven churches, we are shown the heart of a fourth church, the church in Thyatira. The imagery of Revelation chapter one is again used as Jesus reveals Himself as the One **"who has eyes like a flame of fire, and whose feet are like burnished bronze."** Having "eyes like a flame of fire" makes a bit more sense later when Jesus says, **"I am He who searches mind and heart, and I will give to each of you according to your works"** (2:23). What will Jesus commend and rebuke? As we travel 40 miles southeast of Pergamum, to a city that was relatively the least important city economically,[66] we must remember that each local church is very important to Jesus no matter what people think of them or their city. The church is a blood-bought bride for Christ's own possession. This small-town church gets the longest letter of the seven churches. This is partly due to their obedience, but also do to the danger that lies within them.

Jesus begins His commendation in 2:19 by encouraging them for their **"love and faith and service and patient endurance, and that your latter works exceed the first."** When we read such an encouraging commendation from our Lord, we should rejoice if such characteristics are visible among our own churches. Jesus is still pleased with these fruits today and we ought to aim to please Him accordingly. As Mark Jones argues in his wonderful book, *Knowing Christ, "We are able to please our Father in heaven only because Christ pleased his Father by perfectly obeying Him during his earthly ministry."*[67] Or as Paul writes in 2 Corinthians 5:9, *"So whether we are at home or away, we make it our aim to please Him."* This is what the church at Thyatira was aiming to do, and Jesus wanted them to know they were succeeding. We should pray and aim to encourage our own local church to please Jesus in these ways for the rest of our lives.

After His loving encouragement, Jesus' "flame of a fire" eyes see a major issue in His church. In verse 20-23, Jesus exposes a group of people who have tolerated a woman named Jezebel, causing many to fall into the same issues as the church in Pergamum: Idolatry and sexual immorality. Jesus makes clear that He has given her time to repent but she wouldn't. And His just ruling in 2:22 is that He will **"throw her onto a sickbed, and those who commit adultery with her I will throw into the great tribulation, unless they repent of her works."**

To try to get what the Lord is laying down, we must identify who Jezebel is. Unlike Pergamum with a whole group of false teaching from the Nicolaitans, Thyatira is letting an individual woman steer the ship toward hell. To understand the persuasiveness of this woman, we are not meant to see her necessarily as a literal woman named Jezebel but are to let that name drive us back to an Old Testament allusion. 1 Kings 18-19 tells of the prophet Elijah's confrontation with all the false prophets who worshiped Baal and Asherah at the table of Jezebel. In a key moment that was designed by the Lord to show the supremacy of God over all things, Elijah exposes that their gods are mute and dead while God sends a fire and accepts Elijah's offering. This episode proved to all around that the God of Jacob is indeed the only true God. In a similar way, this Jezebel in Thyatira was probably encouraging that people in the church enjoy being a part of the ritual ceremonies offered to

---

[65] Hamilton Jr., *Revelation*, 91.
[66] Derek Thomas, 29.
[67] *Mark Jones, Knowing Christ, 83.*

pagan gods. Among the pagans of Thyatira, this would happen through offering food to idols and practicing sexual immorality as an act of worship. And they were creeping into Christ's church! Amid the great love and service in the church among the band of brothers and sisters worshipping Jesus on the Lord's Day, there were those whoring themselves out to other gods during the week (cf. Hosea 1:2). Our culture in America sadly resembles the wickedness in Thyatira far more than it does the purity there. Richard Phillips lays some heartbreaking statistics before us: "*A 2011 survey by a Christian magazine reported that 80 percent of unmarried Christians had sinned sexually and that two-thirds of unmarried Christians between the ages of eighteen and twenty-nine had been involved in a sexual relationship within the previous year.*"[68] Years ago, the church I pastor at began a class and some counseling meant to help those thinking about dating. The classes and counseling were meant to help fight two areas specifically: Idolatry and sexual immorality. To this day, there has never been so much argument and push back from our congregation, exposing that the idolatry and sexual immorality that are so rampant in the church. Many who attend church may still love sin more than Jesus. We ought not be foolish and think we are too far removed from the seven churches in Revelation. Jesus' eyes of fire see it all. The good news is the same for us today as it was for those dabbling in idolatry and sexual immorality in Thyatira. *Repentance* is the road back home. Even though Jezebel and her followers have not repented, Jesus offers to clean up His dirty bride if they will turn to Him.

Next Jesus addresses the portion of the church that has kept separate from Jezebel and her wickedness. He says to the faithful overcomers in 2:24-25, **"*But to the rest of you in Thyatira, who do not hold this teaching, who have not learned what some call the deep things of Satan, to you I say, I do not lay on you any other burden. Only hold fast what you have until I come.*"** This call seems to simply be saying, 'Keep doing what you are doing.' What follows in verses 26-27 is the root of the message. The alluring aroma of Christ is the power to help the overcomers continue faithfully until the end. The reward far outweighs the temptation when Jesus promises He will give them **"*authority over the nations.*"** As if being co-heirs with the King of glory were not enough, He continues by proclaiming He will rule the nations with **"*a rod of iron.*"** Here, Jesus is using Psalm 2:8-9 in application to Himself as He reigns in the midst of His kingdom people. He is declaring that He is the Messianic King of Psalm 2 who rules the cosmos and promises to give His people the right to judge. He is the One with burnished bronze feet standing victoriously among His faithful saints. This authority rightfully belongs to Jesus, and He dispenses His rule through His saints by calling us to rule with Him in His victory. His kingdom advances as we make disciples of Christ and baptize them in the name of the Father, and the Son, and the Holy Spirit (Matt. 28:18-20).

Jesus closes this letter by promising to give those who overcome the **"*morning star*" (2:28)**. Picking up on another Old Testament allusion, the reader who has an ear to hear (2:29) will likely be transported back to Numbers 24 with Balaam and again. In this story, Balaam sees a star bursting forth from Jacob, a scepter ascending out of Israel to crush Moab (Num. 24:17). Dennis Johnson argues, "*The star-scepter symbolized a warrior king, who identifies Himself in Revelation 22:16…Jesus promises his people not merely dominion but a better treasure, a deeper joy: Himself.*"[69] This morning star is not limited to the context of Numbers 24, but also finds itself beaming through Daniel 12 and Philippians 2. Daniel 12:3 tells of God's suffering people who stay faithful, that they will one day shine like the light of the stars (think Abrahamic Covenant) through resurrection in Christ. This future glory awaiting God's faithful bride is intended to have present implications. Paul picks this up in Philippians 2:15 when he calls

---

[68] Phillips, *Revelation*, 125-26.
[69] Johnson, *Triumph of the Lamb*, 82.

God's gospel-formed people in Philippi to not grumble but be faithful as they "*shine as lights in the world, holding fast to the word of life so that in the day of Christ I may be proud that I did not run in vain or labor in vain.*" Phillips encourages, "*Jesus is promising to give Himself, the Light who shines brightly to cast away all darkness, as the most precious gift to his faithful people. Together with Himself, however, He is promising that we ourselves will enter into that shining brightness of glory through union with Christ in faith.*"[70]

---

[70] Phillips, *Revelation*, 130.

TELEIOS
ACADEMY

WEEK 5
STUDY

REVELATION 3:1-22
Jesus Walks Among His Church: Part II

MEDITATION: As you read to Revelation 3:1-6, pray that it will not be lost on you that you are meeting with God who knows you more thoroughly than anyone. Ask Him for ears to hear His voice.

1. What description of Jesus from chapter one is used in Revelation 3:1? What is the significance of this description?

2. What contradiction is Jesus confronting in the church in Sardis? Can you think of any examples where you may have a reputation of being one thing that is not consistent with the reality?

3. What motive does Christ give to wake up the church at Sardis? What kinds of people will they be joined with if they do wake up?

4. If someone conquers the temptation facing Sardis, what will they gain? Read Matthew 10:32-33 to get further explanation of Revelation 3:5 and the good news of having your name found in the book of life.

APPLICATION: Imagine for a moment what the Day will look like when Jesus joyfully confesses your name before our Father and His angels. What hopeful expectations do you have for that Day?

MEDITATION: God is speaking to you as you read Revelation 3:7-10. Ask Him for ears to hear what He is saying.

1. Unlike the first five churches, the letter to the church at Philadelphia does not open with a vision of Christ from Revelation chapter one. However, in light of Isaiah 22:20-22 write the connections you see to Revelation 3:7.

2. What is Jesus' commendation to the church in Philadelphia? Read 2 Corinthians 12:9-10 and describe what it looks like to stand faithful in the midst of weakness.

3. What does Jesus declare to His faithful ones in Revelation 3:9? What would this mean to you in a time of suffering?

APPLICATION: What are some ways you have been encouraged by other people who have kept the word of Jesus in patient endurance (3:10)? Write down your thoughts and share these encouragements with him/her soon.

MEDITATION: While reading Revelation 3:11-3, keep at the forefront of your mind that the words belong to the One who will come quickly. Ask Him for ears to hear what He is saying.

1. How do you make sense of Jesus' words in Revelation 3:11 that He is coming soon? How do you reconcile that He spoke these words at the end of the first century?

2. Read Revelation 21-22 and make some observations that help you make sense of Revelation 3:12. How would this enable the suffering believer to continue to endure with joy?

3. Is heaven a place in the sky, or something that will come down to us? How does this change the way we should view things of the earth?

APPLICATION: What does it look like to live as a citizen of heaven today (cf. Phil. 3:20)?

MEDITATION: As you read Revelation 3:14-18 prayerfully embrace what God has written.

1. What was written in Revelation chapter one about who Jesus is and what He accomplished that John again has in mind in Revelation 3:14?

2. Of all the rebukes to the seven churches, the one Jesus levels in Revelation 3:15-17 could be the most severe. Why is the root problem in view so critical to understand?

APPLICATION: Are you lukewarm? If so, repent and return to the Lord now. Write out a verse to memorize on page 305.

MEDITATION: Remember as you open to Revelation 3:19-22 you are meeting with the God who knows you. Ask Him for ears to hear what He is saying.

1. What is Jesus' remedy to the lukewarm Laodiceans? Read Isaiah 55:1-2 and list the purchase price of the remedy Jesus offers.

2. Imagine a meal with the glorified Jesus (3:20). Read Revelation 19:6-9 for a jumpstart to your imagination and write a few things you want to converse about with Jesus at His feast.

3. Each of these letters ends with a call to "*let him hear what the Spirit says to the churches.*" Why does Jesus methodically repeat this admonition?

APPLICATION: According to Revelation 2-3 what are some marks of a local church's health?

WEEK 5
COMMENTARY

REVELATION 3:1-22
Jesus Walks Among His Church: Part II

JESUS WALKS AMONG HIS CHURCH: PART II

REVELATION 3:1-6

Imagine with me you are on vacation and visiting a church you have heard great things about. The worship music sounds vibrant, the preacher is dynamic, and the people seem absolutely welcoming. As you are watching this particular body of Christ functioning, you think to yourself, "This church seems so alive!" Imagine, then, that Jesus walks in the church, grabs the microphone (although I don't foresee the need for it), and declares that despite this church looking alive, they are in fact dead. What would you think? How would you process something that appears one way, yet the Word exposes it to be something else? That is the situation with the church in Sardis. Jesus introduces Himself with the picture from Revelation 1:16 and 20 as the One full of the Spirit of God and holding all His churches in His hands. And His first assessment of Sardis is, **"I know your works. You have the reputation of being alive, but you are dead"** (Rev. 3:1b).

Here, Jesus is picking up on a particular historical battle that happened in Sardis as an illustration. Most commentators tell of the story of a king named Croesus who went to war against Cyrus the Great, resulting in the utter destruction of Sardis' army. Years later, visitors entering the town would notice a vista of beautiful rolling hills, appearing to be full of life. They would quickly learn that just feet under the exterior of those hills were burial grounds full of bodies that were slain at the hands of Cyrus the Great. What looked to be alive was indeed dead. This is a reminder of Jesus' warning in John 7:24 when He warned, *"Do not judge by appearances, but judge with right judgment."* This can be so difficult for a lot of us in any form of ministry because we can be tempted to assess the church according to what our eyes see. We ought to give thanks to God for the visible evidences of grace but also be aware that God is often doing an array of works we are not aware of. It might be the stay-at-home mom who labors in faithfulness to be a helper to her husband and lovingly training her kids to know and love Jesus. It might be the member in the body that is faithfully working retail for minimum wage but lovingly sharing Jesus with his co-workers. The dangerous side of this is what Jesus is confronting in Rev. 3:1. We might be doing ministry that is visibly alluring but the heart of people(s) leading that ministry has stopped beating and is a whitewashed tomb.

As we have witnessed in past letters, Christ graciously provides a path back to life. Those who have eyes to see and ears to hear will be struck with Christ's arrows and fall at His feet for true life. This is Jesus' call to repentance (Rev. 1:3). The picture Christ provides is waking up. He says in Revelation 3:2 and 3:3 to **"Wake up!"** Richard Phillips, quoting James Montgomery Boice, writes,

"Revival begins with a few individuals who wake up to the condition of those around them and begin to be concerned for them."[71] The revival necessary in Sardis, and for ourselves today, is not out of the reach of our life-giving God. One might even remember God's faithfulness to breathe life into a bunch of dry bones in Ezekiel 37. Another might recall Jesus' mighty call for Lazarus to wake up from his slumbering death, granting Him life. The great news for Sardis is that if they will humble themselves before God, they will turn to Christ, who is life (John 17:3).

Boice emphasized that a few are awakened in revival, so we find that there is a remnant of believers in Sardis that are not dead but alive. Jesus defines them by saying in verses 4 and 5, **"Yet you have still a few names in Sardis, people who have not soiled their garments, and they will walk with me in white, for they are worthy. The one who conquers will be clothed thus in white garments, and I will never blot his name out of the book of life."** Jesus is pointing out that there are, in fact, some that have not polluted their souls with the filth of the world. This is a foreshadowing of the white garments worn on the Day when Christ's bride will be glorified and made pure in His sight at the wedding supper of the Lamb (Revelation 19:7-8). Dennis Johnson illustrates this by saying, *"This link between purity in the present and white robes in the future shows that the life motivated by hope is shaped by the goal for which we wait. Because victors hope for white wedding garments, they strive for purity here and now."*[72] As 1 John 3:2-3 so clearly agrees: *"We know that when He appears, we will be like Him, because we will see Him just as He is. And everyone who has this hope fixed on Him purifies Himself, just as He is pure."*

Those who repent not only receive cleansing (1 John 1:9) but they also have their names written in the book of life. What a great promise to a people who only have the reputation for being alive. To know that Christ, the Light of Life, would so open the books of life and show them their name! The paradoxical reality of this book of life is that if they repent, they realize their names were written in that book before the foundation of the world (Luke 10:20; Phil. 4:3; Heb. 12:23; Rev. 13:8; 17:8; 20:12; 21:27). As Beale writes, *"If they are genuine believers, then their names, indeed, have already been written down in 'the book of life,' they are destined for a salvific inheritance, and nothing will prevent them from possessing it. In somewhat unusual fashion the positive guarantee of this inheritance is expressed negatively: 'I will not erase his name.'"*[73] On that great Day, Christ will look at you robed in His pure and perfect righteousness, put His arm around you as He looks at our Father in heaven and joyfully confesses your name as one written in the book of life (Rev. 3:5). Are you willing to forsake judging God's work by outward appearances and submit to Christ's "ordinary means of grace" in the preaching of the Word, the Lord's Supper, the prayers, and fellowship with His people? Do not be afraid to commit to the daily and weekly habits of the Christian faith that are far more transformative than the one-time "successes" we often judge things by. Give yourself to the clear God-given habits of loving God and your neighbor and you will find life. Give yourself to Christ the King! As James K.A. Smith spurs us on, *"Every human creature is designed to find his or her telos in the Creator Himself, in the King who has met us in Jesus."*[74]

---

[71] Phillips, *Revelation*, 136.
[72] Johnson, *Triumph of the Lamb*, 84.
[73] Beale, *Revelation*, 280.
[74] James K.A. Smith, *You Are What You Love*, 19.

REVELATION 3:7-13

Throughout the book of Revelation, Jesus' words are likened to the Mount Sinai imagery of roaring waters and peals of thunder. The Word of God is powerful and always accomplishes its intended purpose (cf. Isaiah 55:11). The introduction to the church in Philadelphia highlights this reality. Instead of using a piece of the Christological panorama of Revelation one, this passage instead draws on an Old Testament allusion from Isaiah 22.

In Isaiah 22:20-25 God calls Eliakim to be His mouthpiece. There, God clothes Himself with a robe, overlaid with a sash (Isa. 22:21). This is obviously similar to Jesus having a robe and golden sash in Revelation 1:13. What is key though is that God gives Eliakim *the key of the house of David. He shall open, and none shall shut; and He shall shut, and none shall open*" (Isa. 22:22). This "key" is likened to the ruling power of the Word of God, which is later picked up by Christ when explaining His future authority, which He will grant to His disciples and future church elders (Matthew 16:18-19). The church is meant to be a people ruled by the authoritative word of God. So, why does Jesus open with this imagery to the church in Philadelphia? If you remember in Revelation 1:18, Jesus had the "keys to Death and Hades," revealing that salvation belongs to Him, and Him alone. Beale expands, *"John compares the historical situation of Eliakim in relation to Israel with that of Christ to the church in order to help the readers understand the position that Christ now holds as head of the true Israel and how this affects them."*[75] In short, the church in Philadelphia can entrust themselves to the glorified Christ, knowing He will not waste their suffering nor abuse His authority.

Too rarely do we rejoice as we should in the commendation Jesus gives the church at Philadelphia. If the last church had a reputation for being alive but was dead, this church is commended for looking seemingly weak but really walking in the power of God. As Revelation 3:8b says, **"I know that you have but little power, and yet you have kept my word and have not denied my name."** Imagine again that Jesus were to come to you personally to say, "You look kind of weak!" Would this be an encouragement to you that results in you saying, "Yes! I sure am but I find strength in your power"? Or would you be a bit offended and recount your accomplishments? Do you remember anyone else in Scripture who learned the lesson of strength in weakness? In 2 Corinthians 12:7-8, the great Apostle Paul is given a thorn in his flesh, a messenger from Satan to harass him. In the text, we learn this was a special gift, perfectly tailored, hand-wrapped, and delivered by God Himself to keep Paul humble. As a result, Paul learned the way of his Master through suffering in 2 Corinthians 12:9. Christ sweetly said to Paul, and now to us, *"My grace is sufficient for you, for my power is made perfect in weakness,"* Paul humbly concluded, *"Therefore I will boast all the more gladly of my weaknesses, so that the power of Christ may rest upon me."*

The church in Philadelphia was more than likely a small church, especially through the eyes of a typical citizen in the Roman Empire. Yet, as many of us know, weakness is often the springboard to God's mighty works in the world. Despite their weakness, the church in Philadelphia had something that was of great power: Jesus said, **"you have kept my word and have not denied my name" (3:8b).** While this church might have written itself off as small, weak, and ineffective, they could have hosted a helpful conference for the other seven churches. Christ may call us to the glitz and glamor of "successful" ministry, but what He desires most is our love for Him that leads to us keeping His Word, and not denying His name.

---

[75] Beale, *Revelation,* 284.

In 2016, I had endured a season unlike any other in my life. The Lord sent an 8-month long depression without reprieve. A host of people I had discipled, officiated marriage ceremonies for, and loved left the church, dragging others with them. I entertained leaving the ministry several times to escape the pain, darkness, and criticism. Yet, the one thing that was steadfast and kept me trusting in Jesus was *His Word*. Many of you reading this can find fellowship with me in your own sufferings as you may recall the Rock on which you stand is the only solid thing around you. Rejoice with me; you may be of little power, but King Jesus holds you. Let us not deny His name.

When we continue on to verse 9, we get a glimpse into the people and situation that were making them feel small, weak, and powerless. Revelation 3:9 says, **"Behold, I will make those of the synagogue of Satan who say that they are Jews and are not, but lie—behold, I will make them come and bow down before your feet, and they will learn that I have loved you."** This synagogue of Satan was similar to the Pharisees who crucified Christ, and the Jews who were preaching "another Gospel" in Galatians. But God loves to turn the tables on those that believe they are strong. These same Jews will one day bow at the feet of all who are co-heirs with Christ (Rev. 3:9). Our weakness is not meant to signal defeat, but rather, to make us call on the Almighty One. Douglas Kelly comments that we ourselves, as those fighting to keep Christ's word and not blemish His name, are not in too different of a situation than the church in Philadelphia. He writes that contemporary Christians *"contemplate the aggressive secularism of modern America and Western Europe, with systematic unbelief in high places, such as the universities and the media. Add to that the entrenched Modernism of the educational system, and the precipitous moral decline in once-Christian populations. It is true that over and against them our strength is small. But Jesus says we are not to anxiously to worry about it. 'You have little strength; use what little you have, and I am going to supernaturally multiply it by opening the right doors.'"*[76] If we look around us and conclude that God's faithfulness is synonymous with our circumstances, we have no other choice but to conclude that God is not for us. However, when we remember that the resurrected, ascended, and glorified Christ says He loves us, we ought to press on and never grow weary of hearing:

"To Him who loves us and has freed us from our sins by His blood." - Revelation 1:5

"and they will learn that I have loved you." - Revelation 3:9

Now we come to a dividing subject among some Christians. Revelation 3:10 says, **"Because you have kept my word about patient endurance, I will keep you from the hour of trial that is coming on the world, to try those who dwell on the earth."** There are some faithful and loving Christians who take this verse to mean there is a secret rapture of sorts where Christ will remove His people from suffering tribulation. As I said in the introduction of this study, my main flow of this whole work is to help those intimidated by or unfamiliar with Revelation to better worship the victorious King, even in suffering. For now, I will convey two things that will show my eschatological (end times) position. First, due to the use of "tribulation" in the book of Revelation (especially in 1:9), I find it very difficult to argue that the tribulation is a literal seven-year period of suffering for those that have previously denied Jesus Christ. It seems to me to better be designated as the entire period between the crucifixion of Christ and His Second Coming. Second, throughout all the Scriptures, God tends to use suffering to conform His people to the image of His Son, rather than removing them from suffering. In fact, Romans 8:17 argues that if we do not suffer we are not children of God. I

---

[76] Douglas F. Kelly, *Revelation*, 74.

believe the Scriptures clearly teach that the next event on the redemptive timeline is the Second Coming of Jesus where He will simultaneously save His people and judge those not found in Him. If one does a study of all the times "trumpets" are found in the Bible, it is inescapable that they are most commonly used in reference to a victory of God where salvation and judgment are simultaneously administered. In my humble opinion on this touchy subject, I believe there is no secret rapture or literal seven-year tribulation. No, we are awaiting the last trumpet to sound which will initiate the Second Coming of our Lord. As seen in 2 Thessalonians 1:5-10, salvation and judgement are paired together with the Second Coming.

> *"This is evidence of the righteous judgment of God, that you may be considered worthy of the kingdom of God, for which you are also suffering— since indeed God considers it just to repay with affliction those who afflict you, and to grant relief to you who are afflicted as well as to us, when the Lord Jesus is revealed from heaven with His mighty angels in flaming fire, inflicting vengeance on those who do not know God and on those who do not obey the gospel of our Lord Jesus. They will suffer the punishment of eternal destruction, away from the presence of the Lord and from the glory of His might, when He comes on that day to be glorified in His saints, and to be marveled at among all who have believed, because our testimony to you was believed."*

Continuing to Revelation 3:11-13, Jesus makes a promise that He is "***coming soon.***" As a seemingly weak and suffering church, what greater motivation to stay faithful than the grand promise from Jesus Himself that He is coming soon? Where one might be skeptical about Jesus' words to come soon, seeing that more than two-thousand years have passed, Dennis Johnson reminds us, *"The promise here looks beyond his providential interventions throughout history, focusing instead on that final coming of which all others are precursors. Jesus' promise to the victor blends these present and future dimensions of his protective possessiveness."*[77] Jesus wants to comfort His suffering saints, not as much with a specific time of His return, but with the quality of His return. When He comes back, the weight of present suffering will seem as a fleeing feather in comparison to the weight of glory seen in Christ (cf. Rom. 8:18).

Revelation 3:12 is Jesus lovingly sharing what follows His Second Coming for those who overcome and stay faithful to the end. He promises: "***The one who conquers, I will make him a pillar in the temple of my God. Never shall He go out of it, and I will write on him the name of my God, and the name of the city of my God, the new Jerusalem, which comes out of heaven, and my own new name.***" To say it bluntly, suffering is terrible. Let us not pretend for a second that it is something we joyfully welcome. However, our suffering is not wasted by our Triune God, but is meant to drive us closer to Him. As C.S Lewis famously wrote, *"God whispers to us in our pleasures, speaks in our consciences, but shouts in our pains. It is his megaphone to rouse a deaf world."*[78] Even better than the reality that He does not waste our suffering is the promise to one day take it away for good. Revelation 4:12 is Jesus' promise that a day is coming where suffering will be gone. We will no longer be pilgrims in the world, but we will be sons and daughters who have finally made it home. Derek Thomas writes, *"By becoming pilgrims in this life, Jesus promises that we shall be pillars in the next. The promise concerns our becoming something immoveable and sturdy, part of the very fabric of the city of God."*[79] This city of God is none other than the new heaven and new earth described in Revelation 21-22. The significance of Jesus' comforting words to Philadelphia are better understood in the historical context of this first

---

[77] Johnson, *Triumph of the Lamb*, 89.
[78] C.S. Lewis, *The Problem of Pain* (New York, NY: HarperCollins, 2002), 91.
[79] Thomas, *Let's Study Revelation*, 36.

century city. As Richard Phillips so helpfully shows, Philadelphia was located on a dangerous fault line, causing marring to the city from earthquakes.[80] He expands on this by writing, "*Earthquakes had shattered the city, with aftershocks terrorizing the people for weeks and even years afterward, so that the city suffered from a lack of physical stability. But Jesus promises that his faithful followers will never lack for spiritual stability. The idea is that Christians who endure will be permanent fixtures and beautiful ornaments in the eternal temple, the church of Christ, in which God will dwell forever.*"[81]

Lastly, not only will all who overcome in Christ be found to be pillars in the city of God, they will have Christ's own name on them (3:12). We see this name made clear in Revelation 19:16, "*On His robe and on His thigh, He has a name written, King of kings and Lord of lords.*" The all-glorious ruler of the universe places His very own name upon His blood-bought children as an evidence and declaration that we belong to Him. He owns us, He protects us, and He has our eternal good set in stone and no earthly ruler or oppressor can usurp the rule and decree of the King of kings and Lord of lords. If you are reading this and your life seems to tell a different narrative, rejoice in the future grace of God (1 Peter 1:13). One day, dear pilgrim, you will be standing on the brilliant shores of Christ your King. The suffering of this present world will seem like a distant memory, yet, the scars in the hands of your Lord will remind you of how deep His own suffering was for you. Until that Day, take to heart the precious remedy Samuel Rutherford lays before us when he says, "*Your heart is not the compass Christ saileth by.*"[82] Believe the Promise-keeper who will bring you safely to His shore.

REVELATION 3:14-22

The modern church lives in an age of brilliant minds and technology beyond what many of us ever thought we would experience. We can unlock our phones with our fingerprint, play music while our phones track our speed and mileage as we run, all while keeping our budget in order on another app. Our cars can self-park, get us to any destination we desire by GPS, while we sit comfortably in our heated seats. Our culture has more possibilities at its fingertips than ever before, but are our churches better because of this? We have online giving systems, the most progressive and entertaining worship bands, and you cannot go without the city's hippest coffee in the lobby. This may look "better" to the untrained eye, but if Jesus were to walk among the churches today, would this rouse His delight or incite His gag reflex? Prior to his death John Stott said, "*Perhaps none of the seven letters is more appropriate to the church at the beginning of the twenty-first century than this. It describes vividly the respectable, nominal, rather sentimental, skin-deep religiosity which is so widespread among us today.*"[83] Stott compares our churches today to be most like the church in Laodicea in Revelation 3:14-22 because they, like us, were a wealthy city full of bankers, financiers, and millionaires. Phillips notes that Laodicea was destroyed by a massive earthquake in 61 A.D., "*but was so wealthy that it declined government help for its rebuilding.*"[84] Where Philadelphia was left in ruins by a natural disaster, Laodicea pulled itself up by the bootstraps and got to work.

But Laodicea also had a major problem running through its city: A lack of good water. This resulted in the city having to outsource their water from over five miles away. When the water would

---

[80] Phillips, *Revelation*, 149.
[81] Ibid., 149.
[82] Samuel Rutherford, *Letters* (Carlisle, PA: The Banner of Truth Trust, 2012), 87.
[83] John R. W. Stott, *What Christ Thinks of the Church: An Exposition of Revelation 1-3* (Grand Rapids, MI: Baker Books, 2003), 113.
[84] Phillips, 153.

arrive to Laodicea, it was typically *"tepid and brackish."*[85] This historical backdrop helps set the scene for Jesus' rebuke to the Laodiceans when He cuts deeply by saying, "***I know your works: you are neither cold nor hot! So, because you are lukewarm, and neither hot nor cold, I will spit you out of my mouth***" (Rev. 3:15-16). The imagery is meant to be a very clear picture to the Laodiceans that they make Jesus sick and their works are not satisfying to Him. Imagine being in this congregation and after hearing letters of other churches suffering, you sit there in your comfy prosperity only to find out you make Jesus sick. This ought to jumpstart the cold heart and move people to zeal and love. What about you? Have the glories of Christ become common verbiage to you that no longer stir your affections? Have you defined yourself by your material blessings rather than your union with Christ? Have you forgotten where your true wealth lies, provoking Jesus to become sick? The reality is, there are many in the church today who look to their material blessings, entertainment, and relationships as the assurance that Jesus loves them. This is dangerous ground to walk on. Instead, we should look to God's love for us.

Now, let's return to Revelation 3:14 to see what image of the glorified Christ from Revelation 1 introduces this letter so that we may find a glimmer of hope amongst this lukewarm church. John writes, "***The words of the Amen, the faithful and true witness, the beginning of God's creation.***" If you remember from Revelation 1:5a, we saw Jesus as the Prophet, Priest, and King who is the faithful witness to the world and the firstborn from the dead. Jesus reveals Himself to the Laodiceans as the True Word of God and resurrected King that walks among them. He reveals Himself this way because the Laodiceans have compromised and have not been faithful witnesses themselves, appearing dead and unsatisfying to the onlooking culture. Beale, in summarizing the whole letter, hits the nail on the head; "*The theme of this letter then is that the readers need to be renewed as new creatures in their relationship with Christ by testifying to this relationship in an uncompromising manner. And the creative power of the resurrected Jesus can raise them from their spiritual torpor, strengthen them in faith so that they will repent, and confirm them in their enduring fellowship with him.*"[86] The resurrection of Christ is the power of God that can resuscitate dead hearts who have fallen victim to defining their faith by material blessings. As Paul assures the Corinthians in 1 Corinthians 15:22, "*For as in Adam all die, so also in Christ shall all be made alive.*" As Christ walks in His resurrection power among the church in Laodicea, He does so as the Resurrected King of Glory who outshines all the glitz and glamor in this lukewarm church and city.

Jesus' additional rebuke in verse 17 makes clear how deep the sickness had gone in the hearts of the Laodiceans. Their lukewarmness revealed they believed one thing about themselves although the opposite was true. Jesus confronted them in Revelation 3:17 by saying, "***For you say, I am rich, I have prospered, and I need nothing, not realizing that you are wretched, pitiable, poor, blind, and naked.***" This is a horrifying visual, reminding many readers of Jesus' declaration of the Pharisees being whitewashed tombs. I picture a model church member from Laodicea walking through their house, getting dressed. She imagined herself all cute and fancy. But, after stepping in front of the mirror, she was confronted with a real picture of herself as a filthy creature, almost impossible to look at. The spiritual reality of our world is that we are not what we look like. If we try to make our material blessings define us while our *hearts* are wicked and sick (Jeremiah 17:9), then we need the Light of the world to shine His light upon us and revive our dead hearts. Let me ask you a question: Do you tend to share the gospel primarily with those that seem more likely to believe it? I am thinking

---

[85] Ibid., 153.
[86] Beale, 302.

about those that seem put together, intelligent, and well off. Jesus warned His disciples to not do such a thing when He said, *"Do not judge by appearances, but judge with right judgment."* The right judgment we need is that all are dead in their trespasses and sins apart from the grace of God (Ephesians 2:1-9). This was the problem with Laodicea; they had become so lukewarm that their evangelism would have been completely ineffective. Beale agrees when describing their lukewarm works by saying, *"The particular 'work' which is viewed as ineffective is that of their efforts to witness. The unbelievers of the city were receiving neither spiritual healing nor life because the church was not actively fulfilling its role of witnessing to the gospel of Christ. Two reasons suggest that the issue of witness was the specific concern: 1) this is the issue for which all the other churches are either applauded or condemned, and it would be unusual that the Laodicean situation would be different from the others. 2) Christ introduces Himself as the 'faithful and true witness,' suited to the particular situation of the church."*[87] This ought to make us examine ourselves and see if our Gospel belief is really leading to Gospel witness. Have we seen the Gospel as something to believe "just in case there is a hell," or is it the alluring good news that joyfully causes us to be witnesses to the One who has loved us and freed us from our sins (Rev. 1:5)?

As with the previous six letters, Jesus offers a remedy. He lays a beautiful feast before the Laodiceans if they will repent of their lukewarm faith when He says in 3:18, **"I counsel you to buy from me gold refined by fire, so that you may be rich, and white garments so that you may clothe yourself and the shame of your nakedness may not be seen, and salve to anoint your eyes so that you may see."** What we have here is Christ's remedy as the Great Physician to help the poor, blind, and naked become rich, able to see, and clothed. John is bringing an array of Old Testament allusions into view and laying them on the table for the Laodiceans to feast upon. In regard to Jesus' words to **"buy from me gold refined by fire, so that you may be rich,"** He has in mind the biblical theme of purifying people through His grace (Zech. 13:9; Mal. 3:2-3; 1 Pet. 1:6-9). When Jesus commands them to buy **"white garments,"** might be an allusion to Zechariah 3:1-10 where the high priest, Joshua, is clothed by Christ's righteousness, but the connection to white garments in Sardis (3:4-5), probably is being repeated here as a call for the Laodiceans to be alive and faithful in Christ. Lastly, the counsel to **"salve and anoint your eyes, so that you may see"** was more than likely a reference to the medicinal eye salves that Laodicea were known for.[88] If they would see these eye salves as representative of their spiritual sight, they might see the glory of God again and become alive. We must not be quick to think that we are exempt from becoming blinded. In one of the most beautiful prayers in all of the Bible, Paul prays for *believers* (I say again, for *believers* in Ephesus) that the eyes of their hearts would be enlightened to the realities of Christ and the gospel. None of us are "grace graduates"[89] but are daily in need of God to be with us. Although the Old Testament allusion doesn't seem direct here, the language and concept still apply. Look at this beautiful call from Isaiah 55:1-2:

> *Come, everyone who thirsts,*
> *come to the waters;*
> *and He who has no money,*
> *come, buy and eat!*
> *Come, buy wine and milk*
> *without money and without price.*

---

[87] Beale, 303-304.
[88] Phillips, 158.
[89] Paul David Tripp, https://www.paultripp.com/articles/posts/ministers-of-grace-in-need-of-grace

Why do you spend your money for that which is not bread,
and your labor for that which does not satisfy?
Listen diligently to me, and eat what is good,
and delight yourselves in rich food.

Maybe you are in a season of coldness toward God. Maybe your affections for Christ are slim to none. Christian, come and be satisfied by your Savior. He offers you to buy from Him that which has no price but also eternally satisfies. He is not shaking His head at you in disappointment, but rather, He is moved with mercy to relieve you of your sin. However great your coldness or need feels, listen to the words of Thomas Goodwin on the coat-tail of Isaiah 55:1-2: *"As the measure of any man's need and distress is from sin and misery, accordingly is he affected towards him. And as we have sins of several sizes, accordingly hath he mercies, and puts forth a mediation proportionable; whether they be ignorances, or sins of daily incursion, or else sins more gross and presumptuous. And therefore, let neither of them discourage any from coming unto Christ for grace and mercy."*[90] So come into His presence and receive the mercy and grace you so need.

Jesus belabors this point so that the cold-hearted saint may not be mistaken about the way back into communion with Him. It is not by works, although works will be an evidence of grace. The way back into communion with God is exactly that: communion with God. Jesus calls the lukewarm into His warm and loving presence by inviting them with these words: **"Behold, I stand at the door and knock. If anyone hears my voice and opens the door, I will come in and eat with him, and He with me."** This is not an evangelistic call to unbelievers, but a call from Christ the Lord to His church that has turned their back on Him. Notice the tender display of love. Although they have made Him sick with their lukewarm faith, He wants to be among His people feasting with them in fellowship. What God is this that would not only die for His people, but also after they act coldly towards Him, long to have a meal with them? This is probably an allusion to Luke 12:37 describing how the Master's servants will sprint to the door when He comes knocking and the Master will serve His bride, as if He hasn't served us enough already. This meal is for sinners whom have let Christ into their cold hearts, so they may dine with Him forever. As Hendriksen notes, *"Christ and the believer dine together, which in the East was an indication of special friendship and of covenant relationship."*[91] This meal is enjoyed during the Lord's Supper where we take the body and blood of Christ by faith, but a Day is coming when we will pull up physical chairs, feast on physical food, and be served by Christ by sight (Rev. 19:6-10).

The seven letters conclude with a call to conquer by the victory of the Lamb. Jesus says in 3:21-22, **"The one who conquers, I will grant him to sit with me on my throne, as I also conquered and sat down with my Father on His throne. He who has an ear, let him hear what the Spirit says to the churches."** What great news it is that Jesus so lavishes His people with what He alone deserves. His life, death, and resurrection catapulted Him to His rightful place upon the throne of God (cf. Psa. 110:1). In Him, we are His co-heirs and will reign on the throne. We must finish the race set before us but also do so knowing that our Triune God will finish the work He has begun (Phil. 1:6) before the foundation of the world. Leon Morris says in regard to our overcoming, *"Christ overcame by the way of the cross and this sets the pattern for His followers. They face grim days. But let them never forget that what seemed Christ's defeat was in fact His victory over the world. They need not fear if they are called*

---

[90] Thomas Goodwin, *The Heart of Christ in Heaven Towards Sinners on Earth* (Carlisle, PA: The Banner of Truth Trust, Year not printed), 101.

[91] William Hendriksen, *More Than Conquerors*, 79.

upon to suffer, for in that way they too will conquer."[92] The necessity for us to have ears that are in tune to the voice of the Holy Spirit cannot be overstated. Every letter in Revelation chapters two and three has this command. The first four place it first, while the final 3 place this phrase last. The Spirit of God has come to apply all the benefits of Christ to His people and has made them the temple of the living God (cf. 1 Cor. 6:19-20). Our ears are not our own, and the most glorifying thing we can do with them is hear the Word of God to receive His instructions to overcome to the glory of the King. He who has an ear, let him hear…

---

[92] Leon Morris, *Tyndale New Testament Commentaries: The Revelation of St. John* (Grand Rapids, MI: Eerdmans, 1969), 81.

WEEK 6
STUDY

REVELATION 4:1-7:17
*The Supremacy of Christ
and the Sealed Scroll*

MEDITATION: Worship Jesus along with the four living creatures and twenty-four elders as you read Revelation 4:1-8.

1. What similarities do you see between Revelation 1:10 and 4:1-2? What is happening to John? Whose voice is John hearing? Whose presence is he in?

2. As John is "in the Spirit," what does he see in front of him (Read Revelation 4:2-4)? Knowing this vision of the throne comes from God's perspective, how does it correct/inform your earthly ideas of the throne of God?

3. Read Revelation 4:5-8 and list some of the imagery, scenery, weather, etc. Imagine standing before this throne and having all your senses heightened. What would your response be? Why? (See also Ezekiel 1:5-14; 10:20; Isaiah 6:2-3)

4. What similarities does this vision have with the one recorded in Ezekiel 1:26-2:1? Though the vision is very graphic, look at the last line in Ezek. 1:28, then write out the climax of this passage.

APPLICATION: Is God's Word the high point of your day? Your life? How is it preparing you for the Day you will be before God, no longer by faith but by sight? Write out a verse to memorize on page 305.

MEDITATION: Read and re-read Revelation 4:8-11 asking the Lord to help you offer Him the worship He deserves.

1. As we are given access to the scene of worship in the throne room of God in verse eight, where is the focal point (Read Revelation 1:8 for help)? Think of all the people through all of human history, and this passage reveals only One receiving worship.[93] What does this say of His worth?

2. List the order of events that happen in Revelation 4:9-10. Does each creature in this vision serve the others in directing them to glorify God?

3. Who are the twenty-four elders in Revelation 4:10-11 and what do they do at the sight of Christ?

4. Compare Genesis 1:1; Ephesians 1:11; Colossians 1:15-17, noting your observations below.

APPLICATION: Since Christ is the Creator of all things, what is one way you can better glorify and serve Him as His creature today?

---

[93] Christ is the exalted Mediator we worship. As will be seen in the commentary, the Father (4:5), the Son (4:8b), and the Spirit (4:5b) are all in sight here. As Christians, we do worship the Triune God, but Christ is the one sent by the Father and glorified by the Spirit. The author notes this to make sure you see the worth of all three persons of the Trinity, but also to recognize that Christ is the God-man we see exalted throughout the Scriptures.

MEDITATION: In Revelation 5:1-14 you are treading upon worship-filled and worship-inducing descriptions of Jesus. Ask God to help you see the worth of Christ, and worship Him!

1. List all the parties present in Revelation 5:1-4. As the Father has the scroll, and an angel declares no one is worthy to open the scroll, what is John's response? Why does he react this way?

2. Only Christ our Mediator can open the scroll. What two ways is He depicted in Revelation 5:5-6? Why is Jesus described as "the Lion of the tribe of Judah" (cf. Genesis 49:9)? Why is He described as a "Lamb standing, as though it had been slain" (cf. Ex. 12:5; Matt. 28:5-6)?

3. When the Lamb takes the scroll from the Father, does it remind you of a previous vision (cf. Daniel 7:9-14)? The Kingdom Christ receives is multicultural, full of the beauty of diversity. Read the new song in Revelation 5:9-10 and list how vast the kingdom of heaven will be in ethnicities and cultures.

4. As the Lamb is praised for His worth again in Revelation 5:11-14, write all of the words attributed to the Lion and the Lamb who alone can open the scroll. What does this vision teach us about the connection between Christ's worth and our worship/singing?[94]

APPLICATION: What are some ways you can grow in learning and loving those that are different than you in the kingdom of God?

---

[94] Listen to Andrew Peterson's song on Revelation called, *"Is He Worthy"* https://www.thegospelcoalition.org/article/andrew-peterson-resurrection-letters/

MEDITATION: As you study Revelation 5:1-17 ask God to break open His Word to you.

1. The book of Revelation is a reminder of God's reign to a suffering people. The book of Zechariah had a similar message, as God's people had just returned from exile but did not feel at home. Read Zechariah 6:1-8 and Revelation 6:1-8 together and note the comparisons. What is John trying to communicate?

2. The fifth seal (Revelation 6:9-11) zooms in on the martyrs of the early church. Why were they killed and what is their cry to the Lord? How does the Lord Jesus respond to these faithful saints who gave their lives for Him?

3. As Jesus opens the sixth seal (Revelation 6:12-17), what is unleashed upon the world? What do you make of all the imagery of the moon becoming like blood, stars falling from the earth, the sky being rolled up like a scroll, etc.? Is this imagery literal, symbolic, etc.? Why? See Matthew 24 for more context.

APPLICATION: What are some areas you have compromised in keeping the Word of God this week? Spend some time in repentance and cry out to God for help in further faithfulness.

MEDITATION: Worship the living God of Revelation 7:1-17 today as you listen to Him by glorying in Him.

1. Read Daniel 7:2 and Revelation 7:1 and explain the main difference between the two. With this difference in mind, why is God waiting to unleash His wrath on creation according to Revelation 7:2-3?

2. After reading Revelation 7:4-8, does the 12,000 from each tribe totaling 144,000 seem literal or symbolic of a complete number? Read 7:9 for commentary on 7:4-8. Also, why do you think the tribe of Judah is placed at the top of the list (Hint: Rev. 5:5)? List some people from the tribe of Judah from the Old Testament through whom God kept the Messianic line going despite their sin.

3. Salvation belongs to God (Rev. 7:10). This salvation results in purity and cleanliness from our sins. How do the white robes of the saints in heaven become clean (7:9, 14)? How does the redeemed collective of God's people respond to salvation in heaven (7:11-12)?

4. Read Revelation 7:15-17 and describe the state of the soul of a person who has been redeemed by Christ. John strings together a host of Old Testament allusions, primarily on the Feast of Booths. Read a few and list the significance (cf. Leviticus 23:33-43; Isa. 4:5-6; 49:10; John 7).

APPLICATION: Do you still rejoice that Christ alone has made you clean and acceptable to God? Or do you see that as a past tense work and now the rest is up to you?

WEEK 6
COMMENTARY

REVELATION 4:1-7:17
*The Supremacy of Christ
and the Sealed Scroll*

THE SUPREMACY OF CHRIST AND THE SEALED SCROLL

REVELATION 4:1-8

As we transition to the second angle of the time between Christ's crucifixion and second coming, we will see that the pictures John uses become more and more apocalyptic. In the same way Revelation chapter one used imagery to exalt Christ as King, chapters four and five are a transition into apocalyptic visions for the remainder of Revelation. Where chapters two and three were primarily about Christ walking among His bride on earth, chapters four and five draw us up into the heavenly throne room of God.

Let the reader be reminded that chapters four through seven are to function as *one vision*. Or as Peter Leithart notes, *"This vision is organized as a worship service, a liturgy of word and sacrament. It begins with a summons to enter the throne room (4:1-2). John witnesses an ongoing service of praise."*[95] John, being in the Spirit (*en pneumati*), walks through a door into the throne room of God. Can you imagine? The absolute fear of His holiness, yet a bold confidence that comes from the forgiveness and imputed righteousness of Christ. As John is ushered into the throne room, he not only hears God's thunderous voice (4:1), but sees with his own eyes, **"one seated on the throne."** Whose voice is this that has called John up to the heavenly throne room? When taking the Christ-vision of chapter one into account, it seems to be the voice of Christ. Vern Poythress[96] provides the following chart showing a few of the comparisons:

---

[95] Peter J. Leithart, *International Theological Commentary: Revelation 1-11* (New York, NY: T&T Clark, 2018), 209. I do disagree with Leithart's structure of the book of Revelation, but do agree that there appears to be glimpses into a heavenly worship service throughout the book.

[96] Vern S. Poythress, *Theophany: A Biblical Theology of God's Appearing* (Wheaton, IL: Crossway, 2018), 139. Not only does this show the connections between chapter 1 and chapters 4-5, but strengthens the view that the structure of Revelation is seven angles of the same time period.

FEATURES IN 1:12-16	FEATURES IN 4:1-5:14
in the Spirit (1:10)	*in the Spirit (4:2)*
flame of fire (1:14)	*torches of fire (4:5)*
powerful eyes (1:14)	*powerful eyes (5:6)*
loud noise (1:10, 15)	*loud noise (4:5; 5:2, 12)*
centrality of Christ (1:13)	*centrality of Christ (5:5-6)*

As we notice the details of the throne itself, we are set before a heavenly creation of beauty. Some of us are aware of the specific birthstone attached to our birth-month. These birthstones are beautiful, glimmering stones that attach beauty and significance to our birth. How much more ought the eternal Creator and Redeemer of all things beautify His own eternal throne? As John approaches this holy ground, he sees that the one on the throne "**had the appearance of jasper and carnelian, and around the throne was a rainbow**" (4:3). John has been brought before the throne of God, the very throne previous prophets were ushered to. Ezekiel 1:26 says, "*And above the expanse over their heads there was the likeness of a throne, in appearance like sapphire; and seated above the likeness of a throne was a likeness with a human appearance.*" Also, Ezekiel 1:28 continues, "*Like the appearance of the bow that is in the cloud on the day of rain, so was the appearance of the brightness all around.*" According to G.K. Beale, John is bringing these stones from the throne in Ezekiel into his own vision to show that "*collectively they represent God's sovereign majesty and glory since they appear in OT theophany scenes in which divine glory is manifested and because they are directly linked to God's glory in Rev. 21:10-11, 18-23.*"[97] As John surveys the wondrous vision, he takes a breath and zooms out a bit to see the host of company surrounding the throne. Revelation 4:4-6 says:

> "**Around the throne were twenty-four thrones, and seated on the thrones were twenty-four elders, clothed in white garments, with golden crowns on their heads. From the throne came flashes of lightning, and rumblings and peals of thunder, and before the throne were burning seven torches of fire, which are the seven spirits of God, and before the throne there was as it were a sea of glass, like crystal. And around the throne, on each side of the throne, are four living creatures, full of eyes in front and behind.**"

The scene John witnesses in the Spirit is none other than a preview of what we too will one day see with our eyes. From the throne—showing that God is the source of all things—comes a devastating storm-type revelation. We might picture the throne surrounded by white clouds with nice harp music playing in the background, but this is a sight of holiness where the only proper response is reverence and awe (Heb. 12:28-29). In fact, the storm imagery is meant to take us back to Exodus 19 when the people of God are brought to the base of Mount Sinai and told not to even touch the

---

[97] Beale, *Revelation*, 320.

mountain unless they want to be struck down dead (cf. Ex. 19:12-13). A few verses later, we see what John has in mind when Moses writes, *"On the morning of the third day there were thunders and lightnings and a thick cloud on the mountain and a very loud trumpet blast, so that all the people in the camp trembled"* (Ex. 19:16). As John has been caught up into the glory-cloud of Christ, one must balance the reverence and awe but also remember that he, like us, have not come to Sinai but to Mount Zion (cf. Heb. 12:21-22). John, looking through the throne-storm, sees twenty-four thrones occupied by twenty-four elders. There is a diversity of opinion on whom these elders are, whether human or angelic, but all commentators agree that they are representative of the twelve tribes of Israel and the twelve disciples; a fullness of the history of redemption. William Hendriksen writes:

> *"These twenty-four elders are mentioned first for the simple reason that they are first in importance and in glory of all creatures in heaven (Gen. 1:26; Heb. 2:8). We must not lose sight of the fact that the real reason why these twenty-four thrones with their occupants are mentioned here is to enhance the glory of the throne that stands in the center? Whom do these elders worship? Only the Father? No, the triune God. The Father is seated upon the throne out of which issues flashes of lightning and rumblings and peals of thunder. John also sees seven lamps of fire. They symbolize the ever-active, superlatively wise, and all-seeing Holy Spirit. There is also a sea before the throne. It is glass, like crystal, indicating sanctifying power. We should think of it as containing, symbolically, the cleansing blood of Christ, the Son, in which the saints have 'washed their robes and made them white' (7:14),"*[98]

John is caught up in the midst of the Triune God in all His power, glory, and honor. The One who is due eternal praise and is soon to come.

Not only do the twenty-four elders around the throne reveal the centrality of worship, but the same is true with these four seemingly odd creatures that have eyes in the front and back of their head. John describes them and what he saw when in verses seven and eight. These might seem like an odd alien-like creature if we had no other information about them. But if we return to Ezekiel again, we are given some helpful images to give us a better understanding. Ezekiel 1:5-6 introduces us to *"the likeness of four living creatures. And this was their appearance: they had a human likeness."* Fast-forward to Ezekiel 10 and we see a lot more detail on these four creatures, specifically that they are cherubim (Ezek. 10:5-22).

With all this in mind, John is pressing the point that all humans and all angels ought to see the Triune God of the throne room of heaven as the only one worthy of all worship. Interestingly, Richard Phillips, quoting Iain Duguid, heightens the demand for worship when he describes the faces of these four creatures as representatives of the superlative creations of God. He says, *"Along with man (the highest earthly creature) is 'a lion (the highest wild animal), an ox (the highest domesticated animal), and an eagle (the highest bird)—symbolizing the fact that they embody themselves all of the highest attributes of living creation."*[99] What is more important to John though is what comes out of the mouths of the four creatures. **"Day and night they never cease to say, 'Holy, holy, holy, is the Lord God Almighty, who was and is and is to come'"** (Rev. 4:8b).

---

[98] Hendricksen, *More Than Conquerors,* 86.
[99] Phillips, *Revelation,* 171; quoting Iain Duguid, Ezekiel, 58-59.

Imagine with me you are a first-century suffering saint. Jerusalem and the temple have been destroyed, Christians are mistreated, imprisoned, and killed. As they look around them they see nothing but absolute destruction. Now, imagine you receive this letter from John and as it is read out loud to the congregation, you close your eyes and picture God seated on His throne and all worship is rightly directed toward Him. Representatives from the Old and New covenant are gladly on their faces. Cherubim angels are covering their eyes and crying gladly of God's holiness. As you hear the entire book of Revelation read aloud, you are assured that all evil will one day cease and you yourself will be present in the throne-room, not *only* by faith (as an OT saint), but by sight. The power of these heavenly visions is meant to spur on present faithfulness because of the goodness to come. Like the twenty-four elders and the four creatures, we will also declare the holiness of God forevermore. This song of holiness has some nuanced textual gems to it we might not notice unless we are familiar with the threefold "holy, holy, holy" elsewhere in Scripture. Yet, as Leithart notes, there is something spectacular here: *"The expressions of praise in the heavenly temple are triadically structured. The first praise is an intricate knot of intersecting structures. There is a simple chiasm:*

A. Triple 'holy'
B. Three titles: Lord, God, Pantokrator (Almighty)
A. Triple name: 'He who was, is, comes'

It is a triad of triads, a trinity of trinities, linked with the Triune name: The Father holy, the Son Lord, the Spirit the one who was, is, comes."[100] In short, we are being let in on how the world ought to be. The good news of the gospel declares that one day all who have been purchased by the blood of the Lamb will see our Triune God as the center of all activity in the new heaven and new earth. Everything will be made holy and our tongues will be transformed from the member of fire and poison (Jas. 3:8), to little amplifiers declaring the holiness and glory of our God.

REVELATION 4:8-11

Last week's section ended with Revelation 4:8 and the praise of the twenty-four elders and four creatures. Let us continue in verse 8 so we can rightly recognize the Christ as John intends, and give Him the three-fold holy, holy, holy our King deserves. When John describes the thundering, **"Holy, holy, holy, is the Lord God Almighty, who was and is and is to come,"** he expects our minds to be swiftly drawn back to Isaiah chapter 6. There, Isaiah is ushered, like John, into the heavenly throne room. As he sees the holiness of the Lord with his own eyes, he rightly falls as if dead. Like Revelation 4, the throne is surrounded with angels covering their eyes, saying to one another, *"Holy, holy, holy is the LORD of hosts; the whole earth is full of His glory"* (Isa. 6:3). Isaiah realized his depravity and uncleanliness before the Lord of Glory. The scene in Isaiah is meant to show us that sin is not just a generalization but a sickness that affects the whole person. Even this prophet of God must be cleansed before he is sent to speak on behalf of God. Leithart writes, *"Isaiah recognizes that he cannot even speak to Yahweh without defilement; he cannot join the seraphic song of praise. The organs of communication, confession, praise—his lips—are unclean, and every breath that passes through them pollutes the temple."*[101] In reality, if God left Isaiah here in this position of guilt and sin, He would be just. But the

[100] Leithart, *Revelation*, 245.
[101] Ibid., 243.

scandalous grace of God sends one of the cherubim to Isaiah and cleanses his "organs of communication." In an act of sheer grace, Isaiah is set apart to be the mouthpiece of God to a rebellious generation of people.

So, why is John using this allusion to Isaiah 6 in the book of Revelation? To best answer that question, let's take a detour on our way back to Revelation by stopping in the Gospel of John. In John 12, Jesus is comparing the unbelief of the people in His earthly ministry with the unbelief of Israel in Isaiah's day. With Isaiah 6 in mind, John gives a short yet rich commentary on Isaiah 6 when he says, "*Isaiah said these things because he saw His glory and spoke of Him*" (John 12:41). John is saying that the holy figure that the angels sang to in Isaiah 6 was none other than the Lord Jesus. The supremacy of Christ is not an action put into place at His resurrection, but one that spans back before the creation of the world and will continue for all eternity.

We see the supremacy of Christ and His worthiness to receive worship continuing in verses 9-10. Notice also the domino effect of worship here and the importance of community in worship. John writes,

> **"And whenever the living creatures give glory and honor and thanks to Him who is seated on the throne, who lives forever and ever, the twenty-four elders fall down before Him who is seated on the throne and worship Him who lives forever and ever. They cast their crowns before the throne."**

Track with me on this community effort of praise and worship. The living creatures give glory and honor and thanks, *then* the twenty-four elders fall down and worship, casting their crowns before the throne. Then, the same scenario repeats endlessly. What we have is the centrality of worship for Christ so heightened that every creature around His throne is reminded of their redeemed calling in the new heaven and new earth. Every living creature has become a full man or creature, gladly giving Himself to the eternal praise of God. Notice that they're not envying their position in the throne room, nor are they proud and arrogant of where they stand. Jonathan Edwards, imagining what daily life in the presence of God in a place where sin is a distant memory, says this:

> *"The saints shall know that God loves them, and they shall never doubt the greatness of His love, and they shall have no doubt of the love of all their fellow inhabitants in heaven. And they shall not be jealous of the constancy of each other's love. They shall have no suspicion that the love which others have felt toward them is abated, or in any degree withdrawn from themselves for the sake of some rival, or by reasons anything in themselves which they suspect is disagreeable to others, or through any inconstancy in their own hearts or the hearts of others…And they shall have no jealousy one of another, but shall know that by divine grace the mutual love that exists between them shall never decay nor change."*[102]

In short, Edwards is setting forth the future reality that we will not envy one another, nor will we be arrogant in Heaven. We will never wish we had more, nor be haughty about what we have. We will be loved perfectly and love perfectly. That is exactly what Revelation 4:9-10 is including inviting us into. For all eternity, when one person begins to worship the Triune God, all the saints will follow suit with a full heart and joyful singing.

---

[102] Jonathan Edwards, *Heaven* (Carlisle, PA. The Banner of Truth Trust, 2008), 47-48.

The last part of Revelation chapter four expands on the identity of Christ, as the worshipping myriads rejoice that He is the Creator and sustainer of all things. The redeemed creation sings out in Revelation 4:11, **"Worthy are you, our Lord and God, to receive glory and honor and power, for you created all things, and by your will they existed and were created."** In our western culture, Jesus is often viewed as the God of love in the New Testament, distinct from the Old Testament's God of wrath. This passage, places Christ as the central figure of both covenants worshipped as the Creator of all things. This mirrors the way Paul doxologically broke forth in praise in Colossians 1:16-17, "For by Him all things were created, in heaven and on earth, visible and invisible, whether thrones or dominions or rulers or authorities—all things were created through Him and for Him." Here, we are being reminded that Jesus, our great Savior, is also the Creator of the cosmos. Every atom, every strand of created material owes its existence to Jesus and is held together by Him. This truth should provoke humble fear and jubilant praise. Dennis Johnson expands on this by saying, "Recognition of the supreme worthiness of God evokes a stabbing, sweet sense of awe, to which our modern hearts may be numbed by self-reliance and cynicism. The praises around the throne move from contemplation of who God is in Himself, to His work of creation, and then to the apex of worthiness, the work of redemption accomplished by the Lamb."[103] In Revelation chapter four, God opens the door to His church, saying to us, "This is what I am like and this is what your future looks like. Behold! I am of supreme worth. Keep pressing on, beloved; one day this door will be unhinged, and you will roam freely in my presence forevermore. A little while longer!" The suffering saints who were tempted to be overwhelmed by their circumstances, would have received this text with great joy and thanksgiving. We too should pray in agreement with this beautiful puritan prayer:

"Thy throne of grace
is the pleasure ground of my soul.
Here I obtain mercy in time of need,
here sees the smile of thy reconciled face,
here joy pleads the name of Jesus,
here I sharpen the sword of the Spirit,
anoint the shield of faith,
put on the helmet of salvation,
gather manna from thy Word,
am strengthened for each conflict,
nerved for the upward race,
empowered to conquer every foe;
Help me to come to Christ
as the fountain head of descending blessings,
as a wide open flood-gate of mercy.
I marvel at my insensate folly, that
with such enriching favours within my reach
I am slow to extend the hand to take them.
Have mercy upon my deadness for thy Name's sake.
Quicken me, stir me, fill me with holy zeal.

Strengthen me that I may cling to thee
and not let thee go.
May thy Spirit within me draw all blessings
from thy hand.
When I advance not, I backslide.
Let me walk humbly because of good omitted
and evil done.
Impress on my mind the shortness of time,
the work to be engaged in,
the account to be rendered,
the nearness of eternity,
the fearful sin of despising thy Spirit.
May I never forget that
thy eye always sees,
thy ear always hears,
thy recording hand always writes.
May I never give thee rest until Christ is
the pulse of my heart;
the spokesman of my lips,
the lamp of my feet."[104]

---

[103] Johnson, *Triumph of the Lamb*, 103.
[104] Valley of Vision, *The Throne*, ed. Arthur Bennett (Carlisle, PA: The Banner of Truth Trust, 2013), 272-273.

REVELATION 5:1-14

In Revelation four, John was granted access into God's heavenly throne room. In chapter five, he continues explaining the same vision, zooming in on an object in the hand of God. Meanwhile, the Mediator stands between the people of God. In Revelation 5:1-4, we are spectators of a grand scene, filled with sorrow and helplessness. John writes,

> **"Then I saw in the right hand of Him who was seated on the throne a scroll written within and on the back, sealed with seven seals. And I saw a mighty angel proclaiming with a loud voice, "Who is worthy to open the scroll and break its seals?" And no one in heaven or on earth or under the earth was able to open the scroll or to look into it, and I began to weep loudly because no one was found worthy to open the scroll or to look into it."**

As John is ushered into the presence of God, rather than the resounding, "Holy, holy, holy" moving him to joy and delight, he sees a scroll with seven seals and hears an angel cry out that no one is worthy to open it. John's response is one of tumult and helplessness because, despite the glorious angelic figures and the twenty-four elders he sees, none of them are worthy to open the scroll. The identification of the scroll has several possible interpretations, but I lean toward the view Richard Phillips laid forth in his commentary. Phillips writes, *"The best understanding of the scroll in Revelation 5 is the entirety of God's will for history, both in judging the wicked and in redeeming his people. The scroll is written on both sides, showing that it contains the entire story of God's will."*[105] This scroll, covered with the record of God's redemptive will for humanity, also has an Old Testament allusion in mind. In Ezekiel chapters two and three, God called Ezekiel to prophetic ministry. God's call was accompanied with the command that Ezekiel would be a man bound only to speak what God told him to speak. Ezekiel 2:9-10 captures the scene similar to Revelation five: *"And when I looked, behold, a hand was stretched out to me, and behold, a scroll of a book was in it. And He spread it before me. And it had writing on the front and on the back, and there were written on it words of lamentation and mourning and woe."* Knowing the text of Ezekiel, John's mind is harkened back to the scroll full of words of lamentation and mourning and woe.

John's response, in a sense, is the response of all humanity in the presence of God without Christ. Jesus' beloved disciple was so caught up in the absence of anyone worthy to open the scroll that he forgot the worth of Christ. His immediate response is loud weeping (5:4). Like a thriller movie full of suspense and drama, John is torn with absolute helplessness for himself and humanity. He is moved to loud weeping beneath the prospect that all of history will coming to an end. Hendricksen helps us better understand the weight and severity of John's weeping when he says,

> *"You will understand the meaning of these tears if you constantly bear in mind that in this beautiful vision the opening of the scroll by breaking the seals indicates the execution of God's plan. When the scroll is opened, and the seals are broken, the universe is governed in the interest of the Church. Then, God's glorious, redemptive purpose is being realized; His plan is being carried out and the contents of the scroll come to pass in the history of the universe. But if the scroll is not opened it means that there*

---

[105] Phillips, *Revelation*, 188.

will be no protection for God's children in the hours of bitter trial; no judgments upon a persecuting world; no ultimate triumph for believers; no new heaven and new earth; no future inheritance."[106]

If this were the end of the story, it would be a total letdown for the beloved disciple who gave his life to glorifying his Lord and King, Jesus Christ. However, the vision doesn't end with bitter tears and loud weeping. In fact, he would later write of Christ lovingly wiping away all the tears of His people (Rev. 21:4). In a moment of bitter weeping and desperation, one of the twenty-four elders surrounding the throne says to John, **"Weep no more; behold, the Lion of the tribe of Judah, the Root of David, has conquered, so that He can open the scroll and its seven seals."** There are tied together here two Old Testament allusions that function as a remedy for loud weeping. The first is found in Genesis 49:9-10 when Jacob is blessing his sons and makes clear that the tribe of Judah will be the line that the conquering Messiah will come through (Gen. 3:15). This is the only time that Jesus is referred to as the Lion of Judah, but it's scarcity of citations does not limit the power of the imagery. Lions are fierce and rule their domain. The second Old Testament allusion is found in Isaiah 11:1 and 11:10, foretelling of one who will come from the line of David and rule righteously over the whole earth. What is happening in real time, is that Christ the King is receiving the promised kingdom and authority from the Father to enact and execute the purpose for all creation foretold in Daniel chapter seven. The Ancient of Days has given His Son all the authority in heaven and on earth, and John's weeping has ceased in the presence of the Lion. Beale writes, *"Christ's overcoming of the enemy places him in a sovereign position to effect the divine plan of redemption ion and judgment, as symbolized by the opening of the book and its seals."*[107] Not only is Jesus the righteous Lion that earns salvation for His people by His untarnished righteousness, but He is the Lion that defeats the evil lion who roams around trying to sink his teeth into God's sheep (1 Pet. 5:8).

Yet, what is so interesting in this vision is the difference between what John *hears* and what He *sees*. He heard the comforting and loud declaration that The Lion of the tribe of Judah is present and worthy to open the scroll and the seven seals. But when he turns and looks, he sees **"a Lamb standing, as though it had been slain, with seven horns and with seven eyes, which are the seven spirits of God sent out into all the earth"** (Rev. 5:6). John hears a *Lion* but sees a *Lamb*. Coexisting in one person is both the power and ferociousness needed for victory and righteousness as well as the humility and sacrificial love of a Lamb. Jonathan Edwards describes beautifully the paradox of both the Lion and the Lamb being found in the person and work of Christ. He writes,

> *"Jesus is called a 'Lion'. 'Behold the Lion of the Tribe of Judah'. Jesus is also called 'Lamb'. '...I saw a Lamb'. John saw a Lamb who had prevailed to open the book. The book was John's vision, or visual portrait of God's decrees where the events in time and space were foreordained from the foundation of the world. The Lamb was "as if it had been slain". A lion is a devourer, one that is able and desires to make a terrible slaughter of others. No creature falls more easily prey to a lion than a lamb...The lion excels in strength, and in the majesty of his appearance and voice. The lamb excels in meekness and patience, besides the excellent nature of the creature as good for food, and yielding that which is fit for our clothing, and being suitable to be offered in sacrifice to God. But in Jesus Christ, we see both: Because the diverse excellencies of both the lion and lamb wonderfully meet in him!"*[108]

---

[106] Hendricksen, *More Than Conquerors,* 89.
[107] Beale, *Revelation,* 350.
[108] Jonathan Edwards, *The Excellency of Christ,* https://www.monergism.com/blog/jonathan-edwards-excellency-christ.

The backdrop of the Lamb is found throughout the Old Testament, especially in passages like the Passover Lamb in Exodus 12, the Day of Atonement in Leviticus 16, as well as the Suffering Servant in Isaiah 53.

The unusual description of Christ with "**seven horns and with seven eyes, which are the seven spirits of God...**" (Rev. 5:6) includes elements from Revelation 1:4 and 1:20. Jesus **"went and took the scroll from the right hand of Him who was seated on the throne"** (5:7). Notice carefully that this is a Trinitarian theophany. John is in the presence of the Father (on the throne), the Son (standing as a Lamb), and the Spirit (seven horns and seven eyes). Vern Poythress expands on this by saying,

> "*The ultimate origin of the scene lies in the Trinity. The one God is three persons—The Father, the Son (the Lamb), and the Holy Spirit. Within the Trinity, the Son is the 'exact imprint' of the nature of the Father (Heb. 1:3). He is the image of God (Col. 1:15). The full pattern of reflections has its foundation and its origin in God, and especially the relation of the Father to the Son. The trinity is reflected in the specific vision in Revelation 4-5, which has three persons in three imagistic representations, namely, the one on the throne, the Lamb, and the seven eyes of the Lamb, which represent the Holy Spirit.*"[109]

The response of the myriad of worshippers in chapter five is strikingly similar to chapter four. Every creature in the throne room bows down at the feet of the Lamb as He stands as though slain, holding the scroll and its seven seals. What proceeds is the inner-workings of a redeemed creation expressing their song of delight in the Triune God. Three songs continue one after the other in pure and undistracted worship of the Lamb. All three songs make known the worth of Christ and His power and glory. Every creature in heaven lifts their hearts and their voices to making these things a joyful offering to their Redeemer.

Notice the type of people singing their hearts out. Yes, it is a redeemed people. Yes, it is a myriad of people. But it is also a diverse people. John makes clear that Jesus was slain to bring a multi-ethnic, multi-cultural, diverse people into the new heaven and new earth. This showcases the Lord's multifaceted creativity and unlimited saving power. Around the throne are people **"from every tribe and language and people and nation"** (Rev. 5:9). John is writing to Christians who are suffering at the hands of their persecutors. To them he makes very clear that God's throne is now, and forever will be, surrounded by people from the far reaches of the globe. Nothing will stop the saving purposes of the Lamb from marching forward. The new heaven and new earth will be populated by those who were Republicans and Democrats, rich and poor, popular and unnoticed. The Gospel is a message that can bring terrorists like the Apostle Paul into the eternal kingdom of peace. The kingdom of God and heaven will be people of different degrees of melanin and different languages worshipping a resurrected middle-eastern Man who eternity bears the scars of the racism of His repentant people. The truth of the matter is that some of us need to repent and begin pursuing this loving, gospel-wrought diversity now. Neighbor-love is essential to our love for Christ and His bride and is part of the way we honor His creative beauty. As Trillia Newbell writes, "*Let us strive against partiality in our fallen hearts and toward building homes that celebrate diversity, reflecting the diversity of God's people, all for God's glory. We will see that it benefits not only us but also the entire body of Christ. Diversity is beautiful and necessary for*

---

[109] Vern Poythress, *Theophany*, 132-33.

our good and the good of others."[110] This "new song" can be sung delightfully and eternally because there never has been such a selfless victory than that won by the spotless Lamb of God. A diverse people will be reminded for all eternity of the cost of their redemption as they sing to the King who bears their scars on His hands and feet. Yet, that King will neither guilt nor shame His diverse myriad of saints. Rather, He will gladly smile and accept the praises of redeemed men, women and children from Africa, to China, to the small town of Victorville, California. We worship a diverse Triune God who has broken down every barrier and wall of hostility (Eph. 2:13-16) to bring about a unified collective of grateful worshippers.

REVELATION 6:1-17

After his sight of the Lion and Lamb, John's tears ceased when He realized the worth of the One able to open the scroll and the seven seals (Rev. 5). Then, he witnessed Christ the King open the seven seals one-by-one. Chapter 6 of the Apocalypse reveals Jesus opening the first six seals and showing John what each one contains. We must pay attention to the detail that as these seals are opened individually. Each scroll is a symbolic picture of trouble and persecution. We will see that Zechariah chapter six confirms these are symbolic and apocalyptic in nature. As Hendricksen notes, *"The Lamb has taken the scroll and immediately begins to open the seals. And each seal, when opened, releases its symbolism.*"[111] Not only is Zechariah six in view, but the seals also appear to line up almost directly with the trouble and persecution Jesus preached about in His Olivet Discourse in Matthew 24. As we unpack this text, Zechariah 6 and Matthew 24 will be threaded through Revelation six helping us see its meaning and purpose.

We will set the stage by looking first at Zechariah, then zoom in on Revelation. At the beginning, we notice the order of the horses is different. Zechariah 6:1-8 gives the reader this picture of God going to the ends of the earth on a vicious patrol:

"Again, I lifted my eyes and saw, and behold, four chariots came out from between two mountains. And the mountains were mountains of bronze. [2] The first chariot had red horses, the second black horses, [3] the third white horses, and the fourth chariot dappled horses—all of them strong. [4] Then I answered and said to the angel who talked with me, "What are these, my lord?" [5] And the angel answered and said to me, "These are going out to the four winds of heaven, after presenting themselves before the Lord of all the earth. [6] The chariot with the black horses goes toward the north country, the white ones go after them, and the dappled ones go toward the south country." [7] When the strong horses came out, they were impatient to go and patrol the earth. And He said, "Go, patrol the earth." So, they patrolled the earth. [8] Then he cried to me, "Behold, those who go toward the north country have set my Spirit at rest in the north country."

As we see in Revelation six, John is *not* using Zechariah 6 in the exact way it would have been intended to be read by its original hearers. Rather, John took the concept from Zechariah and applied it through the first century vision he received from Christ

John's vision opened with a look at the first of four horses in Revelation 6:2, saying, **"And I looked, and behold, a white horse! And its rider had a bow, and a crown was given to him,**

---

110 Trillia J. Newbell, *United: Captured by God's Vision for Diversity* (Chicago, IL: Moody Publishers, 2014), 109.
111 Hendricksen, *More Than Conquerors*, 93.

and he came out conquering, and to conquer."The temptation is to read this and immediately associate "white" with Jesus. This seems even more likely when one looks at Revelation 19:11ff and sees the vision of Christ on a white horse. However, the focus of the vision in Revelation six seems to be on the providence of God and how He is capable of using evil for good. As James Hamilton argues, "*The phrase 'a crown was given to him' (6:2) is a divine passive—in other words, God is the unnamed giver of this crown. God is in control of this horseman's activity. This rider on a white horse is not going to do anything other than what God gives him to do. He goes out 'conquering, and to conquer,' and when someone does that, you know there is going to be conflict with the ones he means to conquer. That conflict comes into view when the second seal is opened.*"[112] The white horse seems to be carrying a rider who is pretending to be Jesus, a pseudo-messiah who bears the external similarities of a king but is absent of deity and humility. Matthew 24:4-5 warns of this when Jesus says, "*And Jesus answered them, 'See that no one leads you astray. For many will come in my name, saying, 'I am the Christ,' and they will lead many astray.*'" Some may be unsettled, thinking they are fooled by a false messiah-type figure. But we must remember John's vision reveals that God's people are united to the Lion and Lamb who alone was worthy to open the scroll.

When the second thru fourth seals are opened John sees the following:

> **"another horse, bright red. Its rider was permitted to take peace from the earth, so that people should slay one another, and he was given a great sword. And I looked, and behold, a black horse! And its rider had a pair of scales in his hand."** *(6:4-5b).*

> **And I looked, and behold, a pale horse! And its rider's name was Death, and Hades followed him. And they were given authority over a fourth of the earth, to kill with sword and famine and with pestilence and by wild beasts of the earth."** *(6:8).*

From the first horse to the fourth horse, all are "given" their judgment to pour out upon the earth. None function on their own authority but are steered to-and-fro by the King of kings. As Richard Phillips notes,

> "*Notice that Christ does not have to cause violence, but only to remove his restraint and permit it. It is tragically ironic that a society that has turned from God is surprised by the violence of its people, since the grace of Christ is the only true restraint on sin. Our own society has unleashed the deadliest influences, from violence-glorifying entertainment to sexual 'liberties' that destroy the family. Then, when these sinful forces wreak mayhem and bloodshed in our streets, schools, and homes, secular leaders express dismay. Revelation 6 informs us that the horsemen bring slaughter and judgment by permitting the expression of violent passion within unbelieving mankind.*"[113]

While the red horse appears to be bringing a sort of symbolic religious persecution, the black horse brings an economic persecution where inflation and taxation are used as a means of judgment (6:6). The final horse, being pale in color (sickly-green), seems to be a conclusion or result of the first

---

[112] Hamilton, *Revelation*, 178.
[113] Phillips, *Revelation*, 212.

three when John describes the death and famine that come with it (6:8). John has Ezekiel 14 in mind, showing *"Christ's judgments as a response to idol-worship and unbelief, and indicates that godly people will suffer together with the wicked."*[114] You see this in the continued mention of "wild beasts" and "pestilence," just like Revelation 6:8. The main picture we are to take away from the first four seals and the horsemen is that before Jesus brings His eternal kingdom to earth in holiness, He has to judge and remove all defiling wickedness from the earth. In Matthew 24:8, Jesus said that these judgments are *"the beginning of the birth pains."* That means that these judgments are a picture of the present evil age winding down, but there is also hope in them that *anyone* can turn to Christ for salvation.

The fifth seal moves from the imagery of horses to the souls of the martyrs who have died in faithfulness to Christ. As John sees the souls who had been **"slain for the word of God and the witness they had borne"** (Rev. 6:9). They cried out to God, **"O Sovereign Lord, holy and true how long before you will judge and avenge our blood on those who dwell on the earth?"** (6:10). In a swift rotation of the camera, John's glimpse is taken from the earth back into the heavenly realm. As he sees these saints that were faithful unto death, he is reminded of those in Smyrna who did the same (2:10). Beale exhorts us by saying, *"Such sufferings are not meaningless but are part of God's providential plan that Christians should pattern their lives after the sacrificial model of Jesus. Seen from the heavenly perspective, such sufferings ironically advance the kingdom of God, as was the case with Christ Himself (5:5-6)."*[115] The Gospel reality for those slain for their faithfulness is a "**white robe**" and the command to "**rest a little longer**" (6:11). This white robe is something we have previously seen as a promise to earlier churches (3:4-5; 3:18), as well as something we will see as priestly garments in Revelation 18-19, but the key to this white robe is that it symbolizes, *"that they are being promised a place in the heavenly liturgy before the Father's throne."*[116] Their cries for vengeance are properly placed on the Lord as the Apostle Paul commanded in Romans 12:19, *"Beloved, never avenge yourselves, but leave it to the wrath of God, for it is written, 'Vengeance is mine, I will repay, says the Lord.'"* God's response, knowing that His wrath is being poured out in the seven seals, is to **"rest a little longer."** This rest is a Sabbath-type rest that ceases the from their work as witnesses on earth and awaits the full and unfettered wrath of God to pour out on the wicked. Dennis Johnson writes, *"The mixed experience of the church on earth—liberated, consecrated, and crowned by the Lamb but also assailed by enemies—is reflected in the ambivalent status of the martyrs in heaven who are anxiously awaiting justice now delayed but also celebrating Sabbath rest."*[117]

Lastly, John sees Christ open the sixth seal. As a result, he sees a majority of the signs of the end of the age from Matthew 24 come pouring out upon the earth. Structurally, this makes sense because Revelation 4-7 is one of seven angles depicting the time between the cross and the Second Coming. This means that this sixth seal is edging us closer and closer to the Second Coming of our Lord. However, when one takes Matthew 24-25 as a whole into account, interpretation must be done with caution and generosity. For the sake of this commentary, I will not get into the vast expanse of Matthew 24-25, but will note a couple things that help us with Revelation 6:12-17. First, when Matthew 24 uses the apocalyptic imagery of the sun being darkened, the moon not giving off light, stars falling from heaven, etc., it seems that Matthew is describing the destruction of Jerusalem and the temple in 70 A.D. The amount of times Matthew says, "you" to his original audience places all of these events in Matthew 24:1-28 in the lifetime of that original audience. Second, the topic of Jesus' Second Coming doesn't seem to come into play until Matthew 24:36ff. So, what are we to make of all

---

[114] Ibid., 214.
[115] Beale, *Revelation*, 389.
[116] Leithart, *Revelation 1-11,* 307.
[117] Johnson, *Triumph of the Lamb*, 126.

these pictures? Sam Storms urges us that the "tribulation of those days" in Matthew 24:29, *"refers not simply to the events of 70 A.D. but also to this entire present age between the two comings of Christ."*[118]

In Revelation 6:13-14, John mentions that **"the stars of the sky fell to the earth as the fig tree sheds its winter fruit when shaken by a gale. The sky vanished like a scroll that is being rolled up…"** An Old Testament allusion seems to be at the front of John's mind in regard to all of these things. Isaiah 34 is a chapter describing the Lord's anger and judgment toward the nations, but Isaiah 34:4 specifically says, *"All the host of heaven shall rot away, and the skies roll up like a scroll. All their host shall fall, as leaves fall from the vine, like leaves falling from the fig tree."* Although the quote is a bit lengthy, Richard Phillips brings this all together when he writes,

> *"Isaiah is describing universal judgment in which creation itself is dissolved. This fits Revelation 6:17 description of this event as the 'great day' of God's wrath. Additionally, the sixth seal answers the prayers of the fifth seal, which call for judgment on the entire world (6:10). Moreover, the language used here occurs elsewhere in Revelation to describe the final judgment of all mankind (11:13; 16:18-20; 20:11). Finally, a literal reading of the sixth seal fits Jesus' depiction in the Olivet Discourse. Jesus spoke of the sun being darkened, the moon not giving light, the stars falling, and the powers of heaven being shaken in tandem with His second coming, and the end of the age (Matt. 24:29-32). There, Jesus used the metaphor of the fig tree in the same sense as Isaiah 34:4 and Revelation 6:13, as a lesson of the need to be ready for the end. This literal teaching is confirmed in Peter's second letter: 'The heavens will pass away with a roar, and the heavenly bodies will be burned up and dissolved, and the earth and the works that are done on it will be exposed' (2 Peter 3:10)."*[119]

The Great Day of Wrath will be a terrifying day for those not found in Christ, but, a day of delight and grandeur it will be for the people of God as He shakes all that is wicked and unclean from this world. *"'Yet once more, in a little while, I will shake the heavens and the earth and the sea and the dry land. And I will shake all nations, so that the treasures of nations shall come in, and I will fit this house with glory,' says the Lord of hosts."* (Haggai 2:6-7). *"At that time His voice shook the earth, but now He has promised, 'Yet once more I will shake not only the earth but also the heavens.' This phrase, 'Yet once more,' indicates the removal of things that are shaken—that is, things that have been made—in order that the things that cannot be shaken may remain."* (Hebrews 12:26-27).

REVELATION 7:1-17

Revelation chapter seven continues the vision of chapter six but shows an interruption in the opening of the seven seals. Six seals were opened in Revelation chapter six showing God's judgment upon the earth began pouring out like rain storms on a dry land of unbelief. The interruption in chapter seven prior to the opening of the seventh seal is meant to comfort the seven churches and the people of God. Despite the cataclysmic terrors being poured out on the earth, God comes to His people to assure them that He is their God and they are His people. He reminds them that salvation belongs to the Lord, and He will deliver on all His promises.

---

[118] Sam Storms, *Kingdom Come: The Amillennial Alternative* (Ross-shire, Scotland: Mentor, 2013), 261. I do encourage anyone desiring to better understand this view of Matthew 24, and Amillennialism in general, to read this book by Sam Storms. It is exegetically precise, worshipful, and helpful in better understanding some of the most difficultly texts in the Bible.

[119] Phillips, *Revelation*, 232.

Revelation 7:1-3 begins this important parenthesis.

"After this I saw four angels standing at the four corners of the earth, holding back the four winds of the earth, that no wind might blow on earth or sea or against any tree. Then I saw another angel ascending from the rising of the sun, with the seal of the living God, and he called with a loud voice to the four angels who had been given power to harm earth and sea, saying, 'Do not harm the earth or the sea or the trees, until we have sealed the servants of our God on their foreheads.'"

John beheld a terrifying scene in which a previous generation of God's people were gripped with fear by what they saw. Daniel 7 uses similar apocalyptic imagery to show the aggression and rage of kingdom after kingdom oppressing the saints. Daniel sees four terrifying beasts symbolic of Babylon, Persia, Greece, etc. At the beginning of this vision, Daniel writes, *"I saw in my vision by night, and behold, the four winds of heaven were stirring up the great sea"* (Daniel 7:2). John definitely has this in mind but notice the difference: In Daniel the four winds are stirred up, but in Revelation 7:1 they are being restrained. This is meant to tip off the reader familiar with Daniel's vision that God is restraining evil for the sake of His people. In fact, these four winds are likely synonymous with the four horsemen in chapter six. Beale writes, *"This identification becomes clearer from understanding that the sealing of believers in v 3-8 explains how they can be protected spiritually from the woes of the four horsemen, which they must endure."*[120]

Not only will God's people be spared from harm (eternally), but as Revelation 7:2-4 reveals, they will be *sealed*. The term *"sealed"* (*sphragizo*) is meant to give the picture of ownership and protection. Verse three makes clear that those with the seal are *"the servants of God."* In Revelation 14:1 we will see that the 144,000 saints from chapter seven are shown from another angle, standing with the Lamb on Mount Zion with *"His name and the name of the Father written on their foreheads."* Later we will also see a counterfeit Christ who marks His people on their right hands and foreheads (Rev. 13:16). As Dennis Johnson describes the difference between the seal and the mark, *"The difference in terminology is significant, for the word seal implies security under the protective authority of God. The beast's 'mark' can make no such guarantee. But God's seal on His servants' foreheads does not symbolize a promise that they will be spared physical suffering, for Christ summons to faithfulness, even to the extremity of martyrdom, pervades Revelation (e.g. 2:10; 12:11).*[121]

In Revelation 7:4-8, John hears the voices of those who were sealed from every tribe of Israel. John lists all 12 tribes with 12,000 people from each tribe, totaling 144,000 redeemed. Jehovah's Witnesses are notorious for taking this number literally and claiming that the true and faithful are an exact 144,000. But, verse nine appears to expand on this number as John goes from *hearing* to *seeing*. Revelation 7:9-10 says, *"After this I looked, and behold, a great multitude that no one could number, from every nation, from all tribes and peoples and languages, standing before the throne and before the Lamb, clothed in white robes with palm branches in their hands; and they cry out with a loud voice, saying, 'Salvation belongs to our God who sits on the throne, and to the Lamb!'"* This 144,000 is a symbolic number showing completeness, also explained in verse nine as a *"great multitude that no one could number."* Hendriksen warns readers from

---

[120] Beale, *Revelation*, 406.
[121] Johnson, *Triumph of the Lamb*, 129.

trying to make the 144,000 literal by showing that Revelation 21 describes twelve gates and foundations in the New Jerusalem, which have the names of the twelve apostles, and is 144 cubits high (21:9-14, 17).[122] He goes on to show that the 144,000 also show up again in Revelation 14:3 and we are told that they are "*those who had been redeemed from the earth.*"[123] Hendricksen concludes that "*the 144,000 sealed individuals out of the twelve tribes of literal Israel symbolize spiritual Israel, the Church of God on earth.*"[124]

As mentioned earlier, this sealing of God's redeemed is not a guarantee of His protection *from physical harm*. It is protection *from losing their faith in the face of suffering and persecution*. John may have in mind an Old Testament allusion to the Passover or Ezekiel 9:14-23? Those are seals meant to protect God's redeemed from physical harm. John may just be expanding this to a spiritual protection, but the key to the text is in verse ten, **"Salvation belongs to our God who sits on the throne, and to the Lamb!"** (Rev. 7:10). The point is this: No matter how much God's people suffer, He will always finish the work of salvation He began in the saints (cf. Phil. 1:6).

As we witnessed in chapters 4-5, this great multitude of diverse saints is standing before the throne of the Lamb. They are clothed in white robes (6:11), with palm branches in their hands, as they loudly proclaim the words of Isaiah 4:5-6:

> **"Therefore they are before the throne of God, and serve Him day and night in His temple; and He who sits on the throne will shelter them with His presence.** [16] **They shall hunger no more, neither thirst anymore; the sun shall not strike them, nor any scorching heat.** [17] **For the Lamb in the midst of the throne will be their shepherd, and He will guide them to springs of living water, and God will wipe away every tear from their eyes"** (Revelation 7:15-17).

The palm branches are meant to bring to our minds the Feast of Booths (cf. Lev. 23:33-44; Isaiah 4:5-6; John 7). This celebration existed to remind God's people of their redemption from Egypt, especially during the wilderness wanderings en route to the Promised Land. Once Israel arrived in their new land they lived in tents made of palm branches in remembrance and thankfulness of God's redemption. As Hamilton notes,

> "*The Wilderness/Booths imagery is invoked in Revelation 7:15-17, with language reminiscent of Isaiah 4:5-6. The booths built at the feast were reminders of the tents/tabernacles Israel used through the wilderness, and when Revelation 7:15 says He who sits on the throne will shelter them with His presence, the verb rendered 'shelter' should be translated 'tabernacle' (cf. John 1:14). As water was provided from the rock along with the manna from heaven in the wilderness, so in Revelation 7:16 those who experience the fulfillment of God's protection and provision, which is the fulfillment of the booths, will neither hunger nor thirst, nor will the sun and its heat harm them. The fulfillment of the exodus and the Feast of Passover is fulfilled in the praise of Revelation 5:9-14. The praise in 7:9-17 presents the fulfillment of the wilderness sojourn and the Feast of Booths.*"[125]

---

[122] Hendricksen, *More Than Conquerors*, 110-11.
[123] Ibid., 111.
[124] Ibid., 111.
[125] *Gospel Transformation Bible* (ESV), James Hamilton, Revelation Study Notes, 1735.

John is emphasizing that Christ is the Eternal Shepherd (7:17) who will love and lead His people forevermore. In all our thirsting, He is the shepherd that *"will guide them to springs of living water, and God will wipe away every tear from their eyes."* The reality in this good, but fallen, world is that God's people will suffer. When we look around and it seems the world is falling apart, it's tempting to slump over and give up. But God is calling us through Revelation chapter seven to overcome by the blood of the Lamb, who is shepherding us home and will satisfy the true desires of our hearts. If you are suffering, remember that Christ came all the way to you in His Incarnation, and remains with you now (cf. Matthew 28:20). Rest in Him. In the midst of trials and tribulations, the same One who "tabernacled" (ἐσκήνωσεν) with His people (John 1:14), becomes a continual *"tabernacle"* (σκηνώσει) to His people in this world (Rev. 7:15). You are not alone!

WEEK 7
STUDY

REVELATION 8:1-11:19
The Seven Trumpets of Warning

MEDITATION: Pray that God would open your eyes, heart, and mind to Himself as you study Revelation 8:1-5.

1. Keeping in mind the six seals that were previously opened, what did you expect when the seventh was opened? As you read Revelation 8:1-5, what seems to be the main point of the passage?

2. Why is there silence in heaven after the seventh seal? (cf. Habakkuk 2:20 for context and explanation on the silence).

3. What does the seventh seal and the silence teach us about how God responds to the prayers of His people?

APPLICATION: Read James 1:6-8. What are some prayers that you have prayed, but if honest, did not believe God will answer? Write out a verse to memorize on page 305.

MEDITATION: As you work through Revelation 8:6-13 today, ask the Lord for help in understanding what His judgment entails.

1. As you read about the first four trumpets in Revelation 8:6-13, do they remind you of another important event in redemptive history? (cf. Exodus 7-10)

2. What is the nature of the trumpets and what is their purpose? Are they different than the nature and purpose of the seven seals?

3. If the trumpets have the same/similar purpose as the seals, but from the vantage point of the unbelieving population of the earth, how should the people of God respond to these trumpets?

APPLICATION: Have you ever prayed for God to bring judgment on a person? Why or why not?

MEDITATION: In your study of Revelation 9:1-21 ask the Lord to expose any idols in your heart, or self-righteous work of your hands.

1. As the fifth and sixth trumpets are blown, how does God deal differently with His people and those who do not know and love Him?

2. When you take into account that John is harkening back to Exodus 10-12, what can we expect to come after such ferocious plagues and judgments? How does Joel 2:1-11 shed some light on God's purpose behind such disturbing judgement?

3. Read Revelation 9:13-19. Do these angels seem to be good or evil? Describe how you came to that conclusion.

APPLICATION: When reading Revelation 9:20-21, what idols do you need to repent from worshiping? Share this with a trusted brother or sister and ask them to help you walk in step with the Holy Spirit (Gal. 5:25).

MEDITATION: As you worship God through Revelation 10:1-11 today, ask Him to cause you to taste HIs Word as sweeter than honey.

1. In the same way there was an intermission between the sixth and seventh seal, there is an intermission between the sixth and seventh trumpet. Why are seeing these patterns important to understanding the message of the book of Revelation?

2. List some of the characteristics of the angel in Revelation 10. What similarities does this angel have to someone from previous chapters?

3. Read Revelation 10:8-11 along with Ezekiel 2:9-3:4 and list some similarities. What is the point of John eating the scroll?

APPLICATION: Who in your neighborhood could you befriend and share the Gospel with? Pray for God to give you the boldness and humility to take them His message that is as "sweet as honey."

MEDITATION: Marvel at the majestic God of Revelation 11:1-19 today.

1. Revelation 11 is a difficult passage, and honest and faithful believers have differing views on how it should be interpreted. What are some things that are clear about God in this passage?

2. Read Zechariah chapter four. Is it possible John had this in mind when writing Revelation 11? If so, what similarities do you see, and what is the point of John's vision?

3. In spite of the death of the two witnesses, what does God do that helps us avoid fearing man when sharing the Gospel? Read Ezekiel 37:1-14 for an Old Testament allusion to this passage.

4. What comes with the seventh and final trumpet being blown (11:15-19)? What is the connection to Psalm 2, and how does Jesus fulfill that Psalm?

APPLICATION: When Jesus takes full and final authority over the world, what is one aspect of the brokenness in our world that you most look forward to seeing Him redeem?

WEEK 7
COMMENTARY

REVELATION 8:1-11:19
The Seven Trumpets of Warning

REVELATION 8:1-11:19

THE SEVEN TRUMPETS
OF WARNING

REVELATION 8:1-5

After the first six seals were opened and God comforted and assured His people that He is the Eternal Shepherd, "tabernacling" among them forever. Then, we come to the seventh and final seal. Will we find utter devastation? Will the chaos that ensues be the full and final wrath of God upon the earth? Remarkably, what we witness is, ***"silence in heaven for about half an hour"*** (Rev. 8:1). We are all aware of the eerie silence that precedes a nasty storm. The focus of Revelation 8:1-5 seems to be found in verse 4 when the ***"prayers of the saints, rose before God from the hand of the angel."*** Where we might have been expecting the return of Jesus Christ, this viewpoint is zooming in on the saints of God and their prayers. It seems to be the calm before the storm as John experiences thirty minutes of uninterrupted silence. Think of the continual praise and worship that has been resounding from the depths and diaphragms of God's redeemed. Now, he experiences an abrupt cease of all sound. This would seem like a deafening silence. Dennis Johnson writes, "*Silence is creation's expectant response to the Lord's impending arrival in judgement.*"[126] Or as Hendricksen so eloquently puts it, God's wrath is so "*fearful and awful…that the inhabitants of heaven stand spell-bound, lost for a time—half an hour—in breathless, silent amazement.*"[127] This is not the first time that silence has abounded the people of God. In a chapter of God declaring judgment on the Chaldeans, Habakkuk interrupts the chaos of the idolatry in the world as he declares, "*But the Lord is in His holy temple, let all the earth keep silence before Him*" (Hab. 2:20).

John looks and sees "***seven angels who stand before God, and seven trumpets were given to them***" (Rev. 8:2). These seven angels are more than likely the seven archangels that are continually in God's presence (Isa. 63:9). As Phillips notes, only two of these archangels are named in the Bible: "*Michael (Jude 9) and Gabriel (Luke 1:19). Since the definite article identifies these angels as 'the seven,' it is probably best to understand them as the seven archangels.*"[128] What is more important than the identity of the angels is the trumpets that are given to them. If we were to read Revelation chronologically and literally, we would view these seven trumpets as different judgments than the seven seals. But, we would also run into trouble because the book would start to make less sense as we move forward. We

---

[126] Johnson, *Triumph of the Lamb*, 136.
[127] Hendricksen, *More Than Conquerors*, 117.
[128] Phillips, *Revelation*, 267.

will see that various events and actions are repeated with similar imagery. This leads me to the conclusion that the seven trumpets are the same events as the seven seals, observed by John from a different viewpoint. Not only are they the same in number, and same in their purpose of judgment, but they also have a similar intermission between the sixth and seventh. The seven trumpets that follow the seven seals are followed by seven bowls in Revelation 16. Again, this shows John's repetitive structure, giving support to view each series as the same time period between Christ's cross and the second coming. Richard Phillips explains:

> "Much of what happens when the trumpets are blown, and the bowls are poured obviously precedes the final judgment revealed in the sixth seal. For instance, when the angel blows the third trumpet, a star falls from heaven to poison all the rivers (Rev. 8:10). Under a strict chronology this is impossible, since under the sixth seal (6:13) all 'the stars of the sky' had already '[fallen] to the earth.' Therefore, it is evident that the judgments of the trumpets and the bowls take place chronologically before the sixth seal, which occurs earlier in the text of Revelation. Understood rightly, the seventh seal, the seventh trumpet, and the seventh bowl all depict aspects of the same event: the return of Christ in wrath and salvation."[129]

To best understand the nature of these trumpets, one must understand the use of trumpets throughout Scripture. Biblically, trumpets sound a warning that judgment and salvation will come simultaneously. Think of the story of Jericho and the walls falling at the sound of the seven trumpets blowing on the seventh day after seven laps around the city (cf. Josh. 6). Then consider the sounds of trumpets blown prior to Gideon defeating Midian and God's people being saved (cf. Judg. 7). Or recall the last trumpet of our Lord's coming to inflict vengeance on unbelievers and save His people (cf. 1 Thess. 4:16-17; 2 Thess. 1:5-10; Matt. 24:30-31). *In Scripture, a trumpet either sounds the coming of utter devastation or absolute victory.*

Prior to the trumpet sound of battle in Revelation chapter eight, John experiences a deafening silence. Revelation 8:3-4 shows God's people that their prayers reach all the way to the God of their salvation. Perhaps John is retelling the scene of prayer from Revelation 6:9-10? But his point here is clearly the comfort of the saints. Those who have been praying for God's will to be done on earth as it is in heaven (Matt. 6:9-10), will have those prayers answered in full. This is not just a comfort to the suffering saints of the first century, but an exhortation for all of us to be prayerful. Through this text, we know God will answer our prayers. Each petition lifts as an aroma of incense (cf. Lev. 16) before the Lord. Remember one of the most comforting, yet audacious, realities for the believer: Our weak and feeble prayers move Christ to give His gracious help. Hebrews 4:15-16 says, *"For we do not have a high priest who is unable to sympathize with our weaknesses, but one who in every respect has been tempted as we are, yet without sin. Let us then with confidence draw near to the throne of grace, that we may receive mercy and find grace to help in time of need."* This grace and mercy and help do not come from a weak God, overwhelmed by our neediness. No, it is the same powerful God from Revelation 4-5 whose throne bursts with thunder and lightning. John repeats those same characteristics here in Revelation 8:5 so we will come before God's throne knowing *we are heard by the Almighty.* John reminds us all, **"Then the angel took the censer and filled it with fire from the altar and threw it on the earth, and there were peals of thunder, rumblings, flashes of lightning, and an earthquake."** Let our prayers be those seasoned with confidence, not in ourselves, but in the one who is the Lion and the Lamb. He hears

---

[129] Ibid., 266.

you and sees you, and He will soon be roused from His throne and to answer all your prayers, making all things right.

"Be silent before the Lord God! For the day of the LORD is near" (Zeph. 1:7).

"Be silent, all flesh, before the LORD, for He has roused Himself from His holy dwelling" (Zech. 2:13).

"Then will appear in heaven the sign of the Son of Man, and then all the tribes of the earth will mourn, and they will see the Son of Man coming on the clouds of heaven with power and great glory. And He will send out His angels with a loud trumpet call, and they will gather His elect from the four winds, from one end of heaven to the other." (Matt. 24:30-31)

REVELATION 8:6-13

As we continue to dive into the seven trumpets, viewing the seven seals from another perspective, we see an uncanny resemblance to the plagues in Exodus 7-12. These will continue into Revelation chapter nine (and even a little into chapter 11). We must grasp the theme of the plagues in Exodus to rightly understand what God is revealing to and through John.

The Exodus story is one of redemption and provision. God redeems His people out of slavery by thrusting a brutal onslaught of plagues upon Pharaoh and Egypt so that he will let His people go. This leads to a wilderness journey where God provides water from rocks and bread from the sky. He led Israel by His Spirit through clouds in the day and by a pillar of fire at night. In one sense, it is a period of astounding visible miracles, but in another sense, it is one of great dependence on God. The New Testament picks up this Exodus theme for New Covenant believers. We are identified as those who have been set free from our slavery to sin by the blood of the Lamb. We are now in a type of wilderness generation until we make it to the true and better Promised Land, the New heaven and new earth (cf. Heb. 3-4).[130] As these trumpets are about to be blown by the seven angels we are being called into the Exodus imagery to be reminded that the same God who judged Pharaoh for keeping Israel captive is He who will judge those who persecute His suffering saints. The seven churches in Revelation 2-3 would have found these seals, trumpets, and bowls as the answer to their prayers and longings for judgment. When reading these trumpets, we ought should see them as the time between the cross and the second coming, another angle of the seven seals. Derek Thomas writes, *"The seals view the unfolding of the redemptive purposes of God from the point of view of the Lord's own people, those who are sealed; the trumpets view the same reality from the point of view of the unsealed, those who are not the people of God. The opening of the seals brings great consolation to the people of God. The sounding of the trumpets brings great woes upon those who are not the people of God."*[131]

With this in mind, we are prepared to look at the first four trumpets in Revelation 8:6-13. The initial four trumpets have a common purpose.

---

[130] The book of Matthew traces this same theme as Jesus becomes the faithful Israel in his temptation in the wilderness and leads a people to the Promised Land. In fact, in Luke 9:31, Jesus uses the word "exodus" to explain his departure from this earth. We all, in Christ, follow this pattern of exodus followed by rest, humiliation followed by exaltation.

[131] Derek Thomas, *Let's Study Revelation,* 73.

"And a third of the earth was burned up, and a third of the trees were burned up…" (Rev. 8:7b)

"A third of the living creatures of the sea died, and a third of the ships were destroyed." (Rev. 8:9)

"A third of the waters became wormwood, and many people died from the water, because it had been made bitter." (Rev. 8:11b)

"…and a third of the sun was struck, and a third of the moon, and a third of the stars, so that a third of their light might be darkened, and a third of the day might be kept from shining, and likewise a third of the night." (Rev. 8:12)

The common link between all four trumpets is the destruction of a third of God's good creation. But why? What is the purpose of all of this and what exactly is the point of these pictures? If we understand that the trumpets are the angle of God's judgment directed at unbelievers, especially those who persecute the faithful, then these trumpets are a judgment meant to punish, not bring people to repentance. Beale agrees when writing, *"These judgments are not intended to evoke repentance but to punish because of the permanently hardened, unrepentant stance of the unbelievers toward God and His people."*[132] In the same way that the Exodus plagues resulted in the death of the firstborn of all who did not place their trust in God, so these trumpets are dispensing judgment on the unbelieving population. In his excellent commentary on Revelation, James Hamilton gives us the following table on the use of the Exodus plagues in Revelation's use of trumpets:[133]

TRUMPETS IN REVELATION	PLAGUES IN EXODUS
1st Trumpet: 8:7: hail, fire	**7th Plague:** 9:23-25: hail, fire
2nd Trumpet: 8:8, 9: sea turns to blood, one third of living creatures die	**1st Plague:** 7:20, 21: Nile turns to blood, fish die
3rd Trumpet: 8:10, 11: rivers and springs made bitter	**1st Plague:** 7:19: rivers, canals filled with blood
4th Trumpet: 8:12: one third of sun, moon, and stars darkened	**9th Plague:** 10:21-29: three days of darkness
5th Trumpet: 9:1-11: darkness, locusts like scorpions	**8th & 9th Plague:** 10:21-29: darkness; 10:12-20: locusts

---

[132] Beale, *Revelation,* 472.

[133] Hamilton, *Revelation,* 211. As you can see in the table, this will be used throughout chapter 9 and the beginning of 10 as well. When we get to the seven bowls, I will use Hamilton's table for the bowls and Exodus plagues as well.

6th Trumpet: 9:12-19: angels released, mounted troops, fire, smoke, and sulfur kill one third of humanity	**10th Plague?** 11:1-10; 12:29-32: death angel?
10:1: angel wrapped in a cloud with legs like pillars of fire	Israel led out of Egypt by the pillar of cloud by day and fire by night

These judgments are interspersed throughout the church-age, between the crucifixion of Christ and His second coming. Beale expands on this by showing John's use of the word "plague" throughout Revelation:

> *"The use of plague (plege) of the trumpet woes also indicates that most of the woes occur throughout the latter-day church age (9:20; 11:6; "strike" in 8:12). In 22:18 "plege" is used of a curse that can strike anyone within the church in the late first century and throughout the church age who does not faithfully heed the message of the Apocalypse: 'God will add to him [the disobedient hearer of John's message] the plagues that are written in this book.' This must conclude the trumpet woes. This strongly suggests that some, if not most, of the trumpet judgments happen during the entire period between Christ's first and second comings, not merely at a tribulation period immediately preceding and including the second coming."*[134]

This brings to mind the genre of Psalms known as "imprecatory Psalms." These are Psalms where a psalmist prays for God's judgment to come on evildoers. This can be difficult to balance with Christ's call to love our enemies. Yet, a full-orbed understanding of the counsel of God should allow us to hold both truths simultaneously. On one hand, we ought to long for the conversion of those who continually cause wickedness, yet on the other hand it is righteous to pray for God to bring justice upon those who cause evil. The great news is that vengeance and salvation both belong to the Lord. Therefore, we pray accordingly.

The temptation with these trumpets is understanding what they mean. I am convinced they are not to be interpreted in a literally-only fashion but are especially apocalyptic in nature. However, I am also convinced that some of the plagues have literal aspects to them. While faithful Christians disagree on the interpretation of these texts, one inescapable connection is that John is alluding to Genesis 1-2 and the creation account. My own opinion is that because of the increasing and rampant wickedness that continues to grow, God inflicts a type of "de-creation," climaxing with the New Creation in Revelation 21. Phillips interprets these primarily as images of some greater truth. He argues that the first plague is an image of the loss of life that results from the first trumpet.[135] He sees the second as imagery explaining the cut off of food and economic resources.[136] The third is imagery for the fall of world imperial powers, which he attaches to the Old Testament allusion found in Isaiah 14:12-15.[137] The fourth he argues is imagery for God removing His blessing from His own created order.[138] Phillips argues from the fourth trumpet/plague that it must be taken symbolically because God's

---

[134] Beale, *Revelation*, 486.
[135] Phillips, *Revelation*, 278.
[136] Ibid., 279.
[137] Ibid., 280.
[138] Ibid, 281.

created order couldn't survive a minute with the removal of a third of the sun and moon. Although this is a touchy and difficult section (not the last in this book), Phillips does have the following word of wisdom for us:

> *"We remember that Revelation is not a puzzle book but a picture book. The general impression is therefore most important. Here, the four trumpets bring plagues on the created order—the earth, the seas, the streams, and the stars and the moon—to signify God's judgment on the nations that rise up in idolatry throughout history. These woes are inflicted not by 'nature' but by God, and mankind is completely unable to manage them. This is precisely what a sober view of history shows, with vast portions of the human race suffering and dying at any one time because of tragedies originating from every part of creation."*[139]

This ought to be a sobering message to us all. Those who overcome in Christ are sure to be delivered, but the terrible truth is that many will perish in their sins. Family, friends, and co-workers will suffer the outpouring of God's wrath, enduring eternally because of their eternal debt. This is the seriousness that is the springboard to joyful Gospel proclamation because we ourselves were once citizens of this sinful world before God graciously transferred us to the kingdom of light. Let us share liberally and joyfully the gospel of Jesus so that others may join us in the victory of Christ at the sound of the trumpets. And when that Great Day comes as the last trumpet sounds, let us rejoice in our jealous God who makes all things right.

REVELATION 9:1-21

As we continue John's vision of the trumpets from chapter eight, the descriptions and results of the fifth and sixth trumpets in Revelation nine give a bit more detail than the first four. As the fifth angel blows the fifth trumpet, we are told:

> **"I saw a star fallen from heaven to earth, and he was given the key to the shaft of the bottomless pit. He opened the shaft of the bottomless pit, and from the shaft rose smoke like the smoke of a great furnace, and the sun and the air were darkened with the smoke from the shaft. Then from the smoke came locusts on the earth, and they were given power like the power of scorpions of the earth"** (Rev. 9:1-3).

Now, we must remember that the book of Revelation is meant to be a glimpse into redemptive history from the perspective of God and heaven. That reminder, along with the use of Old Testament allusions are a safe and faithful elixir in grasping what would be the most terrifying and confusing visions if we took them *only* literally. Revelation chapter nine is no exception. My guess is that when you are struggling, you may not initially think to turn to Revelation nine for encouragement? How could the graphic nature and interpretive difficulties produce encouragement? This chapter was breathed out by God as a means of comforting the first century church, as well as believers today.

---

[139] Ibid., 281.

As the fifth trumpet is blown, John saw, **"A star fallen from heaven to earth, and he was given the key to the shaft of the bottomless pit. He opened the shaft of the bottomless pit, and from the shaved rose smoke like the smoke of a great furnace, and the sun and the air were darkened with the smoke from the shaft"** (Rev. 9:1-2). Revelation 9:3-12 follows with the unleashing of a horde of locusts that are given or allowed (1) power like the scorpions of the earth, and (2) power to harm those **"who do not have the seal of God on their foreheads"** (9:4) **for five months, but not to kill them"** (9:5), as well as (3) power to torture people so severely that **"they will long to die, but death will flee from them"** (9:6). It is evident that these are not merely human forces, but some type of demonic forces unleashed at God's will into the world. Two Old Testament allusions are in view here:

> *"The locusts came up over all the land of Egypt and settled on the whole country of Egypt, such a dense swarm of locusts as had never been before, nor ever will be again. ¹⁵ They covered the face of the whole land, so that the land was darkened, and they ate all the plants in the land and all the fruit of the trees that the hail had left. Not a green thing remained, neither tree nor plant of the field, through all the land of Egypt."* (Exodus 10:14-15)

> *"Their appearance is like the appearance of horses, and like war horses they run. ⁵ᵗ As with the rumbling of chariots, they leap on the tops of the mountains, like the crackling of "a flame of fire devouring the stubble, like a powerful army drawn up for battle. ⁶ Before them peoples are in anguish; all faces grow pale. ⁷ Like warriors they charge; like soldiers they scale the wall. They march each on his way; they do not swerve from their paths."* (Joel 2:4-7)[140]

In John's adaptation of these two Old Testament accounts in Revelation 9:7-12, he adds some features which intensify the horror. These warhorse-like locusts have **"crowns of gold; their faces were like human faces, their hair like women's hair and their teeth like lions' teeth"** (Rev. 9:7-8). Phillips says that *"the crowns foretell victory, and the human faces show that they are guided by a rational cunning."*[141] He goes on to explain that *"the pleasing-looking female hair suggests seductive power that in reality bring death."*[142] As you go on and explore the different images of these demonic locusts, we must remember that the repetition of the word "like" is the use of simile, helping us reinforce that these terrifying visions and images often portray a literal reality.

To get a better grasp on John's comparison of the locusts, we need to return to the first part of the vision in Revelation 9:1-4. The star that John saw fall from heaven to earth either seems to be Satan or a demonic archangel. If we look at Luke 10:18, Jesus tells of seeing *"Satan fall like lightning from heaven."* Also, in Revelation 12, Satan is *"thrown down to the earth"* (12:9). Whether it is Satan, or a demonic archangel, we have seen from the seals and the trumpets that God is granting this evil authority to open the "bottomless pit," or better translated, "the abyss of hell." Here lies the reality we see with God's absolute sovereignty throughout the Scriptures: *The God who has unleashed this fifth trumpet controls the evil one and all of his schemes.* God can use the most ferocious evil assault to be an offensive tool of his own character, whipping it into a means of inflicting vengeance and justice upon evil itself. The entire imagery of Revelation 9:1-4 is God allowing Satan to unleash the demonic forces from the pit of hell to ultimately bring judgment upon the evil one and his demons. As Hendricksen

---

[140] See all of Joel 2 for the proper picture and the depth of calamity pictured in Revelation 9.
[141] Phillips, *Revelation*, 287.
[142] Ibid.

writes, *"The power to bring this about is 'given' to the devil; that is, by God's permissive decree he is not prevented from carrying out his wicked designs in the hearts of the children of men, a wickedness for which he—not God—is responsible."*[143] It is challenging to wrap our minds around how a good God can allow such suffering. That is, until we grasp the gospel, which leads us to respond, "How can God allow one ounce of good toward such a wicked person as me?" And that is exactly what we see in Revelation 9:4 when these demonic forces of Satan are **"told not to harm the grass of the earth or any green plant or any tree, but only those people who do not have the seal of God on their foreheads."** In the positive sense, while God's people are persecuted for their faith, they cannot be harmed by the judgments poured out on the unbelieving population. The suffering saint does not see these judgements and puff of his chest in pride, but instead knows that it was only sheer grace that has allowed us to overcome by the blood of the Lamb. And as they look on, perhaps God's people will pray with Paul, *"that I have great sorrow and unceasing anguish in my heart. For I could wish that I myself were accursed and cut off from Christ for the sake of my brothers, my kinsmen, according to the flesh"* (Romans 9:2-3)?

These judgments of God are horrendous, yet also deceptive. We might picture an Apocalypse-type movie where things are destroyed visibly all around the cast of characters. Yet, I think John has more subtle things in mind, with devastating results to the soul. In Revelation 9:11, John says, **"They have as king over them the angel of the bottomless pit. His name in Hebrew is Abaddon, and in Greek he is called Apollyon."** Phillips notes,

> *"Both of these names mean "Destroyer," which shows his evil servitude to Satan, if he is not Satan Himself, as well as the result of his activity. The name Apollyon derives from the same verb as the name if the Greek god Apollo. Since the Roman emperor Domitian considered Himself an incarnation of Apollo, John may be tying the imperial persecution facing the churches of Asia to the tormenting plane unleashed by this trumpet."*[144]

The point of this text is not so much on identifying the exact ways these evil forces bring judgment, as much as they are to teach us that God is making things right. We can tend to think that the evil in the world is not attached to Satan. But from texts like this, we can see that every evil on earth has a direct tie to the evil one. For example, I would argue that the epidemic plague of pornography, even in the church, is part of Satan's evil war on this world. Racism is an evil that is continuing to bring division in America and causing people to take sides rather than rejoice in the God of grace. Narcissism through social networking, the intolerance of tolerance, you name it, Satan has a way of sneaking his evil hands into everything. Anything that has the capability for good, Satan distorts for evil. If we are not aware of the way evil is often crouched around every corner, we can find ourselves slowly spiraling downward into this abyss. We must be Spirit-led people, aware of the schemes of the evil one (cf. 1 Pet. 5:8). And we must be on guard, arm in arm, in the midst of a community of those *unified* and *overcoming* until we see Christ face-to-face.

The sixth trumpet is quite similar to the fifth, except the focus is on wars which kill a third of mankind. John writes,

"The number of mounted troops was twice ten thousand times ten thousand: I heard their number. And this is how I saw the horses in my vision and those

---

[143] Hendricksen, *More Than Conquerors,* 120.
[144] Phillips, *Revelation,* 288-89.

who rode them: they wore breastplates the color of fire and of sapphire and of sulfur, and the heads of the horses were like lions' heads, and fire and smoke and sulfur came out of their mouths" (Rev. 9:16-17).

This destruction is widespread and does not lead those to repent for those who experience it (9:20-21). I am under the impression, within the structure of Revelation, that these wars are the satanic forces working behind common men and women throughout history, which bring about actual war. This would mean that the rise of Hitler and his evil regime were a result of Revelation chapter nine and the sixth trumpet. Henricksen agrees when he writes, *"The sixth trumpet describes war; not one particular war is indicated but all wars, past, present, and future."*[145] Likewise, Phillips writes pastorally,

"The history of mankind shows nations repeatedly turning away from God in order to raise up their own glory. Every empire promises its own salvation on earth with peace and prosperity. History records them all as crashing before invading forces of unforeseen seen ferocity. Usually the origins of these conquerors are either surprising or unexplainable. Historians struggle to explain the source of the Gothic invasions that destroyed the Roman Empire under mighty leaders such as Attila the Hun. Centuries later the hordes of Islam swept across North Africa with virtually no warning. In the early thirteenth century, the Mongol armies, led by the charismatic leader Temujin, also known as Genghis Khan, rose up with unexplained genius and vigor, conquering from China in the East to the Danube in the West. The Mongols so resembled the riders of the sixth trumpet that Christians viewed them as the literal fulfillment of Revelation, labeling them the 'devil's horsemen.' In the fourteenth century, the armies of England were suddenly equipped with invincible longbowmen. Historians do not know how this prowess for archery was developed in England and Wales or why it suddenly died out, but military advantage granted to the Edwardian kings resulted in the Hundred Years' War. The twentieth century witnessed the shocking scourge of the Nazi panzer divisions, which so many people understandably compared to Revelation 9's horsemen. In the twenty-first century, a bloody passion has enflamed Islamic jihadists in a way that defies logic. These otherwise unexplainable conquerors, whose bows, swords, and bombs have killed great swaths of humanity, are hard to explain from the sixth trumpet's vision of warfare let loose on earth from the pits of hell."[146]

The overall theme of Revelation must stay in view as we read the details of these trumpets, and the following chapters. We need to remember that while the world is getting worse and worse, while evil seems to be gaining ground on us, Jesus is the victor who will return at the final trumpet blast to judge the wicked and save His dearly loved, blood-bought people (Rev. 1:5).

REVELATION 10:1-11

As we saw in Revelation 6-7, there was an intermission of sorts between the sixth and seventh seals. Likewise, Revelation 10 repeats the intermission between the sixth and seventh trumpets. Just as the intermission in the seven seals was a means of comforting the people of God with the victory of Christ, so also is the intermission in the seven trumpets. John writes,

---

[145] Hendricksen, *More Than Conquerors*, 122.
[146] Phillips, *Revelation*, 291-92.

"Then I saw another mighty angel coming down from heaven, wrapped in a cloud, with a rainbow over His head, and His face was like the sun, and His legs like pillars of fire. He had a little scroll open in His hand. And he set His right foot on the sea, and His left foot on the land, and called out with a loud voice, like a lion roaring. When he called out, the seven thunders sounded. And when the seven thunders had sounded, I was about to write, but I heard a voice from heaven saying, 'Seal up what the seven thunders have said, and do not write it down'" (Rev. 10:1-4).

The imagery played out before us is a reminder of the true victor and comforter of the saints. The angel coming down from heaven is **"wrapped in a cloud, with a rainbow over His head, and His face was like the sun, and His legs like pillars of fire,"** an almost exact repeating of Christ's description in Revelation chapter one, and of His throne in Revelation four. Whether this angel is an image of Christ, or a created angel reflecting the glory of God, Poythress writes,

> *"My own opinion is that the angel in 10:1-2 is a created angel, who reflects the glory of God and of Christ. But some interpreters think that the description refers to Christ directly—that the angel is Christ. And indeed, Christ in 1:12-16 is described as having a face 'like the sun shining in full strength,' and 'His feet were like burnished bronze,' corresponding to the angel's 'legs like pillars of fire' (10:1; cf. Ezek. 1:27; Dan. 10:6)."*[147]

Whether we interpret this as Christ or an angel, the imagery is clear that God is comforting His people by sending them a heavenly message. The first thing this divine message entails is the command for John to **"Seal up what the seven thunders have said, and do not write it down" (Rev. 10:4).** This is an allusion to Daniel 8:26, where an angel from heaven tells Daniel, *"The vision of the evenings and the mornings that has been told is true, but seal up the vision, for it refers to many days from now."* Daniel was in the midst of a vision of conquering kingdom after conquering kingdom. But this command for Daniel to seal up this prophetic vision is also followed by an intermission of prayer. John is taking the imagery from Daniel and applying it to the command God has given him. And the shocking part of John's vision is that he will be commanded to eat the same scroll that he previously wept over when no one was found worthy to open it. You would think the great scroll of Christ would be set in a galley in heaven as a precious relic, but instead, John is commanded to chomp it up and swallow it like good BBQ on a Sunday afternoon. As this angel stands straddling the earth and the sea (a picture of the message being for all people, Jew and Gentile alike), John approaches the angel and is told:

> *"'Go, take the scroll that is open in the hand of the angel who is standing on the sea and on the land.' [9] So I went to the angel and told him to give me the little scroll. And he said to me, 'Take and eat it; it will make your stomach bitter, but in your mouth, it will be sweet as honey.' [10] And I took the little scroll from the hand of the angel and ate it. It was sweet as honey in my mouth, but when I had eaten it my stomach was made bitter. [11] And I was told, 'You must again*

---

[147] Poythress, *Theophany*, 142.

prophesy about many peoples and nations and languages and kings'" (Rev. 10:8-11).

John receives the scroll of Christ from the angel and proceeds in his prophetic role to taste, eat, and devour the Word of God and take it to the nations. As in many Old Testament allusions used throughout Revelation, God is showing He exists outside of time. He takes something He said to the prophet Ezekiel 700 years earlier and applies it to John's particular situation. In a mysterious sense, John is transported back to Ezekiel's time, while the words God said to Ezekiel are transported and retold to John on the little island of Patmos. Obviously, John would have recognized and identified with the sufferings of Ezekiel, but also the grandeur of the message that he is commanded to take to the nations. The Word of God is often sweet to one person and very bitter to another. In this case, John experiences both. Sweet to the taste, bitter to the stomach. More than anything, John is being validated as a true prophet. Ezekiel 2:9-3:4 is filled with striking similarities:

> *"And when I looked, behold, a hand was stretched out to me, and behold, a scroll of a book was in it. And He spread it before me. And it had writing on the front and on the back, and there were written on it words of lamentation and mourning and woe. And He said to me, "Son of man, eat whatever you find here. Eat this scroll, and go, speak to the house of Israel." So I opened my mouth, and He gave me this scroll to eat. And He said to me, "Son of man, feed your belly with this scroll that I give you and fill your stomach with it." Then I ate it, and it was in my mouth as sweet as honey. And He said to me, "Son of man, go to the house of Israel and speak with my words to them."*

The use of Ezekiel in Revelation is inescapable and is meant to drive home the point that in the same way Ezekiel brought the Word of God to Israel, so John is now to take it and prophesy about the consummation of world history.[148] Hamilton shows the connection between Ezekiel and Revelation by saying,

> *"The structure of the whole book of Ezekiel is roughly paralleled by the book of Revelation. In Ezekiel 1, Ezekiel has a vision of God's indescribable glory. Then in Ezekiel 2, Ezekiel is commissioned to go and prophesy to the children of Israel. This is matched in Revelation as John has a vision of the indescribable glory of God and Christ in Revelation 1-5, then the scroll is unsealed in Revelation 6-8, the trumpets sound in Revelation 8, 9, and now John is commissioned to prophet in Revelation 10. Ezekiel prophesied of God's judgment (Ezekiel 4-32), and then he prophesied of God's future salvation (Ezekiel 33-48). Similarly, John will prophesy of God's judgment (Revelation 11-18), and then he will prophesy of the salvation God will bring in Christ (Revelation 19-22)."[149]*

Imagine being a member of one of the seven churches in Revelation and hearing this read publicly. That God could take the Word He declared to Ezekiel centuries earlier and redeclare it to John in a little prison cell on a tiny island. Then, you hear that the prophetic nature of the Word of God sent to your little church as a comfort to *you*, that the glorious Christ has won the victory and is using a bound prophet to unleash the message of the scroll to the world. Oh, what a comfort! God, in His grace, pauses between the seals and trumpets to remind His people that His decree for history

---

[148] Hamilton, *Revelation*, 229.
[149] Ibid.

cannot be stopped. Likewise, the King of kings is ruling over history and He will soon stand visibly over all of creation, judging the wicked and bringing final salvation to His people.

REVELATION 11:1-19

In England in 1555, there was a man named Rowland Taylor who, along with other faithful Protestants, was experiencing persecution at the hands of the Roman Catholic Church. As a pastor in the city of Hadley, he was continuing to preach the Word of God, making it more accessible for all. As his friends urged him to flee the persecution, Taylor replied, *"God will not forsake His Church. As for me, I believe, before God, I shall never be able to do God so good service, as I may do now; nor shall I ever have so glorious a calling as I now have, nor so great mercy of God offered to me as now. So, I ask you, and all other of my friends, to pray for me; and I know God will give me strength and His Holy Spirit."* Taylor was taken before the bishop and Lord Chancellor. After being condemned and thrown in prison for two years, he once again stood before his accusers. Keeping faith in Christ, he was condemned to death by burning at the stake in his hometown of Hadley. Along the way he was so joyful and merry that, had they not known otherwise, those watching could have thought he was going to a banquet or wedding. His words to his guards caused them to weep as he earnestly called them to repent from their evil and wicked living. In front of a crowd of hecklers and fellow parishioners, he loudly prayed, *"I have taught you nothing but God's holy Word and those lessons that I have taken out of God's blessed book, the holy Bible. I am come here this day to seal it with my blood."* At that, the fire was lit. Dr. Taylor held up both his hands and called upon God, saying, *"Merciful father of heaven, for Jesus Christ my Savior's sake, receive my soul into Thy hands."* He stood in the flames without either crying or moving, his hands folded together.[150]

Throughout Revelation we have seen that Christ's people are a suffering people. They are victors in Him, though often sufferers. Revelation 11 is a case study and picture of this theme in detail. As we start to conclude the third of John's seven perspectives describing the period between the cross and the second coming, we also find ourselves in a chapter that is *"widely regarded as one of the most difficult passages in this challenging book."*[151] Although it is quite difficult, and the author confesses that chapters 11-14 are particularly difficult, if we keep our emphasis on Revelation being a picture book of visions, we can minimize the difficulty to some degree. My own view is that, while the visions can be hard, the main points are usually quite clear.

Out of the gate I think Revelation 11 is a picture of the True and Faithful Church throughout the period we have looked at over and over again: the time between the crucifixion and second coming of our Lord. Bauckham writes,

> *"Two individuals here represent the church in its faithful witness to the world. Their story must be taken neither literally nor even as an allegory, as though the sequence of events in this story were supposed to correspond to a sequence of events in church history. That the two witnesses symbolize the church in its role of witnessing to the world is shown by the identification of them as lampstands (11:4)."*[152]

---

[150] DC Talk and the Voice of the Martyrs, *Jesus Freaks vol. 1* (Tulsa, OK: Alsbury Publishing, 1999), 111-13.

[151] Phillips, *Revelation,* 318.

[152] Richard Bauckham, *New Testament Theology: The Theology of the Book of Revelation* (New York, NY: Cambridge University Press, 2013), 84-85.

To grasp this text, we must look at the Old Testament allusion John has in mind. The imagery is taken from an apocalyptic vision in Zechariah chapter eleven. In this vision there are two lampstands/olive trees (11:4, 11) described as *"the two anointed ones who stand by the Lord of the whole earth"* (Zech. 11:14). Reading through the entire chapter reveals the two olive trees are prince Zerubbabel (a king) and Joshua the high priest (an anointed priest). The key to the Zechariah passage is found not in the people, but in the person of the Spirit. 4:6 says, *"Not by might nor by power, but by my Spirit, says the Lord of hosts."* In Zechariah's day, the Spirit of God was working through His Word, using both kings and priests as His witnesses to Israel.

Likewise, in Revelation 11 there are two lampstands/olive trees (11:4) who are called to bear witness to God. If they were harmed, God would bring judgment. Yet, God makes clear that their ministry would end in death by Satan at the same spot of Jesus' crucifixion (11:5-8). These two witnesses would **"have the power to shut the sky, that no rain may fall during the days of their prophesying, and they have power over the waters to turn them into blood and to strike the earth with every kind of plague, as often as they desire"** (11:6). Those familiar with the Old Testament will quickly be ushered to 1 Kings 17, where Elijah prayed for the skies to be shut for three and a half years,[153] and Moses turning the Nile into blood in Exodus 7:7ff. Likewise, when John says, **"if anyone would harm them, fire pours from their mouth and consumes their foes"** (11:5), it harkens back to 2 Kings chapter one, when Elijah calls down fire on soldiers trying to arrest him. With all these passages in mind, God is revealing that the two witnesses will be used by Him to declare His Word by His Spirit. Remember, we are still in the intermission between the sixth and seventh trumpet, which are designed to bring assurance to the people of God. In Revelation 11:1-2 we see how God is separating His people from the rest of humanity:

> **"Then I was given a measuring rod like a staff, and I was told, 'Rise and measure the temple of God and the altar and those who worship there, but do not measure the court outside the temple; leave that out, for it is given over to the nations, and they will trample the holy city for forty-two months.'"**

In Revelation 1:12, 20, we saw that the lampstands were the seven churches. The same applies here. Yet, in Revelation 11 these lampstands are in the same vision as the actual temple, leading me to believe this is a picture of the true church, the people of God purchased with the blood of Christ (cf. 1 Cor. 3:16-17; 2 Cor. 6:16; Eph. 2:21). In support of this view, the language of verse 8 directs us to interpret this symbolically when John writes, **"and their dead bodies will lie in the street of the great city that symbolically is called Sodom and Egypt, where their Lord was crucified."**[154] All of this is a comfort to God's people, reminding us that God has marked us for salvation, and that we dwell in the true temple, Christ Himself.

Even so, we are reminded that faithfulness doesn't always mean security on this earth. Sometimes we wonder, especially in seasons of glad gospel proclamation, how God could allow us to suffer. Rather than faithfulness and suffering being incompatible, they are often two sides of the same coin. If you are an adopted child of God, you will suffer (cf. Rom. 8:15-17). The two lampstands/olive trees that represent the True Church are no exception. Revelation 11:8 reminded us that **"their dead**

---

[153] Note the same time reference to Revelation 11:9. 1 Kings 17 is three and a half years, while Revelation 11:9 is there and a half days, but the picture is parallel.

[154] The use of πνευματικῶς (*pneumatikos*) can be understood figuratively. From the context of the passage, it seems that John is driving us to a symbolic or figurative meaning that Jerusalem is now identified with Sodom and Gomorrah.

bodies will lie in the street of the great city." And while the unbelieving world will look on in glad agreement at the death of Christ's faithful martyrs (11:9-10), God will raise them victoriously the same way He raised His Son. John writes,

> *"But after the three and a half days a breath of life from God entered them, and they stood up on their feet, and great fear fell on those who saw them. ¹² Then they heard a loud voice from heaven saying to them, "Come up here!" And they went up to heaven in a cloud, and their enemies watched them"* (Rev. 11:11-12).

This miraculous and victorious resurrection is for all the unbelieving world to see, drawing our eyes back to Ezekiel 37 when God breathed life into dead and decrepit bodies. Ezekiel 37:5 states, *"Thus says the Lord God to these bones: Behold, I will cause breath to enter you, and you shall live."* Even more similar language to Rev. 11:11 is founded in Ezekiel 37:10, which says:

> *"So I prophesied as He commanded me, and the breath came into them, and they lived and stood on their feet, an exceedingly great army."* Beale comments on this, *"It seemed that had deserted the witnesses by leaving them in a subdued condition. But He vindicates them by delivering them and demonstrating that He is their covenantal protector. The deliverance in 11:11-12 could be literal resurrection from the dead. But that appears not to be the focus, since the conquering of the witnesses did not entail all of their literal deaths. Rather, as parallels to this episode elsewhere in Revelation show, a community of believers still exists, and God vindicates them by destroying their oppressors (so 20:7-10, which is based on Ezekiel 38). At the least, the ascent of the witnesses figuratively affirms a final, decisive deliverance and vindication of God's people at the end of time."*[155]

These two faithful witnesses—symbolizing the True Church— *"went up to heaven in a cloud"* (11:12) with the same one that came down out of a cloud in 10:1. This shows divine approval of the faithful bride. This is reminiscent of 1 Kings 2:11 when Elijah was taken up into heaven in the midst of a storm-wind. Both instances of faithful prophets taken up in the clouds are echoes of the Prophet (Deut. 18:15), on whom a cloud descended, and God voiced His approval (Matt. 17:5), who also ascended back to the Father on the clouds (Acts 1:9-11). This same faithful Prophet, the Lord Jesus, will return on the clouds bringing judgment and salvation (Dan. 7:13; Matt. 26:64).

Revelation 11:13 tells of simultaneous judgment on the wicked. It says, *"And at that hour there was a great earthquake, and a tenth of the city fell. Seven thousand people were killed in an earthquake, and the rest were terrified and gave glory to the God of heaven."* The language here is almost directly taken from Ezekiel 38:19, *"where seismos megas (great earthquake) is used of final judgment of Gog at the end of history, when Gog attempts to exterminate restored Israel."*[156] This means that the pattern of resurrection and judgment in Ezekiel 37-38 are at the forefront of the vision in Revelation 11. While the context of Revelation 11 focuses on Jerusalem, we are reminded that John is using Jerusalem symbolically for the whole world.[157]

---

[155] Beale, *Revelation*, 597.

[156] Ibid., 602.

[157] Beale concludes that those who do not die in the earthquake and give glory to God uses similar wording from Daniel 4 when Nebuchadnezzar gives glory to God; we are not sure if he was authentic or generally acknowledging Daniel's God. The same may be true here in Rev. 11:13.

Then the intermission ceases, and we proceed to the seventh trumpet in Revelation 11:15-19. The entire passage appears to bring in the kingdom of God in its fullness. Revelation 11:15b makes this most clear when a myriad of loud voices in heaven say, *"**The kingdom of the world has become the kingdom of our Lord and of His Christ, and He shall reign forever and ever.**"* Not only is this evidence that the second coming is in mind but notice an earlier phrase that is repeated in 11:17 and what is missing: *"**We give thanks to you, Lord God Almighty, who is and who was, for you have taken your great power and begun your reign.**"* Do you see what is missing? The original phrase was, *"who is and who was and who is to come"* (1:4, 8), but in 11:17 the *"who is to come"* is omitted. This is a grammatical clue that the seventh trumpet ushers in the second coming who no longer *"is to come"* but He is here!

Sam Storms agrees when saying, *"With the seventh trumpet we have reached the consummation. There are loud voices in heaven speaking. There is lightning, sounds, and peals of thunder. The temple of God is mentioned, as is the throne. Divine wrath comes upon unbelievers."*[158] Upon the arrival of this great Day in Rev. 11:18, we get an Old Testament connection to Psalm 2. This Psalm is about the eternal reign of God's anointed, the same King described in Daniel 7:13-14. Psalm 2:8 also makes clear the vastness of the kingdom when it says, *"Ask of me, and I will make the nations your heritage, and the ends of the earth your possession."* Christ the King brought the kingdom during His Incarnation (Mark 1:15). He will bring the fullness of the kingdom at His second coming. His kingdom was secure and limitless at His first coming. But we will experience the fullness of the kingdom at His second coming. In the famous words of Abraham Kuyper, *""There is not a square inch in the whole domain of our human existence over which Christ, who is Sovereign over all, does not cry, Mine!"*[159]

As this vision begins to conclude, John sees *"**God's temple in heaven was opened, and the ark of His covenant was seen within His temple**"* **(11:19a).** This is no small detail. It ought to cause our hearts to burst with delight. The Old Covenant speaks of an ark that is hidden behind the veil. It was hidden from sight and represented the presence of God in His holy Temple. The vision John sees is one of *full access* to the presence of God. How could this be possible? Hebrews 10:19-20 declares, *"Therefore, brothers, since we have confidence to enter the holy places by the blood of Jesus, by the new and living way that He opened for us through the curtain, that is, through His flesh."* The loving and substitutionary sacrifice of Christ grants us access into the presence of God forever! Hendricksen says, *"That ark of the covenant is the symbol of the superlatively real, intimate, and perfect fellowship between God and His people—a fellowship based on the atonement."*[160] This is why John wrote to the seven suffering churches. This is why we are blessed to read this book today (Rev. 1:3). The second coming of our Lord, the high king of heaven, will tear down all the doors that stand between us and the unfiltered presence of Christ. No longer by faith, but by sight! *"Beloved, we are God's children now, and what we will be has not yet appeared; but we know that when He appears we shall be like Him, because we shall see Him as He is."* (1 John 3:2)

"High King of Heaven, my victory won,
May I reach Heaven's joys, O bright Heav'n's Sun!
Heart of my own heart, whatever befall,
Still be my Vision, O Ruler of all."[161]

---

[158] Sam Storms, *Kingdom Come*, 401.

[159] Abraham Kuyper, https://www.goodreads.com/quotes/99035-there-is-not-a-square-inch-in-the-whole-domain.

[160] Hendricksen, *More Than Conquerors*, 133.

[161] Dallan Forgaill, *Be Thou My Vision,*

WEEK 8
STUDY

REVELATION 12:1-14:20
Christus Victor &
The Demise of the Dragon

MEDITATION: Pray that God would shine His light in your heart as you study Revelation 12:1-6.

1) What is happening in the imagery of Revelation 12:1-6? List the three characters in this text and who they most likely symbolize. According to the structure of Revelation who should we identify with in this conflict?

2) Read Psalm 2:9 along with Revelation 12:5. What are some characteristics of this "child?" With the whole of Psalm 2 in mind, why would this be a comfort to the seven churches in Revelation?

3) The conflict beginning in Revelation 12:1-6 is seen throughout the history of the Old Testament. How far back does this conflict go? Does it ever get resolved? (See Gen. 3:15; Col. 2:13-15)

APPLICATION: Should Satan be feared? Why or why not? What are some ways he has deceived you recently? What does the end hold for him?

MEDITATION: Be mindful as you study Revelation 12:7-17 that you are meeting with the Great Conqueror and Deliverer.

1. Read Revelation 12:7-12 as one symbolic vision, and 12:13-17 as another symbolic vision. What similarities and differences to these visions have with 12:1-6?

2. When reading Revelation 12:7-17, what can we conclude about Christ and His people? What can we conclude about the dragon?

3. Read Revelation 12:10. As a first century believer, suffering at the hands of the evil one, how would this verse have comforted its original hearers? How does this comfort you?

APPLICATION: As you consider your posture before God, does your identity in Christ ring louder than Satan's accusations against you? Summarize what God says about a Christian's identity? Write out a verse to memorize on page 305.

MEDITATION: Praise God, that there is none like Him, as you read Revelation 13:1-18.

1. How are Satan and the beasts mimicking the Trinity? How do the followers of the evil one mimic the people of God?

2. What are the main agendas of the beasts according to Revelation 13:4 and 13:7? Have you ever noticed yourself being drawn into this first agenda or experiencing the second agenda?

3. What is the mark of the beast according to Revelation 13:16-18? Consider this week's commentary notes to help you see the deceitful ways of the evil one. How must we be awake and aware of wolves dressed like sheep (Matt. 7:15)?

APPLICATION: The false trinity in Revelation 13 is a reminder that Satan doesn't typically tempt us with things we would usually avoid. Read James 1:13-15. Write an honest confession below that you will also share with a trusted brother or sister and ask for their help, prayer and accountability.

MEDITATION: Pray that you will listen and obey to the voice of heaven as you read Revelation 14:1-13.

1. What earlier scene does Revelation 14:1-5 seem to repeat? Why do you think the author places this directly after the brutal onslaught of deception in Revelation 12-13? See 14:4 for help.

2. What makes the gospel "eternal" (Rev. 14:6)? When you think of the power of the gospel, do you tend to think of it as something you believed in the past, or something you are believing today?

3. Read Revelation 14:6-13. Would you agree that the messages of the angels are summarized in 14:12? Why or why not? Are these first century divine warnings still applicable for you today?

4. According to Revelation 14:7, what is the route to avoiding the pitfalls of false worship?

APPLICATION: What do you fear most (honestly)? If it is not God, why?

MEDIATION: Pray that you will not be one who trifles with God as you read Revelation 14:14-20.

1. If Revelation 12-14 is another angle of the time period between the cross and the second coming, what event is in view in Revelation 14:14-20? Read Revelation 14:20 and 19:15. Can this be different events or do you think John retelling these events from different angles?

2. Read Matthew 3:12. Do Jesus' words seem to match what is happening in Revelation 14:14-20?

3. The imagery of Revelation 14:20 should be appalling. Why is John writing with such graphic descriptions?

APPLICATION: We are called to live each day as if Jesus were returning. If so, who should you share the glorious and eternal gospel with today? Do you need help doing so? Ask a brother or sister to come alongside you in prayer and evangelism.

TELEIOS
ACADEMY

WEEK 8
COMMENTARY

REVELATION 12:1-14:20
Christus Victor &
The Demise of the Dragon

CHRISTUS VICTOR AND THE DEMISE OF THE DRAGON

REVELATION 12:1-6

Near the beginning of history, not long after God's good creation erupted forth from His love, the serpent slithered his way into the Garden of Eden, testing God's Word. Genesis 3 tells of the downfall of humanity as sin entered the world, radically tarnishing all creation. Yet, in the midst of the brokenness and sorrow, the mercy of God was radically present. God walked Adam and Eve to the edge of the Garden, before they head east of Eden, and declared a promise to them. More specifically, the promise was directed toward the serpent, but would benefit all of God's people. God said, *"I will put enmity between you and the woman, and between your offspring and her offspring; he shall bruise your head and you shall bruise his heel."* Way back then, God was promising He would send a Hero to strike a death blow to the serpent. In this victory, the Hero would suffer a wound as well. The crucifixion of Christ was this deathblow. Satan, the serpent, was put to open shame, and the cross freed the people of God from slavery and started the countdown to the serpent's final demise. The author of Revelation is taking us further behind the curtain of this heavenly reality. We would be wise to look with the faith-filled eyes of a child. As G.K. Chesterton famously said, *"Fairy tales are more than true — not because they tell us dragons exist, but because they tell us dragons can be beaten."*[162]

If we were to take Revelation 12:1-6 as a literal picture of things to come, building doomsday would be the logical approach. But, like the rest of Revelation, this is a *picture* of something literal. Thus, we continue to press forward as overcomers by the blood of the Lamb. Yes, the vision is frightening. John means it to be. We are shown three different characters in 12:1-6. We'll take them one at a time before concluding what this apocalyptic and prophetic picture is designed to communicate.

First, we have the radiant woman. John writes, ***"And a great sign appeared in heaven: a woman clothed with the sun, with the moon under her feet, and on her head a crown of twelve stars. ² She was pregnant and was crying out in birth pains and the agony of giving birth"*** **(Rev. 12:1-2).** This first character sign bears witness to a woman who appears as some type of goddess at first glance. We should keep in mind that chapter divisions were not original to the text. Chapter 11 ended with God's temple being opened for all of His people. John saw a symbol pointing

---

[162] G.K. Chesterton, https://www.goodreads.com/quotes/403140-fairy-tales-do-not-give-the-child-his-first-idea.

to greater meaning and significance. Some scholars believe this refers to Mary, the mother of Jesus. In another view, which I also embrace, this image points to the church. Phillips argues, "*The woman, therefore, is the covenant community of God's faithful people, through whom God brought His Son, the long-promised Savior, into the world.*"[163] An Old Testament allusion might help us here. Consider John's description of this sign including the sun, moon, and a crown of twelve stars. Genesis 37:9-11 invites us to listen to Joseph tell his family about his dream:

> "*Then he dreamed another dream and told it to his brothers and said, "Behold, I have dreamed another dream. Behold, the sun, the moon, and eleven stars were bowing down to me." But when he told it to his father and to his brothers, his father rebuked him and said to him, "What is this dream that you have dreamed? Shall I and your mother and your brothers indeed come to bow ourselves to the ground before you?" And his brothers were jealous of him, but his father kept the saying in mind.*"

In this dream, Jacob is the sun, Rachel is the moon, and Joseph's twelve brothers are the eleven stars. The point John is trying to make about this sign is that the church, the people of God in its entirety from Genesis to Revelation, brought forth the Messiah through a band of rebels and sinners (cf. Matthew 1). As Douglas Kelly so wonderfully words it, "*Old Testament Israel was being used as a womb from which the Messiah would be born.*"[164]

The second sign in Revelation 12 is described like this:

> **"And another sign appeared in heaven: behold, a great red dragon, with seven heads and ten horns, and on his head seven diadems. [4] His tail swept down a third of the stars of heaven and cast them to the earth. And the dragon stood before the woman who was about to give birth, so that when she bore her child he might devour it"** (Rev. 12:3-4).

Revelation 12 is a shift from the first 11 chapters. Although it is another angle to the same time period, chapters 12 and following seem to highlight the battle between the Trinity and the evil forces led by Satan. It's as if we are sitting in a theatre and the curtains are drawn. The lights turn off and the auditorium is filled with the sounds of beasts charging, armor clashing, and pandemonium on a grand scale. The author of the story calls you on stage and pulls the curtains back just a smidge, and you see a great red dragon waging war against the precious bride of Christ. But what are we to make of his **"Seven heads and ten horns, and on his head seven diadems"**? This appears to be harkening back to Daniel 7:7 and 7:24. In Daniel's vision of the four beasts, he writes,

> "*After this I saw in the night visions, and behold, a fourth beast, terrifying and dreadful and exceedingly strong. It had great iron teeth; it devoured and broke in pieces and stamped what was left with its feet. It was different from all the beasts that were before it, and it had ten horns*" (Dan. 7:7) and again, "*As for the ten horns, out of this kingdom ten kings shall arise, and another shall arise after them; he shall be different from the former ones, and shall put down three kings*" (Dan. 7:24).

---

[163] Phillips, *Revelation,* 343.
[164] Douglas F. Kelly, *Revelation,* 216.

The red dragon is the serpent who began waging war with Adam and has been ever-present in deceiving and tempting the people of God ever since. He was driven to **"devour"** the Messiah from that first gospel promise in Genesis 3:15. Leithart writes,

> *"He casts stars from heaven with his tail, then stands before the woman to receive the child and devour it. He knows that the woman bears the promised Seed, knows that the Seed owns the future, and knows that if the Seed comes, he is doomed. He must stop the Seed before it can be planted and grow (a doomed project, since killing and burying is planting). This is the archaic serpent in the garden, attacking Eve. The dragon waits to devour the newborn child."*[165]

The imagery of horns and seven heads, and so on, are meant to be a picture of power and aggression. But if you add up the number of heads on Daniel's beasts, you end up with seven, which this *one* dragon has. He is the picture of pure unadulterated evil and is out to destroy Christ and His bride at all costs. This ought not shock us because, as Jesus said about the evil one, *"You are of your father the devil, and your will is to do your father's desires. He was a murderer from the beginning, and does not stand in the truth, because there is no truth in him. When he lies, he speaks out of his own character, for he is a liar and the father of lies"* (John 8:44).

The third character is described like this: **"She gave birth to a male child, one who is to rule all the nations with a rod of iron, but her child was caught up to God and to His throne,** **⁶ and the woman fled into the wilderness, where she has a place prepared by God, in which she is to be nourished for 1,260 days"** (Rev. 12:5-6). Verse five is a summary statement of Christ's incarnate life on earth. John writes elsewhere that the whole world could not contain the books of Christ's work on earth (John 21:25). But here, he sums up the life of Christ in one verse! Beale agrees, *"Now a snapshot of Christ's entire life—his birth, his destiny of kingship, and his incipient fulfillment of that destiny in his ascent to God's heavenly throne after his post resurrection ministry—is given in one line."*[166] Beale goes on to show that the purpose of this, especially that John omits any mention of Christ's death, is to highlight His *"victory and ascension."*[167] When His kingship is described, it is an Old Testament allusion to Psalm 2:9; *"You shall break them with a rod of iron and dash them in pieces like a potter's vessel."*

Imagine you are back in the auditorium again. As you have felt the fire from the mouth of the dragon, and heard the sweep of his tail, all of a sudden you look up above the stage into the rafters. There you see a child, snickering and giggling at the dragon. While the people of God are terrified at its ensuing wrath against them, the child-king laughs and holds them in derision (cf. Psalm 2:4). Christ the King has woven throughout the drama of Scripture a story where the deceiving dragon just will not win. We no longer have to see this drama as life-threatening. While we may be tempted to think that the worst that can happen is death, the gospel takes the sting of death away and tells us that the new worst that can happen is life here. But even life here, as Paul says, is fruitful labor for the church (cf. Philippians 1:21-23). In the face of the dragon and all his deception and temptation, we can sing Romans 8:31-39 with the saints:

> *"What then shall we say to these things? If God is for us, who can be against us? ³² He who did not spare His own Son but gave Him up for us all, how will He not also with Him graciously give us all things? Who shall bring any charge against God's elect? It is God who justifies. Who is to condemn?*

---

[165] Peter J. Leithart, *Revelation 12-22*, 23.
[166] Beale, *Revelation*, 639.
[167] Ibid.

Christ Jesus is the one who died—more than that, who was raised—who is at the right hand of God, who indeed is interceding for us. Who shall separate us from the love of Christ? Shall tribulation, or distress, or persecution, or famine, or nakedness, or danger, or sword? As it is written, 'For your sake we are being killed all the day long; we are regarded as sheep to be slaughtered.' No, in all these things we are more than conquerors through Him who loved us. For I am sure that neither death nor life, nor angels nor rulers, nor things present nor things to come, nor powers, nor height nor depth, nor anything else in all creation, will be able to separate us from the love of God in Christ Jesus our Lord."

The King has risen in victory over the Serpent and we are intimately bound to Him. Let us sing,

"He's alive, He's alive!
Heaven's gates are opened wide.
He's alive, He's alive!
Now in heaven glorified."[168]

REVELATION 12:7-17

In Job 1 and Zechariah 3, we are given glimpses into the heavenly courtroom where Satan stands accusing God's people of their sin and filth before the throne of God. In both instances, God declares His servants justified and clean. With our heavenly throne scene in Revelation 4-5, we can conclude that this justification and cleansing are a result of the Lion and Lamb that stands as Mediator between His people and His Father. Revelation 12:7-17 is a picture into this throne room again, but this time something final and decisive happens: Satan is thrown down out of heaven. He can no longer accuse Christ's blood-bought people. Again, imagine being a persecuted believer in the first century and hearing this declaration:

> **"Now war arose in heaven, Michael and his angels fighting against the dragon. And the dragon and his angels fought back, but he was defeated, and there was no longer any place for them in heaven. And the great dragon was thrown down, that ancient serpent, who is called the devil and Satan, the deceiver of the whole world—he was thrown down to the earth, and his angels were thrown down with him"** (Rev. 12:7-9).

The archangel Michael and his subordinates wage war on the evil one and defeat him. The one who seemed to persevere in a brutal onslaught against Christ and His people, finds Himself falling from the courtroom of heaven. In his fall, it's as if he sees the "No vacancy" sign forever posted in glory. The serpent is tossed out with his whole band of deceiving angels and the history of redemption nears its end. Daniel 10:13, 21 and 12:1 are clearly in John's mind. There, Michael wages war against the earthly kingdoms and will one day fight the final battle against the father of lies. Daniel portrays Michael fighting on behalf of the Son of Man (Dan. 7), so here in Revelation 12, Michael is fighting on behalf of the Son of Man. The question is, when did this great eviction take place? According to what

[168] — KEITH GETTY, KRISTYN GETTY, AND ED CASH; *Christ is Risen, He is Risen Indeed,* © 2012 GETTYMUSIC AND ALLETROP MUSIC (BMI) (ADM. BY MUSICSERVICES.ORG)

we have seen throughout Revelation, and leaning also on Colossians 2:13-15, it seems biblically accurate to believe that Satan was cast out of the heavenly throne room and stripped of his ability to accuse believers at the cross and resurrection. Beale writes, *"The parallelism of these two OT prophecies (Dan. 2:35 and Psalm 2) supports our view that Rev. 12:7-12 depicts a heavenly version of what transpired on earth at the time of Christ's resurrection."*[169] This has very encouraging and practical implications for us because, while Satan and his evil army can still seek to deceive us, those deceptions and accusations no longer have one ounce of weight. Hendricksen says,

> *"Whereas Christ was born and rendered satisfaction for sin, Satan has lost every semblance of justice for his accusations against believers. True, he continues to accuse. That is his work even today. But no longer is he able to point to the unaccomplished work of the Savior. Christ's atonement has been fully accomplished; complete satisfaction for sin had been rendered when He ascended to heaven."*[170]

What a comfort to know that even when the vilest of accusations have truth to them, the final word is our Savior's cry from Calvary, "It is finished!" When I said that Satan's eviction was applied at the cross and resurrection, such a conclusion comes from the heavenly declaration in verses 10-12. John writes,

> **"And I heard a loud voice in heaven, saying, 'Now the salvation and the power and the kingdom of our God and the authority of His Christ have come, for the accuser of our brothers has been thrown down, who accuses them day and night before our God. And they have conquered him by the blood of the Lamb and by the word of their testimony, for they loved not their lives even unto death. Therefore, rejoice, O heavens and you who dwell in them! But woe to you, O earth and sea, for the devil has come down to you in great wrath, because he knows that his time is short!'"**

It is the atoning and resurrecting work of the Lord Jesus Christ that causes the angels of God to act like bouncers and cast Satan out of the heavenly party. Revelation 12:7-12 is a complementary vision to 12:1-6, making clear that Christ's victory over the evil one is definitive, from which the people of God gain confidence and comfort. Where Daniel 7 foretold of God the Father giving the kingdom to His Son, John shows us a heavenly picture of that taking place. Dennis Johnson writes, *"The dragon's banishment from heaven to earth marks the coming of God's kingdom and of His Christ's authority."*[171] In the unfolding narrative of Scripture, especially between the resurrection and Pentecost, we see the Christ pouring out the Spirit. This is especially meant to empower us to proclaim His kingdom, through which Christ ushers others in. *"From heaven's perspective, it is the coming of the kingdom that produces unmitigated joy, for the accuser's authority to prosecute 'our brethren' has been nullified by the shed blood of the Lamb."*[172] What is interesting, and an intentional phrase for John, is that the blood of the Lamb has conquered, but it is also **"the word of their testimony"** that conquers, referring to the accused brothers in verse 10. This means that that Christ's people are to walk in the expectation of effort with confidence they will overcome. As Reformed-type folks, we are not opposed to effort, but to earning.

---

[169] Beale, *Revelation*, 655.
[170] Hendricksen, *More Than Conquerors*, 141.
[171] Johnson, *Triumph of the Lamb*, 184.
[172] Ibid.

This means that being loved and freed by Christ (1:5b), will naturally result in Spirit-empowered obedience that longs to hold fast to the word. We cling to who Christ is and what He has done for us. Satan knows he has lost, but he creeps around in the shadows deceiving the world. When I was in the United States Army, almost all of my job was conducted at night. We were a team of highly-trained soldiers that could go into an extremely volatile conflict to accomplish our mission without many people knowing we were even there. Satan is the deceptive black-ops technician of the heavenly realm, sneaking around looking for people to devour (cf. 1 Pet. 5:8). But, when we bear witness to Christ's person and work, we are waging the offensive against him and reminding him that he lost the war 2,000 years ago at Golgotha. D.A. Carson wrote,

> *"How else can we push back against Satan and his forces? We will be defeated if we simply keep silent. If you never share the gospel with anybody else, you yourself are defeated. You are not pushing back the frontiers of darkness. This is how Satan is defeated—by the blood of the Lamb and by the word of your testimony."*[173]

So, we are to be glad people declaring the glad news of a glad Savior. The evil one knows his time is short (12:12), so let us be diligent. Diligence is needed is because of the serpent's response to being cast out of heaven. Notice in verses 13 and verse 17, Satan turns to an aggressive pursuit to destroy Christ's bride.

> **"And when the dragon saw that he had been thrown down to the earth, he pursued the woman who had given birth to the male child. But the woman was given the two wings of the great eagle so that she might fly from the serpent into the wilderness, to the place where she is to be nourished for a time, and times, and half a time. The serpent poured water like a river out of his mouth after the woman, to sweep her away with a flood. But the earth came to the help of the woman, and the earth opened its mouth and swallowed the river that the dragon had poured from his mouth. Then the dragon became furious with the woman and went off to make war on the rest of her offspring, on those who keep the commandments of God and hold to the testimony of Jesus. And he stood on the sand of the sea"** (Rev. 12:13-17).

Although his accusing credibility has been falsified, Satan is like a roaring lion with rabies seeking to devour Christ's people. In the final passage of Revelation 12, God shows us our own situation. That is, we stand between Christ's ascension and second coming. We are victorious in Christ, and at the same time we are at war against the evil one. Although the victory has been won, Satan is determined to deceive and destroy as many souls as he can before he is cast into the Lake of Fire (Rev. 20:1-6). Richard Phillips gives a historical comparison with Hitler that helps illuminate this text. Describing the months after victory had been won, he writes,

> *"In his mad rage against his enemies, he did all that he could to hurt them. One example is the V-2 rocket campaign that Hitler rained on the cities of England in the last months of the war. Until the*

---

[173] D.A. Carson, "This Present Evil Age," in *These Last Days: A Christian View of History*, ed. Richard D. Phillips and Gabriel Fluhrer (Phillipsburg, NJ: P&R Publishing, 2011), 35-36.

rocket-launch sites were finally overrun, over a thousand V-2 rockets had landed in England, killing many people and badly damaging London. Why did Hitler do this even though the war had been lost? Revelation 12:12 answers: 'Woe to you, O earth and sea, for the devil has come down to you in great wrath, because he knows that his time is short!'[174]

The imagery John uses in the next couple verses is meant to direct God's people to a place of refuge in the midst of Satan's chaos. In 12:14 the woman (the church) is given ***"the two wings of the great eagle"*** as a means of safety and nourishment from the serpent. This would have drawn the original audience quickly back to the Old Testament, especially of God's sovereign protection and provision like Exodus 19:4-6 and Deuteronomy 32:10-11. As Satan tempts them, and us, we are nourished for ***"a time, times, and half a time,"*** which is symbolic for the same age the whole book of Revelation represents between the death and resurrection of our Lord and His second coming.[175] This is the fulfillment of Daniel 12:5-7. Trying everything he possibly can, Satan floods the saints with a symbolic river from his mouth. I understand this text as harkening back to when Pharaoh tried to drown Israel, but I admit this is not absolutely clear.

When ***"the earth opened its mouth and swallowed the river that the dragon had poured from his mouth"*** (Rev. 12:16) this is an allusion to Numbers 16:26-33, where God opens a gaping crevasse in the earth to swallow up false witnesses who opposed Moses. So, false witnesses are swallowed up while those who bear witness to Christ are protected under the loving care of their God. Revelation 12 ends with Satan continuing his uncontrollable rebellion against God and His people. For current readers, we should understand ourselves as part of this age-old battle that began in Genesis 3. But, we now stand in the victory of Christ. His banner of love and righteousness follows us wherever we go. Even in moments of failure and sin, we are not doomed. Instead, we must look up with great gratitude and rejoice our Christ with the repentance that leads to salvation without regret (cf. 2 Cor. 7:10). We gladly declare the good news of the gospel to our neighbors knowing that our Sovereign can pluck them, too, from the fire. We bear witness to the testimony of Christ as those who are under the loving care of God. One day we will stand with our feet planted on Mount Zion as co-heirs with our Great King and friend.

The great hymn writer, Charles Wesley, had gone through an extensive season of spiritual doubt and weakness. Through a friend, God encouraged him and renewed his faith. One year later, Wesley wrote an 18-stanza hymn called "*O For A Thousand Tongues to Sing.*" The song describes the way we are called to conquer through the word of our testimony. Consider singing this portion, and rejoice in the freedom we have to bear witness to the glory of God and all He has done for us:

"O For a thousand tongues to sing
My dear Redeemer's praise!
The glories of my God and King,
The triumphs of His grace!

My gracious Master and my God,
Assist me to proclaim,

---

[174] Phillips, *Revelation*, 360.

[175] The interpretation of this period of time is highly debated between premillennial and amillennial convictions. However, let that not move your affections away from the clear point of the text that God Himself is the refuge and provider for His people in the midst of Satan's last hoorah.

To spread through all the world abroad
The honors of Thy name.

Jesus! the Name that charms our fears,
That bids our sorrows cease;
'Tis music in the sinner's ears,
'Tis life, and health, and peace.

He breaks the power of cancell'd sin,
He sets the prisoner free;
His blood can make the foulest clean,
His blood avail'd for me."

REVELATION 13:1-18

At the end of Revelation 12 Satan, the deceiving serpent-dragon, was booted out of heaven. He was determined to destroy as many followers of Christ as possible even though he had lost the war against Christ the King. Chapter 13 describes Satan's assault on the collective band of believers. Being the deceiver, his plan is to divide the people of God by a "false trinity" opposed to the true Triune God and his people. Although God's people walk by faith, not by sight (cf. 2 Cor. 5:7), we can be deceived by what we see and hear. In 2001, John Travolta starred as a man named Gabriel in a movie called "Swordfish." After a moment of absolute deception, he says to another character, *"Have you ever heard of Harry Houdini? Well he wasn't like today's magicians who are only interested in television ratings. He was an artist. He could make an elephant disappear in the middle of a theater filled with people, and do you know how he did that? Misdirection. What the eyes see, and the ears hear, the mind believes."*[176] Jesus calls us not to judge by appearances (7:24), but we are all guilty.

Satan's deceptive strategy is to draw people to Himself through two beasts:

"And I saw a beast rising out of the sea, with ten horns and seven heads, with ten diadems on its horns and blasphemous names on its heads" (Rev. 13:1).

"Then I saw another beast rising out of the earth. It had two horns like a lamb and it spoke like a dragon" (Rev. 13:11).

The first beast **"out of the sea"** reminds us of Leviathan (cf. Job 41:1) who ruled out of the sea, while the second of the beast that ruled **"out of the earth"** (cf. Job 40:15). Reading Daniel 7 reveals that John also has the four beasts of that chapter. The beasts in Daniel are of the sea and of the earth. They are powerful kingdoms and oppress God's people. They deceive and terrorize.

The first beast has **"blasphemous names"** on all if its heads. This shows it is full of deception and anti-Christ behavior. Derek Thomas writes, *"The background here may well be the fondness of the Roman emperors for being referred to by divine names. Domitian, for example, demanded to be called 'our Lord and our God'. The first readers of Revelation were familiar with ships coming to shore bearing the divine names of Roman*

---

[176] John Travolta, *Swordfish*, 2001.

emperors and establishing worship in the local port-cities."[177] Part of the deception is to mimic the True King, particularly as the Lamb who was slain. In Revelation 5:6-10, we were taken into the throne room and saw Christ standing as a Lamb who was slain. Alive from the dead, He alone was worthy to open the scrolls. Revelation 13:3-4 tells of the deceitful mimicking of the beast when John writes,

> **"One of its heads seemed to have a mortal wound, but its mortal wound was healed, and the whole earth marveled as they followed the beast. And they worshiped the dragon, for he had given his authority to the beast, and they worshiped the beast, saying, "Who is like the beast, and who can fight against it?"**

Thomas makes a great grammatical and exegetical observation: "*The use of the language 'seemed to have' in the ESV rendering of verse 3, 'One of its heads seemed to have a mortal wound', is not meant to cast doubt on its reality or even in its eventual fatality. It is a parallel—perhaps a deliberate parody of John's vision of 'a Lamb standing as though it had been slain' (5:6).*"[178] Or as Phillips uncovers, "*Parallels in the Greek text make clear the connection with Christ's death and resurrection. The same word is used to say that both Jesus and the beast were 'slain,' and the same word is used to say that Jesus 'came to life' (2:8) and the beast 'yet lived' (13:14).*[179] The sad and terrifying result of such parody is that "***they worshipped the beast,***" just as the evil one desires. Ironically, the multitude of unbelieving worshipers marvel at the wound and healing of this wicked beast, yet deny the Lamb who was slain and raised to the glory of God his Father. Beale writes,

> "*The multitudes likewise worship the beast because of his purported incomparability: they proclaim in their worship 'who is like the beast and who is able to make war with him?' The expression of Satanic incomparability is an ironic use of OT phraseology applied to Yahweh (Exod. 8:10; 15:11; Deut. 3:24; Isa. 40:18, 25: 44:7; 46:5 Ps. 35:10; 71:19; 86:8; 89:8; 113:5; Mic. 7:18). This is a further attempt at Satanic imitation of God.*"[180]

Not only does the beast blaspheme God in his self-exaltation and deception, we see that God allows him to do so:

> **"And the beast was given a mouth uttering haughty and blasphemous words, and it was allowed to exercise authority for forty-two months. It opened its mouth to utter blasphemies against God, blaspheming his name and his dwelling, that is, those who dwell in heaven. Also, it was allowed to make war on the saints and to conquer them. And authority was given it over every tribe and people and language and nation, and all who dwell on earth will worship it, everyone whose name has not been written before the foundation of the world in the book of life of the Lamb who was slain"** (Rev. 13:5-8).

Here, the Satanic pseudo-Lion and pseudo-Lamb draws a line in the sand as he calls people to worship the Serpent rather than the Christ. In a mysterious way we see that God allows this (13:5, 7).

---

[177] Derek Thomas, *Let's Study Revelation*, 110.
[178] Ibid., 111.
[179] Phillips, *Revelation*, 366-67.
[180] Beale, *Revelation*, 694.

The Serpent's intent is to pretend he has the authority (13:5, 7) so all will worship him. We get a peek at God's motives when John described that none of these false worshipper's names are written in **"the book of life of the Lamb who was slain"** (verse 8). While the beast's authority is expressed only in talk, the Lion and Lamb has extensively exercised his authority throughout human history in word and deed. Who is this beast? If Revelation's structure shows different perspectives of the same period in history, then this beast can be represented throughout the time between the cross and the second coming. Quoting Vern Poythress, Richard Phillips writes, "*In democratic countries, Satan wants people to look to the state as if it were the messiah. When the government is set forth as the remedy for all ills—economic, social, medical, moral, and even spiritual—then the idolatry of the state usurps the place reserved for God alone.*"[181] Not only is the deceiving false messiah driven to blaspheme God with a host of faithful followers, he is on an all-out mission to persecute the people of God. Thankfully, those whose names are written in the Lamb's book of life will be preserved to rejoice in the victory of Christ. In a foretelling of the defeat of the beast, Isaiah eloquently proclaims, "*In that day the LORD with his hard and great and strong sword will punish Leviathan the fleeing serpent, Leviathan the twisting serpent, and He will slay the dragon that is in the sea*" (Isa. 27:1).

We need to be aware of the second beast as well. Where Satan is the pseudo-Father, and the first beast is the Pseudo-Christ, this second beast functions as a pseudo-spirit-prophet using its deception to drive people's worship back to the first beast. Dennis Johnson writes, "*It is a counterfeit John the Baptist, simulating but not sharing the spirit and power of Elijah (cf. Luke 1:17; Matt. 11:14; Mal. 4:5-6).*"[182] We see these characteristics when the beloved disciple writes,

> **"It performs great signs, even making fire come down from heaven to earth in front of people, and by the signs that it is allowed to work in the presence of the beast it deceives those who dwell on earth, telling them to make an image for the beast that was wounded by the sword and yet lived. And it was allowed to give breath to the image of the beast, so that the image of the beast might even speak and might cause those who would not worship the image of the beast to be slain"** (Rev. 13:13-15).

In the same way that the Holy Spirit directs all worship to Christ, so the second beast deceives the masses into worshipping the first beast, who mimics Christ the Lamb.

What are we to make of this second beast in regard to its work in the church-age? Where the first beast was a symbol of political and military power, the second beast is a symbol of Satan's deceptive use of religious idolatry. Joel Beeke put it like this:

> "*As the second beast, the Roman imperial powers did not oppose the worship of various gods, so long as those worshippers honored the Emperor. In fact, in Asia Minor there were priests and temples devoted specifically to the worship of the genius of the Emperor. One such temple in Ephesus housed a large statue of Domitian. Christians in Asia Minor felt increasing pressure to publicly offer worship to the Emperor, and refusal to participate could result in economic exclusion from commerce, and worse yet, capital punishment from the civil authorities.*[183]

---

[181] Vern Poythress, *The Returning King: A Guide to the Book of Revelation* (Phillipsburg, NJ: P&R Publishing, 2000), 139, quoted in Richard Phillips, *Revelation*, 369.

[182] Dennis Johnson, *Triumph of the Lamb*, 195,

[183] Joel R. Beeke, *Lectio Continua: Revelation* (Grand Rapids, MI: Reformation Heritage Books, 2016), 362.

This understanding of the beasts might be foreign for some of us, but if we are to interpret Revelation within the structure throughout the book, it is not hard to see these beasts as symbolic for oppressive regimes throughout history. Phillips agrees and says, *"The beast from the sea is a secular political power, while the beast from the earth is a religious institution fostering worship of the first beast."*[184] In fact, is this too hard to imagine in our own culture? Many in our society are drunk with sexual idolatry, and the blood sacrifice of abortion. Masses are labeled intolerant unless you agree with their version of tolerance. Media has a deceitful drive to push what sells and ignore the truth. We are actually not too far removed from Rome and the first century believers, except that Christians have yet to face death for their faith in Jesus here in our land. As the decline continues, true believers will be set apart from false professors of salvation. Yes, this is sobering. But, what an exciting time to be alive. We have a great Christ and the good news of the gospel to offer to those whose current idols are failing and leaving them hopeless.

The last part of Revelation 13 has led to much speculation and different interpretations over the last 100 years. If we look at it in the larger context of Revelation, it can actually appear quite simple. Revelation 13:16-18 says,

> **"Also it causes all, both small and great, both rich and poor, both free and slave, to be marked on the right hand or the forehead, so that no one can buy or sell unless he has the mark, that is, the name of the beast or the number of its name. This calls for wisdom: let the one who has understanding calculate the number of the beast, for it is the number of a man, and his number is 666."**

We have all encountered fanatics in our age who tend to assign every political leader as the antichrist. Or others who propose dates for a secret rapture and build doomsday bunkers. There are others who are quick to jump to conclusions about the mark of the beast and 666. Some have used the numbers 666 to be a symbol for Nero or some other evil world leader.

Revelation uses the number seven for completion or perfection, which would make six the number of incompletion or imperfection. Also, in context, the false trinity with the second beast drawing worship toward the first beast, the number 666 seems to be exposing the wickedness of the beasts and their man-centeredness. Or as Thomas says,

> *"According to 13:18, the number 666 is a 'number of a man,' and, tempting as it is to identify with a particular individual, it is more in the spirit of this chapter as a whole that it should signify something broader. The reference could be to man considered universally, that is, man without God, religious man without God!…It is likely that John intends 666 to be a parody of 777. A number short of completeness repeated three times is a trinity of imperfection. The beast of the earth bears the spirit of utter imperfection. Despite his lofty claims he bears a deadly flaw."*[185]

Carefully consider the mark of the beast. This mark cannot be a credit card chip, or something implanted in the skin, but imagery of ownership. Where the people of God have their names written in the book of the Lamb (13:8) and are sealed by God (7:3; 14:1), the false trinity of Revelation 12-14

[184] Phillips, *Revelation*, 376.
[185] Thomas, *Let's Study Revelation*, 113.

is marking false worshippers whose names are not written in the book of the Lamb. Interestingly, Phillips shows an example of this from 3 Maccabees,

> *"which recounts how the Egyptian tyrant Ptolemy IV Philopater demanded that the Jews offer pagan sacrifices. Those who refused were put to death. Those who relented were branded with an ivy-leaf symbol for Dionysus, the Greek god of wine and sensual indulgence. Bearing this mark afforded willing Jews all the privileges of citizenship in Ptolemy's realm (3 Macc. 2:28-30).[186]*

Whether or not this is the exact instance John has in mind, we can see the cultural practice of marking people out as something John is using to illustrate people's ultimate allegiances. Satan and his two beasts are on a mission to mark out anyone willing to turn away from Jesus Christ due to their suffering. He marks them as citizens of darkness. This means that John's call for wisdom in Revelation 13:18 is a call to wisely choose who to follow. It is a call to count the cost and see if the call to daily death to self (Luke 9:23) is worth it. And the vision from the heavenly realm is saying that it will always be worth it because once the Lord returns, you are either associated with the Trinity of love, or you are associated with the false trinity of deception and hatred. The former will eat at the marriage supper of the Lamb (19:6-10), while the latter will be judged by the rider on the white horse and thrown into the lake of fire (19:11-21).

REVELATION 14:1-13

Revelation 12-14 closes with a gripping scene of assurance for the people of God. The scene recapitulates what we saw in chapter seven with the 144,000, and the myriads of worshippers. John knows Satan's strategic warfare, side-by-side with his two beasts, could frighten Christ's blood-bought people. He therefore assures the redeemed that those for whom the Lamb dies, He also resurrects. Or as Paul says in Romans 6:3-5,

> *"Do you not know that all of us who have been baptized into Christ Jesus were baptized into his death? We were buried therefore with Him by baptism into death, in order that, just as Christ was raised from the dead by the glory of the Father, we too might walk in newness of life. For if we have been united with Him in a death like his, we shall certainly be united with Him in a resurrection like his."*

As the false worshippers of the false trinity in Revelation 13 were marked with ownership by Satan, the perfectly-numbered people of God in Revelation 14 are marked with ownership by God. Revelation 14:1-5 explains,

> **"Then I looked, and behold, on Mount Zion stood the Lamb, and with Him 144,000 who had his name and his Father's name written on their foreheads. And I heard a voice from heaven like the roar of many waters and like the sound of loud thunder. The voice I heard was like the sound of harpists playing on their harps, and they were singing a new song before the throne and before**

---

[186] Phillips, *Revelation*, 381.

the four living creatures and before the elders. No one could learn that song except the 144,000 who had been redeemed from the earth. It is these who have not defiled themselves with women, for they are virgins. It is these who follow the Lamb wherever He goes. These have been redeemed from mankind as firstfruits for God and the Lamb, and in their mouth no lie was found, for they are blameless."

John is being shown an image of the martyrs and faithful overcomers who are the first fruits of the Lamb. Just as Jesus was raised victoriously from the dead, so will be the myriad of His saints—symbolically numbered 144,000. While Satan and his pseudo-trinity persecute believers from generation to generation, God will bring the faith of his saints to completion (cf. Phil. 1:6). Although the world looks at Christians as wilted sprouts, barely surviving in the harsh elements of the world, God sees us in our finished form, as strong and sturdy fruit-bearing branches attached to the Vine (cf. John 15:1-11).

This vision explains the end-result for those who unashamedly believe the gospel (cf. 1 Cor. 15:1-6; Rom. 1:16-17). This is a picture of those who heed what Paul wrote to the Colossians, *"Therefore, as you received Christ Jesus the Lord, so walk in Him"* (Col. 2:6). The Christian life *does not* begin by the gospel and continue by our own hard work. Rather, it is a life of being conformed to Christ through the daily and habitual *work of believing* the gospel. Years ago, my wife shared a quote with me about the power of the gospel that delights me every time I think of it. Imagine this quote being read to the suffering and persecuted believers in first century Rome:

> *"Outside of heaven, the power of God in its highest density is found inside the gospel. This must be so, for the Bible twice describes the gospel as 'the power of God.' Nothing else in all of Scripture is ever described in this way, except for the Person of Jesus Christ. Such a description indicates that the gospel is not only powerful, but that it is the ultimate entity in which God's power resides and does its greatest work. Indeed, God's power is seen in erupting volcanoes, in the unimaginably hot boil of our massive sun, and in the lightning speed of a recently discovered star seen streaking through the heavens at 1.5 million miles per hour. Yet in Scripture such wonders are never labeled 'the power of God.' How powerful, then, must the gospel be that it would merit such a title! And how great a salvation it could accomplish in my life, if I would only embrace it by faith and give it a central place in my thoughts each day."*[187]

According to John, this powerful gospel is an eternal gospel. He writes,

"Then I saw another angel flying directly overhead, with an eternal gospel to proclaim to those who dwell on earth, to every nation and tribe and language and people. And he said with a loud voice, 'Fear God and give Him glory, because the hour of his judgment has come, and worship Him who made heaven and earth, the sea and the springs of water'" (Rev. 14:6-7).

What does this first of many angels in Revelation 14 have in mind when proclaiming "*an eternal gospel?*" Because Revelation is a glimpse into the heavenly realities of the eternal God, I am

---

[187] Milton Vincent, *A Gospel Primer for Christians: Learning to See the Glories of God's Love* (Self-published, 2008), 14-15.

inclined to believe (and rejoice!) that the Spirit of God wants us to know the gospel message *does not have an expiration date*. It is a message rooted in God, who decided to lavish His love on His people before the foundation of the world. The *eternal gospel* will produce *eternal* praise from the saints. Indeed, in God's wisdom, the gospel will cease to have *converting power* at Christ's Second Coming, but the joy it brings to the saints will never cease. For God, and for His people, the gospel will be the epicenter of our eternal joy. James Hamilton writes,

> *"Have you contemplated the majesty of the truth of the gospel? This is not just some old story—it is the eternal gospel. Let me encourage you to let your mind contemplate this until the grandeur of it rests on you with a weight that will change your life. If you know the gospel, you know truth that is true from eternity past and that will still be true in eternity future. If you know the gospel, you know the good news—everlasting good news."*[188]

The eternal Gospel is in view in Revelation 14:7 when the angel proclaims (preaches), **"Fear God and give Him glory, because the hour of his judgment has come, and worship Him who made heaven and earth, the sea and the springs of water."**

In Revelation 14:6-13 we are confronted with a vision containing two of the many angels in chapter 14. While the first angel declared the eternal gospel, together these heavenly messengers are sent to declare God's judgment. As with the previous cycles in the structure of Revelation, this vision is nearing the second coming of Christ. In chapter 14, as in the previous sections, judgment comes *before* Christ's return. The second of four angels declares, **"Fallen, fallen is Babylon the great, she who made all nations drink the wine of the passion of her sexual immorality"** (Rev. 14:8). Most scholars agree that "Babylon" in Revelation are references about Rome. This becomes clearer in light of 1 Peter 5:13, which says, *"She who is at Babylon, who is likewise chosen, sends you greetings."* In Revelation 14, the second angel is unequivocally declaring the imminent destruction of the great world-power. The reason of judgment is owing to Rome's culture of wickedness and sexual immorality. Friends, is our culture any different today? Absolutely not. This is why we should all pay heed to the message of Revelation. Masses of people surrounding us are steeped in the lie that sexual pleasure (outside of marriage) is a creature-comfort to which they entitled. The downfall of marriage, the rapid spread of disease, broken families, result from, and are perpetuated by, this cycle which has continued for generations. We, nor Babylon/Rome, were the first culprit of a culture of sin and sexual immorality. This is an evil fruit produced by unredeemed human hearts. Such degradation transcends places and times. *"Babylon is the spirit of godlessness which in every age lures men away from the worship of the Creator."*[189]

The third angel trumpets judgment against all who have been marked by the false trinity of Revelation 12-13. The angel declares,

> **"If anyone worships the beast and its image and receives a mark on his forehead or on his hand, he also will drink the wine of God's wrath, poured full strength into the cup of his anger, and he will be tormented with fire and sulfur in the presence of the holy angels and in the presence of the Lamb. And the smoke of their torment goes up forever and ever, and they have no rest, day or**

---

[188] Hamilton, *Revelation,* 284.
[189] Phillips, *Revelation,* 401.

night, these worshipers of the beast and its image, and whoever receives the mark of its name." (Rev. 14:9-11).

This is a strategic offense to rid the earth of false worshippers. This is the final pronouncement of judgment upon those whose names are not written in the book of the Lamb. These are permanently set aside to be vessels of wrath (cf. Rom. 9:19-24). If the camera lens were to zoom back from this scene, it would reveal a worldwide epidemic of idolatry, and focus on the eternal punishment for all who reject the blood of the Lamb. The wrath of God is being executed upon those who reject Christ, who endured their hell and torment on the cross. Instead of fleeing to Him for mercy, they have chosen to pay the price of utter wrath and destruction…*forever.*

Sometimes we are told that this is "eternal separation from God." However, Revelation 14:10 reveals the torment of the ungodly will take place *"in the presence of the holy angels and in the presence of the Lamb."* Indeed, the holy angels and the Lamb are present at the initial judgment. But Scripture is clear that God is present in wrath toward the judged forever. If God is omnipresent, everywhere at once, then hell must be a place God is present. Instead of His mercy, hell only experiences His power and wrath.

John's main point seems is that all will eventually realize the Lamb is who He says He is. All who rejected Him will see the glorious Lamb face-to face. But many will only receive His just judgment. As Phillips notes, *"This statement seems to indicate not only that the suffering of hell is physical, but that it also involves the anguish of seeing Christ, the Savior they had warred against in rebellion, exalted in triumph as Lord."*[190] The eternal results are so devastating: **"And the smoke of their torment goes up forever and ever, and they have no rest, day or night, these worshipers of the beast and its image, and whoever receives the mark of its name." (Rev. 14:11).** This is an allusion to Isaiah 34:9-10, which reads, *"And the streams of Edom shall be turned into pitch, and her soil into sulfur; her land shall become burning pitch.* [10] *Night and day it shall not be quenched; its smoke shall go up forever. From generation to generation it shall lie waste; none shall pass through it forever and ever."* Like God's dealing with Edom, the judgment in Revelation 14 is irreversible and final.

Although this judgment is laser-focused on the unbelieving population, the primary purpose is to motivate God's people to endure to the end. Carefully consider John's words:

> **"Here is a call for the endurance of the saints, those who keep the commandments of God and their faith in Jesus. And I heard a voice from heaven saying, 'Write this: Blessed are the dead who die in the Lord from now on.' 'Blessed indeed,' says the Spirit, 'that they may rest from their labors, for their deeds follow them!'"** (Rev. 14:12-13).

This is God's loving way of saying, *"You are almost there, the end is near."* Even those who die are *instantly* with the Lord. Really, as my friend Thomas Aschinger says in regard to Philippians 1:21, "The worst that can happen is that they stay alive."[191] The eternal gospel of Revelation 14:6 ushers in eternal rest for all who endure and overcome the schemes of the evil one, including his political and cultural divisiveness with which he tempts God's people. Revelation 12-14 exists to explain this to us in advance. Satan seeks to use even our secret desires as springboards to evil. Money, power, politics,

---

[190] Phillips, *Revelation,* 405.

[191] Thomas Aschinger is a father in the faith to me and a deacon at Kaleo Church. He has been a steady encouragement to me for years and said this to me after I preached on Philippians 1:21. http://kaleochurch.com/sermons/?sermon_id=16.

sex, etc. Satan knows how to take good things and turn them in to avenues of false worship. But the day coming at the return of Christ when this daily battle of faith will end in perfect rest. As Leithart so poignantly put it, *"Those who keep God's commandments and hold the faith of Jesus will be followed into the Lord's presence by their works (14:13). They have followed the Lamb wherever He goes, all the way to the cross (14:4), and their works trail along behind them."*[192]

REVELATION 14:14-20

We now approach the actions of the fourth and final angel in this vision. This passage places John's sights right up against the coming of Jesus. Before the angel obeys the commands of the Lord to bring judgment and salvation, we are given another glimpse of the exalted Christ with imagery from Daniel chapter seven. Joel Beeke writes,

"This cloud is the same cloud that filled the temple in the days of Solomon (1 Kings 8:10). It is the same cloud that people saw leaving the temple when the glory departed from Israel (Ezek. 10:18). It is the cloud that enveloped Christ on the Mount of Transfiguration when His garments became glistening white and his face shone like the sun (Matt. 17:15). It is the shekinah cloud—the cloud of God's glory. Isn't this how Jesus Himself puts it in the Gospels, answering his disciples' questions about the signs of His return and the end of the world? Christ's answers conclude on this high note: 'And they shall see the Son of man coming in the clouds of heaven with power and great glory' (Matt. 24:30."[193]

John writes, **"Then I looked, and behold, a white cloud, and seated on the cloud one like a son of man, with a golden crown on his head, and a sharp sickle in his hand"** **(Rev. 14:14).** Where Revelation 12-13 was filled with a false-trinity frolicking around as a parody of the Trinity, in Revelation 14 Jesus bursts upon the scene as the true King of kings and Lord of lords. He enters the scene on a cloud (cf. Dan. 7:13), as symbol to the entire world that He has come to judge all evil and gather His kingdom children. The kingdom belongs to Him, and there is no comparison to the force and power He yields. He holds a sickle to work the soil of every person, whether good or bad. This is the final harvest and the Master Gardener is now rolling up His sleeves. He will dig out and burn all that doesn't bear fruit. He will aside all the glorious produce He raised between the first creation and new creation. In a single moment, the Son of Man will come and divide all of humanity into two groups: those who will see Him in his glory and soil themselves under his weighty hand of wrath, and those who will with great joy and expectation declare, *"My God and my King!"* On one hand this text reveals the most extreme severity toward unbelievers, and on the other hand the day for which Christ's people eagerly await (cf. Heb. 9:28).

The King of the Harvest will wield the sickle of salvation and judgment with the aid of holy angels. John writes,

"And another angel came out of the temple, calling with a loud voice to Him who sat on the cloud, 'Put in your sickle, and reap, for the hour to reap has come, for the harvest of the earth is fully ripe.' So He who sat on the cloud swung his sickle across the earth, and the earth was reaped. Then another

---

[192] Leithart, *Revelation 12-22*, 103.
[193] Joel Beeke, *Revelation*, 407.

angel came out of the temple in heaven, and he too had a sharp sickle. And another angel came out from the altar, the angel who has authority over the fire, and he called with a loud voice to the one who had the sharp sickle, 'Put in your sickle and gather the clusters from the vine of the earth, for its grapes are ripe.' So the angel swung his sickle across the earth and gathered the grape harvest of the earth and threw it into the great winepress of the wrath of God" (Rev. 14:15-19).

The symbolism and imagery here is focuses primarily on the judgment of unbelievers. We know from Revelation, as well as the whole Bible, that at this time believers will be saved. But this vision focuses on the angels' arrival with Christ to gather the wild grapes and throw them into the great winepress of his wrath. This reminds us of what The Harvester experienced. The Garden of Gethsemane, where Jesus agonized in prayer, was an olive orchard. The produce from that orchard would be crushed to harvest the oil. Similar imagery comes to mind when we read in Luke 22:44, *"And being in agony He prayed more earnestly; and his sweat became like great drops of blood falling down to the ground."* Our humble Servant-king was under the weight of bearing the wrath of the sins of his people. As the olives produced oil under pressure, so the body of Jesus produced blood under the extreme pressure of His coming crucifixion.

All individuals are either in Christ—and all God's wrath for our sin has been graciously put on the Son of man; or are in Adam—and for all eternity will bear the great winepress of the wrath of God. What a terror that Day will be for some. And what great joy the believer will have when our faith becomes sight, and we behold our King face to face (cf. 1 John 3:2).

At the coming of Jesus, His sickle ought not surprise us. John the Baptist warned in Matthew 3:12, *"His winnowing fork is in his hand, and He will clear his threshing floor and gather his wheat into the barn, but the chaff He will burn with unquenchable fire."* The good news of the gospel not only frees us from fear of judgment, but it also enables us to joyfully declare this good news. Jude 22-23, *"And have mercy on those who doubt; save others by snatching them out of the fire; to others show mercy with fear, hating even the garment stained by the flesh."* Jude calls God's people to save others *with mercy* because our garments were once stained by the flesh also. Christ clothed us with His perfect robe of righteousness. His blood has cleansed us. We must tell others how they can be spared from judgment. Otherwise, at the harvest, His robe will be soaked in the blood of those that did not believe.

In a horrific visual scene, John writes, **"And the winepress was trodden outside the city, and blood flowed from the winepress, as high as a horse's bridle, for 1,600. stadia."** The image here is of *total victory*. The enemies of God will be dealt with. Imagine, if this were a literal scene. Who could stomach the smells and sights? Many faint at the sight of blood from a small cut, but here we have deeply flowing rivers of blood for 184 miles (1,600 stadia). This should remind us of the flood in Noah's day, only far more cataclysmic. John is alluding to Isaiah 63:1-2, which says;

"Who is this who comes from Edom, in crimsoned garments from Bozrah, He who is splendid in his apparel, marching in the greatness of his strength? 'It is I, speaking in righteousness, mighty to save.' Why is your apparel red, and your garments like his who treads in the winepress?"

About this allusion, Vern Poythress says, "*The picture of might is reminiscent of a warrior theophany. But the specific visual picture is the imagery of a man treading a winepress. Fulfillment is found in Revelation 14:20 and 19:13, 15.*"[194]

---

[194] Poythress, *Theophany*, 315.

TELEIOS

ACADEMY

WEEK 9
STUDY

REVELATION 15:1-16:21
The Seven Bowls & the Greater Exodus

MEDITATION: Sing to the Lord of His great worth as you study Revelation 15:1-4.

1. What Old Testament passage does John quote? What is the connection between the two? (cf. Rev. 5:6, 9-10)

2. Read the Song of Moses in Exodus 15. What do the people of God celebrate? How were they delivered from bondage?

3. What connections do you see between the Red Sea in Exodus 14, and the sea of glass in Revelation 15:2?

APPLICATION: If we are a type of wilderness people, currently making our journey as pilgrims between the cross and second coming, what are some temptations and pitfalls we can avoid that Israel's generation *failed* to avoid?

MEDITATION: Ask God to fill you of His fullness as you meditate on Revelation 15:5-8.

1. Considering the seven seals (Chs. 6-8) and the seven trumpets (Chs. 8-11), what might we expect the seven bowls in chapters 15-16 to contain?

2. Read Revelation 15:8 along with Habakkuk 2:4. What are the people of God awaiting? What will God do *before* ushering in His world-covering glory?

APPLICATION: Write five things you long for at the coming of Jesus. Share some of these with your spouse, kids, friends, neighbors, co-workers, and/or small group. Write out a verse to memorize on page 305.

MEDITATION: Humbly meet with "the Lord God the Almighty" as you study Revelation 16:1-7.

1. Where the seven trumpets announced judgments similar to the plagues in Exodus, are the first three bowls similar or different? Explain.

2. According to Revelation 16:1, who commands these bowls to be poured out? Does this challenge your view of God? Why or why not?

3. What Old Testament passages are quoted in Revelation 16:5-7? What does John have in mind?

4. How would a first century church member who was present at the original reading of Revelation be comforted by Revelation 16:1-7? What about you?

APPLICATION: If you believe you have insight or understanding into God's purpose for one of the instances of suffering in your life, what was it? (Don't worry if God's purpose in your suffering is unclear to you. He will make it plain at the right time!).

MEDITATION: As you read Revelation 16:8-16 ask the Lord to search your heart and examine your mind.

1. What does the fourth bowl of judgment contain? (cf. Daniel 5:22-23)

2. What does the fifth bowl judgment contain and upon whom is it poured out? Do these judgments seem to be intensifying toward a finality?

3. What comes to mind when you hear the term "Armageddon?" Does the sixth bowl judgment agree or disagree with your original thoughts? Why or why not?

4. Is the false trinity in 16:13 staging its final battle against God and His bride? Explain.

APPLICATION: What are some ways you need to "stay awake" *today* (cf. Matt. 24:42; Rev. 16:15)? How do you plan on doing this faithfully, to the glory of God?

MEDITATION: Ask the Lord to help you better understand His wrath, and increase your zeal for evangelism as you study Revelation 16:17-21

1. Immediately after the angel pours out the seventh bowl, whose voice does John hear and what does he herald?

2. According to 16:19-21, what are the results of the seventh bowl being poured out?

3. How does the unbelieving population respond to the final judgment of God in chapter 16? How is this different from what the people of God will experience according to Rev. 21:1-4?

APPLICATION: If the severity of these judgments increases between Christ's cross and the second coming, how should we view our unbelieving friends, family, and co-workers? What is keeping you from heralding the gospel to them?

WEEK 9
COMMENTARY

REVELATION 15:1-16:21

The Seven Bowls & the Greater Exodus

REVELATION 15:1-16:21

THE SEVEN BOWLS AND THE GREATER EXODUS

REVELATION 15:1-4

As we delve into the next angle of the period between the cross and second coming of Christ, John identifies Christians as exodus people. In the same way Moses led the people out of slavery into the wilderness after being "covered" by the blood of an innocent Lamb, so Christ leads us out of slavery to sin by His own blood. And like Israel, we too are led into a wilderness. Christians today are still awaiting the true Promised Land, the new heavens and the new earth. John begins this cycle by writing,

> *"Then I saw another sign in heaven, great and amazing, seven angels with seven plagues, which are the last, for with them the wrath of God is finished. ² And I saw what appeared to be a sea of glass mingled with fire—and also those who had conquered the beast and its image and the number of its name, standing beside the sea of glass with harps of God in their hands. ³ And they sing the song of Moses, the servant of God, and the song of the Lamb, saying,*
> *'Great and amazing are your deeds,*
> *O Lord God the Almighty!*
> *Just and true are your ways,*
> *O King of the nations!*
> *⁴ Who will not fear, O Lord,*
> *and glorify your name?*
> *For you alone are holy.*
> *All nations will come*
> *and worship you,*
> *for your righteous acts have been revealed.'"* (Rev. 15:1-4)

With this vision, John gives another vantage-point into the seven seals and seven trumpets, but here they are called seven bowls. In the same way that the book of Revelation grows in intensity, so do the seven bowls. That is why John said in verse 1 that **"for with them the wrath of God is** *finished."* These bowls mirror and expand upon the Exodus plagues against Pharaoh and Egypt. But first, John opens his readers' eyes to the fact that they have been delivered by the blood of an innocent Lamb (5:6). Therefore, we can sing in unison with the wilderness generation that the victory is ours in Christ. In Exodus 15, Moses and the people of God stand on the edge of the Red Sea rejoicing in God's victory over Pharaoh and his army. Israel celebrated their freedom in their Savior as the Egyptian army was drowned in the chaotic waters of God's wrath. John makes this connection clear, not only by quoting Moses' song but also by writing, **"And I saw what appeared to be a sea of glass mingled with fire—and also those who had conquered the beast and its image and the number of its name, standing beside the sea of glass with harps of God in their hands"** (15:2). The false trinity of Revelation 12-14 is conquered by the blood of the Lamb and all who are in Christ are conquerors with Him. They stand, as it were, on the eschatological shores of the new heaven and new earth rejoicing that God's wrath has poured out upon the false trinity of Satan, the beast, and the false prophet.

Helping us grasp this scene, Richard Bauckham writes,

"John's use of the new exodus imagery shows that for him the decisive eschatological event has already occurred: the new Passover Lamb has been slaughtered and He has ransomed a people for God. The goal of the new exodus is still to be attained, when Christ's people will reign with Him as priests on earth (20:4-6; 22:3-5), attaining their theocratic independence in the promised land." [195]

That is where John is going next, to the glorious reality of the new heaven and new earth. Here, Christ's people stand on the glimmering shores of victory declaring that He is the Victor. As H.B. Swete says, *"The saints exodus from the spiritual Egypt has led them through the Red Sea of Martyrdom, which is now exchanged for the Crystal Sea of Heaven."* [196]

REVELATION 15:5-8

Not only is this exodus theme applied to the New Covenant people of God, but John also applies Old Testament tabernacle imagery. He writes,

"After this I looked, and the sanctuary of the tent of witness in heaven was opened, and out of the sanctuary came the seven angels with the seven plagues, clothed in pure, bright linen, with golden sashes around their chests. And one of the four living creatures gave to the seven angels seven golden bowls full of the wrath of God who lives forever and ever, and the sanctuary was filled with smoke from the glory of God and from his power, and no one could enter the sanctuary until the seven plagues of the seven angels were finished." (Revelation 15:5-8).

Where the tabernacle was a replica in the wilderness of the heavenly temple, this vision is of the heavenly reality. That is what John has in mind when he says that the **"the sanctuary of the tent of witness in heaven was opened."** Likewise, Hebrews 10:1 describes the function of the law and

---

[195] Bauckham, *The Theology of the Book of Revelation,* 72.
[196] Henry Barclay Swete, *Commentary on Revelation,* 2 vols. (1911; reps., Grand Rapids: Kregel, 1977), 2.195.

sacrifices being a mere shadow to the realities in heaven when the author writes, *"For since the law has but a shadow of the good things to come instead of the true form of these realities, it can never, by the same sacrifices that are continually offered every year, make perfect those who draw near."*

This whole idea—that much of the good things that God has created on earth are but mere shadows of the realities of those things in heaven—is absolutely astounding. As C.S. Lewis said in the Chronicles of Narnia,

> *"It is as hard to explain how this sunlit land was different from the old Narnia as it would be to tell you how the fruits of that country taste. Perhaps you will get some idea of it if you think like this. You may have been in a room in which there was a window that looked out on a lovely bay of the sea or a green valley that wound away among mountains. And in the wall of that room opposite to the window there may have been a looking-glass. And as you turned away from the window you suddenly caught sight of that sea or that valley, all over again, in the looking glass. And the sea in the mirror, or the valley in the mirror, were in one sense just the same as the real ones: yet at the same time they were somehow different - deeper, more wonderful, more like places in a story: in a story you have never heard but very much want to know. The difference between the old Narnia and the new Narnia was like that. The new one was a deeper country: every rock and flower and blade of grass looked as if it meant more."[197]*

As John witnesses this heavenly tabernacle, it is also **"filled with smoke from the glory of God and from His power."** John is continuing his exodus theme, alluding to when the glory of God visibly fell upon the tent of meeting in Exodus 40:34-35. Moses wrote, *"Then the cloud covered the tent of meeting, and the glory of the LORD filled the tabernacle. And Moses was not able to enter the tent of meeting because the cloud settled on it, and the glory of the LORD filled the tabernacle."*

John was helping first century readers, and us, see that God is about to unleash his final and full wrath on the false trinity of Satan and all those who are marked out by him. Once the bowls are poured out, repentance and faith will be a thing of the past. This ought to sober us, and also give us a boldness to share the gospel. Not only will repentance and faith soon cease, but so will evangelism. Whatever it is that intimidates us from sharing the gospel, we should realize that the darkness of the bad news is what makes the goodness of the good news shine so bright. Phillips applies the great news of Revelation 15:3 and the Song of Moses this way:

> *"This heavenly song urges believers to be preoccupied not with the changing events of earth but rather with the glory and might of the unchanging and holy God. What is true of the saints above should increasingly be true of believers here below: 'They sing the song of Moses, the servant of God, and the song of the Lamb, saying, 'Great and amazing are your deeds, O Lord God the Almighty! Just and true are your ways, O King of the nations!' (Rev. 15:3)."[198]*

---

[197] C.S. Lewis, *Chronicles of Narnia: The Last Battle* (New York, NY: HarperCollins Publishers, 1998), 759.
[198] Phillips, *Revelation*, 439.

REVELATION 16:1-7

Where Revelation 15 was an introduction to the seven bowls, Revelation 16 is a heavenly vantage point of the bowls being poured out in succession upon those that belong to the false trinity. John tells of God ordering his mighty angels to dispense His wrath on the unbelieving world in verse 1: ***"Then I heard a loud voice from the temple telling the seven angels, 'Go and pour out on the earth the seven bowls of the wrath of God.'"*** As we witness throughout the book of Revelation, God is the initiator in pouring out wrath on all those marked by the beast. As John follows his exodus theme we traced in chapter 15, he now applies the Exodus plagues to the time between the cross and the second coming. As with the trumpets earlier in Revelation, James Hamilton provides the following overview chart of the use of the plagues in Revelation[199]:

BOWL IN REVELATION	PLAGUE IN EXODUS
1st Bowl: 16:2 sores	6th Plague: 9:10: boils/sores
2nd Bowl: 16:3: sea to blood, all living things die	1st Plague: 7:17-21: Nile turns to blood, fish die
3rd Bowl: 16:4-7: rivers and springs turn to blood	1st Plague: 7:17-21: rivers and springs turn to blood
4th Bowl: 16:8, 9: sun burns people	
5th Bowl: 16:10, 11: darkness	9th Plague: 10:21-29: darkness
6th Bowl: 16:12-15: Euphrates dries up, and the demons prepare for battle	10th Plague: 11:1-10; 12:29-32: death angel; Red Sea parted
7th Bowl: 16:17-21: earthquake, hail	7th Plague: 9:13-35: hail

The temple has been opened and these plague-bowls come pouring out. Each bowl is full to the brim with the pure wrath of God. As Christ died on the cross for His people, He drank the horrors of this very wrath down to the last drop. Now, it is too late for others. We see in 16:8-16, no one repents as these bowls of wrath are unleashed. They have stood with their heads held high and chests puffed up in full allegiance to Satan and his false trinity. Richard Phillips argues that Revelation 16 teaches *"four aspects of God's wrath that are worthy to be praised: the holiness of wrath, the vengeance of wrath, the justice of wrath, and the benefits of God's wrath."*[200] As we continue through Revelation 16, we see why God's wrath is something the believer ought not fear. Instead, God's wrath is a cause for us to give Him praise.

In verses 2-3 we are given the vision of the first two angels and the bowls of wrath they pour out. John writes,

---

[199] Hamilton, *Revelation,* 211.
[200] Phillips, *Revelation,* 444.

"So the first angel went and poured out his bowl on the earth, and harmful and painful sores came upon the people who bore the mark of the beast and worshiped its image. The second angel poured out his bowl into the sea, and it became like the blood of a corpse, and every living thing died that was in the sea."

As these plague-bowls are poured out, not only are they like the plagues in Egypt, but they are also eerily similar to the seals and trumpets. Again, that is because the structure of Revelation is giving us different angles of the same time period. Hendricksen says,

> *"A very definite connecting link is established between the vision of the trumpets (chapters 8-11) and that of the bowls (chapters 15-16). Trumpets warn; bowls are poured out. These impenitent men receive the mark of the beast (13:16). They worship the dragon and are the friends of the two beasts and of the harlot, Babylon. Thus conceived, we notice that the vision of the bowls of wrath runs parallel with all the others and like them covers the entire dispensation."*[201]

These first two bowls are laser-focused on the unrepentant, bringing sores and boils upon their bodies, turning the sea to blood and killing everything in it. Although the imagery might bring the horrors of blood to mind, the vision is mainly about the *effects* of these plagues. Imagine what a detriment all the fish in the sea would be to a culture. Imagine all the jobs that would be cut off. As Beale argues,

> *"As with the second trumpet, the similar imagery of the second bowl may indicate famine conditions and economic deprivation, though more severe because of the wider APPLICATION. Therefore, the sea being turned to 'blood' in 16:3 is figurative, at least in part, for the demise of the ungodly world's economic life-support system."*[202]

John continues describing the vision by showing the next angel and its bowls of wrath in Revelation 16:4-7:

> *"The third angel poured out his bowl into the rivers and the springs of water, and they became blood. And I heard the angel in charge of the waters say,*
> *"Just are you, O Holy One, who is and who was,*
> *for you brought these judgments.*
> *For they have shed the blood of saints and prophets,*
> *and you have given them blood to drink.*
> *It is what they deserve!"*
> *And I heard the altar saying,*
> *"Yes, Lord God the Almighty,*
> *true and just are your judgments!"*

---

[201] Hendricksen, *More Than Conquerors,* 158.
[202] Beale, *Revelation,* 815.

As the second angel focused on the greater bodies of water, this third angel obliterates all other water sources with blood. Any means of water-life left has now been cursed and death has prevailed. No fish, no water. Notice how the angel proclaims God's holiness in 16:5, while alluding to Jeremiah 12:1, a passage about evil people *seemingly* prospering. But not here. Evil has had its day and the Holy One has brought His judgment. One might read Revelation 16 and question what is so praiseworthy about God's wrath? How can one delight in such audacious pain and judgment? Let us return to Richard Phillips as he so clearly and pastorally guides us:

> *"The holiness of God, the wrath of God, and the health of the creation are inseparably united. God's wrath is His utter intolerance of whatever degrades and destroys. He hates iniquity as a mother hates the polio that takes the life of her child. Here, the wrath of God is linked to his love, since he does not simply walk away in disgust from his fallen creation. The world belongs to him and was created for the display of his glory. God in his love for his own work is utterly, irreconcilably opposed to sin, is resolved to stamp it out, and through his wrathful judgment is determined to cleanse the world for its holy destiny in the glorious return of Jesus Christ (Rom. 8:19-21)."[203]*

It is only in this grasp of the purpose of God's holiness and wrath that we can see the visions of these bowls as good and just. In fact, Revelation 16:6 quotes Isaiah 49:26, a blunt description of God judging the wicked and leaving them with only blood to drink and God declares, *"It is what they deserve."* Likewise, Revelation 16:7 quotes Psalm 119:137, a quote from the altar of God declaring that these judgments and wrath are indeed *good*! As a first century hearer, probably with PTSD from seeing other believers publicly tortured, this vision would give hope that God does not sit idly by, but will make all things right. We will sing with them one day,

> *"'Til on that cross as Jesus died,*
> *The wrath of God was satisfied*
> *For ev'ry sin on Him was laid*
> *Here in the death of Christ I live."[204]*

REVELATION 16:8-16

As the theme of the exodus and its plagues continue to be poured out on the satanic trinity and all their followers (16:2), we will now look at bowls four, five, and six. The fourth bowl—poured out by God (16:9) at the hands of the fourth angel—is poured out on the sun:

"And it was allowed to scorch people with fire. [9] They were scorched by the fierce heat, and they cursed the name of God who had power over these plagues. They did not repent and give Him glory" (Rev. 16:8-9).

In Greek mythology, there was a god for virtually everything. One of these was Ra, the sun god. In all of the Exodus plagues, God was flexing His might and showing Himself as the one true

[203] Phillips, *Revelation*, 446.

[204] Keith Getty & Stuart Townsend, *In Christ Alone*, Copyright © 2002 THANKYOU Music(PRS) ADM Worldwide at CapitolCMGPublishing.com

God of all creation. Likewise, in Revelation, God is pouring out these bowls in wrath and judgment on those who follow the satanic trinity. They are designed to wake up the pagan worshipers and turn their worship from the false trinity and to God. But as we will see throughout the rest of the bowls, **"They did not repent of their deeds"** (16:9, 11). This is the opposite effect of what God promised His people in Revelation 7:16 when He said, *"the sun shall not strike them, nor any scorching heat."* At the same time, God is protecting His people and pouring out wrath on all who are aquatinted with the evil one. There is a clear line in the sand. The wheat is placed one side and the chaff on the other. The chaff are unrepentant even under this severe judgment. Instead of turning from sin, they **"cursed the name of God."** The more proper translation is that they "blasphemed, or slandered, the name of God" (*eblasphemesan ta onoma tou theou*). The judgments are a purifying fire that bring out what is already in the heart of those being judged. There are allusions here to Daniel 5:22-23, where the idolatrous and vile king names Belshazzar had purposely set Himself against Yahweh and did not honor Him as he ought. Yet, this is just one picture of the many hearts throughout human history who failed to follow God and praise Him with the lips He made.

In the fifth bowl, God takes precise aim at the throne of the beast. John writes,

> **"The fifth angel poured out his bowl on the throne of the beast, and its kingdom was plunged into darkness. People gnawed their tongues in anguish and cursed the God of heaven for their pain and sores. They did not repent of their deeds"** (16:10-11).

This, in one sense, is a continuation of the fourth bowl with the darkness that follows. However, it is also aimed at the false trinity the same way God attacked the throne of Pharaoh in Exodus. Derek Thomas writes,

> *"The very seat of his government is challenged, plunging his kingdom into darkness. It is reminiscent of the plague of darkness over Egypt. In the Exodus story, the plague was a direct attack upon Pharaoh who was believed to be an incantation of the sun god, Ra. The fifth bowl identifies God's total sovereignty over Satan and his forces. Again, despite the intense imagery of pain and suffering, there is no repentance (16:11)."*[205]

The beast is not the only one affected by such wrath. Satan's followers also gnaw their tongues and blaspheme God again. These are people with hardened hearts, setting their allegiance fully on evil. They will never taste and see that the Lord is good (Psalm 34:8). And, as Beale says, *"The temporal judgment here is a precursor of the final judgment, when unbelievers will be 'cast into the outer darkness,' where 'there will be weeping and gnashing of teeth' (Matt. 8:12; 22:13; 25:30)."*[206] It is absolutely clear in the text that God pours out His wrath on those that are not sealed by the blood of his Son and the Spirit.

When the angel is sent forth from God with the sixth bowl, we learn,

> **"The sixth angel poured out his bowl on the great river Euphrates, and its water was dried up, to prepare the way for the kings from the east. And I saw, coming out of the mouth of the dragon and out of the mouth of the beast and**

---

[205] Thomas, *Let's Study Revelation,* 129.
[206] Beale, *Revelation,* 824.

out of the mouth of the false prophet, three unclean spirits like frogs. For they are demonic spirits, performing signs, who go abroad to the kings of the whole world, to assemble them for battle on the great day of God the Almighty. ("Behold, I am coming like a thief! Blessed is the one who stays awake, keeping his garments on, that he may not go about naked and be seen exposed!") And they assembled them at the place that in Hebrew is called Armageddon" (16:12-16).

This sixth bowl brings us to what is commonly known as the "Battle of Armageddon." God providentially uses this bowl to bring history nearer to His intended end. When the Euphrates is dried up, bringing forth the kings of the east, it leads to the great assembly of demonic troops for the Battle of Armageddon. Again, Exodus imagery is in view. John has in mind the pursuing army of Pharaoh after the people of God. In a last-minute display of His power and provision, God splits the Red Sea to save His people and judge His enemies. Likewise, in Revelation 16, John is recapitulating the Exodus to comfort the suffering church. He looks ahead to 17:1, where these "kings of the east" are seen as the great prostitute that are seated on the waters. All of the imagery with the frogs and the false trinity show the effects and rebellion that come with following the evil one. Hamilton notes,

> *"So here Satan and the beast the false prophet are a false trinity, a twisted parody of the Father and the Son and the Holy Spirit. And these 'unclean spirits like frogs' that come from their mouths (16:3), 'demonic spirits, performing signs' (16:14), are the powers that produce the world's network of assumptions and conclusions. These are the demonic powers that teach the world the common set of 'given facts' that convince 'the kings of the whole world, to assemble them for the battle on the great day of God the Almighty.'*[207]

In short, Satan and his evil schemes are at war primarily within the social structures of this world. These schemes form and shape the mind of people, convincing them to blaspheme God and go to war against Him. It is what David summarized of the unbelieving person when he wrote, *"The fool says in his heart, 'There is no God.' They are corrupt, they do abominable deeds, there is none who does good"* (Psalm 14:1). Yet, at the end of history, John shows these fools are not only void of good, but are purposely at war against the God who created them.

In regard to Armageddon, there have been many fictional books trying to show what this battle may look like. To discern John's point, we should understand this is *the same war* we read about in Revelation 11:7 from a different angle. Evil and demonic spirits of the world wage war against the Almighty. But as we saw earlier, this war was providentially set in place by the Almighty to bring an end to the evil trinity and his host of marked followers. Some interpreters place this battle after a secret rapture and literal millennial (1000 year) kingdom. Others take an opposite extreme and place this battle during the destruction of the temple in 70 A.D., resulting in a golden age where Christianity flourishes. However, as we have seen in every cycle in Revelation, things get progressively worse closer and closer to the return of Christ the King. As Beale says, *"The nations are deceived into thinking that they are gathering to exterminate the saints, but they are gathered together ultimately by God only in order to meet their own judgment at the hands of Jesus."*[208] John has Old Testament war imagery in mind when he says,

---

[207] Hamilton, *Revelation*, 319.
[208] Beale, *Revelation*, 835.

"Armageddon." This is a combination of Hebrew words referring to Mount Megiddo. This was the fortress Israel often fought from against its opponents. Battles from Deborah and Barak, to Saul being slain, to Elijah conquering Baal's false prophets, to Gideon having victory over the Midianites, etc. each took place at Megiddo. As Phillips notes about this Armageddon not being a physical and literal war, he writes,

> *"Some scholars envision a literal battle taking place in the future at Megiddo, in which the armies of the entire earth will be gathered to assault a future Jewish state. This approach does not fit the symbolic nature of Revelation's visions. Moreover, large as the plain around Megiddo was for ancient warfare, it could not hold even a single large military formation today, much less the combined armies of the world. Moreover, Revelation specifies the symbolism at work in this passage. Chapter 17 states that the reference to the Euphrates River was a symbol for 'peoples and multitudes and nations and languages (17:5).*[209]

In conclusion, the Battle of Armageddon is less about the destruction of the temple in 70 A.D., or about a literal future wide-scale war. Instead, Revelation 17 is about the spiritual reality of the final struggle of Satan and his followers attempting to kill the people of God. At this point our assurance ought to be bolstered because we know that Christ has already won the victory through His life, death, and resurrection. The only event left is His second coming, when all evil will be dealt with for good.

REVELATION 16:17-21

In previous parts of Revelation, especially the seven seals and the seven trumpets, there was a vision of encouragement for the people of God in the midst of the chaos and judgment. The opposite happens with John's telling of the seven bowl judgments. Instead of an interlude, John goes straight from the sixth to the seventh bowl. Not only that, he also brings the exodus pattern to completion in 16:17-21.

As the seventh angel pours out the seventh and final bowl a loud voice declares from the throne, ***"It is done! And there were flashes of lightning, rumblings, peals of thunder, and a great earthquake such as there had never been since man was on earth, so great was the earthquake"*** **(16:17-18).** This has imagery of Mount Sinai from Exodus 19:16-18, but with one massive difference. In Exodus, God was giving people the Law and sending them out as a kingdom of priests. Here, it is God's final verdict on the evil forces of the world. In this final verdict, you are either under the declaration of Christ's gracious "It is finished" (John 19:30)—which frees you from sin and death; or you are under His wrathful "It is done" (Rev. 16:17)—condemning you to eternal torment forever and ever.

The destruction is cataclysmic, and John makes that clear through the following vision:

> ***"The great city was split into three parts, and the cities of the nations fell, and God remembered Babylon the great, to make her drain the cup of the wine of***

---

[209] Phillips, *Revelation*, 459.

the fury of his wrath. And every island fled away, and no mountains were to be found. And great hailstones, about one hundred pounds each, fell from heaven on people; and they cursed God for the plague of the hail, because the plague was so severe."

Whether imagery of the earthquake and its results, the drained cup of wrath, or the storms and plagues that bring more people to blaspheme God, this is clearly and end of another cycle zooming in on the second coming of the Lord. Of course, as the context would suggest, this aspect of the second coming is on the judgment of unbelievers. God will shake out all that is not pure from the world. As the Spirit declared in Haggai 2:6, *"Yet once more, in a little while, I will shake the heavens and the earth and the sea and the dry land."* All of these symbols of permanence (mountains, islands, etc.) are swept away in destruction.[210] Nothing will be left for people to trust in, no place for them to hide. You will either be found safe in the refuge of Christ or left open to the brutal onslaught of God's wrath. All safety will be swept away by the Word of God. All unbelievers will be naked and exposed with nowhere to hide. Everyone will acknowledge Christ as Lord (Phil. 2:9-11), but many will do so only with shrieks of terror. As Leithart so vividly puts it, *"When all creation has been drenched with holy blood, all the phenomena originally associated with the throne come down to earth: Lightning flashes, thunder, sounds (4:5)."*[211]

Christ the King will dispense His holy angels to bring forth His holy power upon all who are not found holy and blameless in Him. Indeed, God will cleanse the earth and make room for the new heaven and new earth (Rev. 21-22).

But we are not there yet. This is good news for our unbelieving friends, family, and co-workers. The ensuing terror could be minutes away and we are called to be ready for Christ's return. Will we be a loving and obedient people declaring the greatest news of all, or will we shrink in shame because someone might not approve of us? We already have approval and acceptance in Christ (cf. Rom. 5:1-2) and are called to be heralds of the good news. We have freedom in evangelism because we are not responsible for saving people. We simply tell the good news of the gospel. Salvation belongs to the Lord. We are to be a joyful people, sharing who God is and what He has accomplished in Christ. As Dennis Johnson writes,

> *"Neither the backwash of sin's bitter aftertaste nor the first fruits of its lethal harvest can soften hearts of stone. Only God's Spirit, applying the gospel of grace, can turn stony hearts into hearts of tender flesh, but the bowls show us a moment in time when the Spirit's gentle and irresistible wooing is complete, the Son's sheep have been gathered, and the Father's patience has waited long enough."*[212]

God's people are in need of more preaching and singing about Christ's second coming. This will cause us to fix our eyes on future grace and create present trust and endurance.

"Lo! He comes, with clouds descending,
  Once for favored sinners slain:
Thousand saints attending
  Swell the triumph of His train:
    Hallelujah!

---

[210] Phillips, *Revelation*, 466.
[211] Leithart, *Revelation 11-22*, 159.
[212] Johnson, *Triumph of the Lamb*, 239.

Jesus now shall ever reign.

Every eye shall now behold Him
    Robed in dreadful majesty;
Those who set at nought and sold Him,
    Pierced, and nailed Him to the tree,
      Deeply wailing,
    Shall the true Messiah see.

Every island, sea, and mountain,
    Heaven and earth, shall flee away;
All who hate Him must, confounded,
    Hear the trump proclaim the day:
      Come to judgment!
    Come to judgment! Come away!

Yea, amen! let all adore Thee,
    High on Thine eternal throne:
Savior, take the power and glory,
    Claim the Kingdom for Thine own:
      O come quickly,
    Hallelujah! come, Lord, come![213]

[213] Charles Wesley, *Lo! He Comes with Clouds Descending,* https://hymnary.org/text/lo_he_comes_with_clouds_descending_once.

WEEK 10
STUDY

REVELATION 17:1-20:15
Bye-bye Dragon and the Celebratory Supper

MEDITATION: Marvel afresh at the majesty of God and the beauty of Christ as you study Revelation 17:1-18 today.

1. List some of the characteristics of Babylon and the great prostitute from chapter 17. How (with whom, or what) have you identified Babylon and the harlot?

2. Regarding the great prostitute, read 17:1-6 more slowly and identify:

   a. Her location

   b. Her mount

   c. Her adornment

   d. Her cup of abominations

   e. Her name

3. According to 17:13-14, all people are associated with one of two people. Who are these two people and what does allegiance to each one look like?

APPLICATION: How could/should we communicate the spiritual realities going on every day to our unbelieving neighbors who are associated with the Dragon?

MEDITATION: As you read of Babylon's demise in Revelation 18:1-24 consider your own heavenly citizenship and the resulting benefits.

1. Basing your response on the text, does Babylon appear to be an actual city or symbolic for something else? Explain.

2. In Revelation 18:4, John quotes Isaiah 48:20. Read both verses and explain John's purpose and the significance of this connection.

3. In Revelation 18:11-18, what things seem to be affected by the cataclysmic judgment? What similarities do you see to the effect of the plagues in Revelation 15-16?

4. Revelation 18:19-24 gives a very clear picture of the final fall of Babylon. According to this passage, how do the people of God respond?

APPLICATION: Do the realities of the judgment of the wicked bring you *joy*? Why/why not?

MEDITATION: Feast on the God of the Bible and what He is saying from Revelation 19:1-21. Worship Him!

1. Now that Babylon has fallen, what are some of the responses of the heavenly host of God's redeemed?

2. Describe what takes place at the Marriage Supper of the Lamb. Why is so much emphasis put on the clothing and attire?

3. Read Revelation 19:11-21. Those in the previous passage eat with the Lamb, who is doing the eating in this passage?

4. Does the punishment of sin and evil pictured in verses 20-21 seem to fit the crime of what the beast and all its followers had done? Why or why not?

APPLICATION: When you think of the Marriage Supper of the Lamb, what excites you most about that coming feast?

MEDITATION: As you study Revelation 20:1-10 be mindful, thankful, and hopeful in the victory to be had in Christ's finished work on the cross.

1. When reading 20:1-6, what is John's main point when you consider his original readers are a suffering people? Does this clash with any presuppositions you typically bring to this passage?

2. If Revelation is structured around seven angles of the same time period, what does the "thousand years" probably refer to? Have numbers in Revelation been literal or symbolic so far?

3. Read 20:5-6 and explain when the first resurrection and the second death take place. Read John 5:25-28 and 1 Corinthians and 15:50-57 for help.

4. If Satan and his followers were destroyed in Revelation 19:11-21, how is it that they could be destroyed again in 20:1-10? Or is it more likely that John is retelling the same event from a different viewpoint?

APPLICATION: How does the reality that the Satan has already been defeated at the cross give you freedom to depend on the Spirit rather than the flesh? Write out a verse to memorize on page 305.

MEDITATION: As you open the Bible to Revelation 20:11-15 thank and praise God if your name is written in His book.

1. The Second Coming ushers in one last major event. According to Revelation 20:11-15, what enemy is done away with once and for all?

2. What does the book of life contain? What do the other books seem to contain?

3. Read 1 John 5:4-5 and describe how that passage coincides with Revelation 20:11-15.

APPLICATION: Because the "death of death in the death of Christ" (John Owen) was fully dealt with, why do Christians fear anything other than God? How can we grow in healthy fear of the Lord?

WEEK 10
COMMENTARY

REVELATION 17:1-20:15

Bye-bye Dragon and the Celebratory Supper

REVELATION 17:1-20:15

BYE-BYE DRAGON AND THE CELEBRATORY SUPPER

REVELATION 17:1-18

In Daniel 4:30 the Babylonian King, Nebuchadnezzar, looked from his balcony and said, *"Is not this great Babylon, which I have built by my mighty power as a royal residence and for the glory of my majesty?"* The super-power in Daniel's day was known for its wickedness and evil, but even more, for its oppression of God's people. In Revelation, John uses Babylon as a picture of Rome and all the evil world powers ruled by Satan and the false trinity. As we approach the final section Revelation highlighting the war between the true Trinity and the false, John draws our attention to a new character in Satan's evil regime.

In 17:1-6, John writes:

> **"Then one of the seven angels who had the seven bowls came and said to me, "Come, I will show you the judgment of the great prostitute who is seated on many waters, with whom the kings of the earth have committed sexual immorality, and with the wine of whose sexual immorality the dwellers on earth have become drunk." And he carried me away in the Spirit into a wilderness, and I saw a woman sitting on a scarlet beast that was full of blasphemous names, and it had seven heads and ten horns. The woman was arrayed in purple and scarlet, and adorned with gold and jewels and pearls, holding in her hand a golden cup full of abominations and the impurities of her sexual immorality. And on her forehead was written a name of mystery: "Babylon the great, mother of prostitutes and of earth's abominations." And I saw the woman, drunk with the blood of the saints, the blood of the martyrs of Jesus. When I saw her, I marveled greatly."**

A heavenly picture of the unbelieving world is laid before John. At first glance, he "**marveled greatly.**" That is because the world, or Babylon, is a seductress. John calls her the great prostitute because she is the epitome of that which draws the people of the world to the evil one. She is sitting on the beast showing her foundation is the evil one. She represents all that he represents. Her clothing is alluring, and her motive is seduction. Contemporary artist, Carrie Underwood, unwittingly describes this situation when she sings, "His lips are dripping honey, but he'll sting you like a bee."[214]

King Solomon had the same idea in mind when he warned, *"For the lips of a forbidden woman drip honey, and her speech is smoother than oil,* [4] *but in the end, she is bitter as wormwood, sharp as a two-edged sword"* (Proverbs 5:3-4). This evil seductress is no ordinary prostitute though. As Joel Beeke writes,

> *"She is the mother of prostitutes. She is the queen bee in the hive of prostitutes. She is not the woman from Revelation 12, who is chased into the wilderness by the dragon…This woman is a prostitute, not an adulteress. The word in Greek is 'porne,' from which we get our word pornography. This woman has never been married to Christ. This woman is not an adulteress; she is a temptress, a harlot. Her titles identify her as an immoral woman and a wicked city. She is seen as 'the mother of harlots' and as 'Babylon the Great.'"[215]*

John explains this prostitute is located in the wilderness, a place typically inhabited by demons (cf. Matt. 4:1; 12:43). John later shares that Babylon will be turned into a wilderness (cf. Rev. 18:2). She is also mounted on the beast with seven heads and ten horns, the same persecuting tyrant from revelation 13:1. As Phillips notes, *"The fact that the harlot rides the beast shows an alliance in which the aims of sinful debauchery and the aims of violent tyranny are bound together."[216]* She is adorned with royal colors and cloaked in fine jewelry (17:4), parading these things as outward symbols of her inward immorality. Beale writes, *"She is the symbol of a culture that maintains the prosperity of economic commerce as well as reflecting the outward attractiveness by which whores try to seduce others."[217]* One cannot help but think of the fascination the world has with celebrities such as the Kardashian family, and how they parade their bodies, their expensive clothing and vacations, all while their rise to fame was founded on porn. The world approves of these things, and the harlot is attempting to seduce as many as possible by making empty promises to those that would trust her and join her on the back of the beast.

In her hand, she holds **"a golden cup full of abominations and the impurities of her sexual immorality."** This is the alluring world-system that entices the senses and tastes sweet at first but will lead to an eternal sickness that cannot be satisfied (cf. Jeremiah 51). And on her forehead lies the key to her identity: **And on her forehead was written a name of mystery: "Babylon the great, mother of prostitutes and of earth's abominations."** Mysteries in the Scriptures are revealed to the people of God. They are veiled and cloaked to the unbeliever, but the believer has eyes to see. John is revealing the mystery that this woman is none other than Babylon. She is the opposite of the church that has been cleansed and purified by the blood of the Lamb.

After John marveled at her, the angel gently rebukes John while making known the mystery in further detail (Revelation 7:7-14).

> **But the angel said to me, "Why do you marvel? I will tell you the mystery of the woman, and of the beast with seven heads and ten horns that carries her. The beast that you saw was, and is not, and is about to rise from the bottomless pit and go to destruction. And the dwellers on earth whose names have not been written in the book of life from the foundation of the world will marvel to see**

[214] Carrie Underwood, *Good Girl,* Sony/ATV Music Publishing LLC, Warner/Chappell Music, Inc., 2012.

[215] Beeke, *Revelation,* 455.

[216] Phillips, *Revelation,* 479.

[217] Beale, *Revelation,* 854.

the beast, because it was and is not and is to come. This calls for a mind with wisdom: the seven heads are seven mountains on which the woman is seated; they are also seven kings, five of whom have fallen, one is, the other has not yet come, and when he does come he must remain only a little while. As for the beast that was and is not, it is an eighth, but it belongs to the seven, and it goes to destruction. And the ten horns that you saw are ten kings who have not yet received royal power, but they are to receive authority as kings for one hour, together with the beast. These are of one mind, and they hand over their power and authority to the beast. They will make war on the Lamb, and the Lamb will conquer them, for He is Lord of lords and King of kings, and those with Him are and chosen and faithful."

The angel's rebuke is telling the readers that despite her alluring beauty, it will thrust all who taste of her into eternal torment. The angel also makes absolutely clear that this harlot and the beast she rides on are antichrists. Where Jesus has been continually called the one "who was and is and is to come," John is told that **"the beast you saw was, and is not..."** Again, in verse 8, the parody continues as the beast is described as one whom **"was and is not and is to come."** He is an antichrist and will draw people to death. All those who associate themselves with the beast will marvel at him, but their names are not written in the book of life.

The next description from the angel **"calls for a mind of wisdom"** (17:9). We must have wisdom because we are being let in on the mystery of what the beasts seven heads and ten horns are symbolize. We must admit, this is a difficult passage. In fact, I am pausing and praying for wisdom before proceeding.

The "seven mountains," more than likely, refer to what the original audience would have identified as Rome. Rome was called the city of seven hills.[218] John probably has in mind how Domitian was using his role as emperor to demand worship from all people. This calls for wisdom so that the people of God won't be allured by the great prostitute nor bow down to an antichrist.

What comes next demands incredible God-given wisdom. What does the reader make of verse 10 when John says, **"they are also seven kings, five of whom have fallen, one is, the other has not yet come, and when he does come he must remain only a little while"**? After showing some of the weaknesses in the historical approaches to this passage, Phillips argues that it is meant to be taken primarily as symbolic when he writes,

> *"Seven stands for completeness and here would represent the totality of antichrist government throughout history. Picture a beast with seven horns, five of which have been cut off. The idea is that Christ's first coming inflicted a deadly blow to Satan and his beast, who continues fighting undaunted, employing the power of his deadly sixth head, with a seventh to come. The point is that war is getting closer to the end."*[219]

Again, John shows the reader we are nearing the end of history. The cycles in Revelation 17-20 continue to progress toward the end of all evil. We know this is the case because chapters 21-22 primarily concern God and His people *without the presence of evil.*

---

[218] Phillips, *Revelation,* 491.
[219] ibid., 493.

This winding down of history finds its climax and purpose in verses 13-14. In short, a war is coming but the Lamb will strike the final blow and all enmity between the Lamb and the Serpent will cease forever. Between the cross and the second coming, it is primarily those united to the Lamb that suffer. But the final blow to the Serpent's head will be justice for all the saints. This will be played out as evil turns against evil:

> **"And the ten horns that you saw, they and the beast will hate the prostitute. They will make her desolate and naked and devour her flesh and burn her up with fire, [17] for God has put it into their hearts to carry out his purpose by being of one mind and handing over their royal power to the beast, until the words of God are fulfilled"** (Rev. 17:16-17).

The key to this passage is love. Where the people of God are called to love one another, those associated with the evil one hate one another and have no ethic of love. Not one ounce running through their cold veins is truly loving. The beast has used the harlot and is done with her. She will go into the lake of fire, where he soon will follow.

REVELATION 18:1-24

The book of Daniel is full of visions of the rise and fall of world kingdoms. They usurp one another's authority and oppress the people of God. Yet, Daniel is told that a kingdom is coming that will be greater than all other kingdoms and its King will rule the whole earth (cf. Dan. 2:31-35; 7:13-14). What we have in Revelation 18 is the final fall and demise of all world systems that are opposed to God and His Kingdom. All economic, religious, and political agenda that is not under the authority of King Jesus comes crumbling down. As we learned in Revelation 17, John lumps all of these anti-Christian kingdoms into one designation: "Babylon."

In the Old Testament, especially during the exile, Babylon was the pinnacle of wickedness and idolatry. Isaiah 21:9 sums this up with imagery also used in Revelation: *"'And behold, here come riders, horsemen in pairs!' And he answered, 'Fallen, fallen is Babylon; and all the carved images of her gods he has shattered to the ground.'"* John takes this verse from Isaiah and strings together a few different sentiments about Babylon when he writes,

> **"Fallen, fallen is Babylon the great! She has become a dwelling place for demons, a haunt for every unclean spirit, a haunt for every unclean bird, a haunt for every unclean and detestable beast. For all nations have drunk the wine of the passion of her sexual immorality, and the kings of the earth have committed immorality with her, and the merchants of the earth have grown rich from the power of her luxurious living"** (Rev. 18:2-3).

Chapter 18 is a cacophony of Old Testament judgments on Babylon, stringing them together beneath the Judge's final verdict on all wickedness and rebellion. It appears that the imagery of wilderness from chapter 17 is being filled up again, but now with demons. Leithart comments, *"Turning Babylon into a demonic zoo only makes obvious what was already the case. But now, the demons have settled in for the long haul.*[220] Or as Douglas Kelly writes, *"When a culture turns its back on God, the Holy Spirit, to some degree, is withdrawn, leaving a vacuum. Guess who rushes in to fill it? The evil one and those fallen created beings, former angels, who now are demons."*[221] While this may bring to mind terrifying images that seemed only possible at some future time, we must remember that God is peeling back the curtains of reality, so we can see His perspective from the throne. When we remember this, we can see how the world has been invaded by demons throughout history. The corruption of the institution of marriage, the breakdown of embracing our God-given gender, pervasive racism, and the fleeting notion of objective truth are current expressions of this warfare. The serpent has sunk his venomous teeth into God's good and created order, affecting every single sphere. But, the fall of Babylon will come!

John strings together a host of Old Testament verses, giving us a glimpse into the fall of Babylon. In Revelation 18:4-9, John writes:

> **"Then I heard another voice from heaven saying,**
> **"Come out of her, my people,**
> > **lest you take part in her sins,**
> **lest you share in her plagues;**
> **for her sins are heaped high as heaven,**
> > **and God has remembered her iniquities.**
> **Pay her back as she herself has paid back others,**
> > **and repay her double for her deeds;**
> > **mix a double portion for her in the cup she mixed.**
> **As she glorified herself and lived in luxury,**
> > **so, give her a like measure of torment and mourning,**
> **since in her heart she says,**
> > **'I sit as a queen,**
> **I am no widow,**
> > **and mourning I shall never see.'**
> **For this reason her plagues will come in a single day,**
> > **death and mourning and famine,**
> **and she will be burned up with fire;**
> > **for mighty is the Lord God who has judged her."**
> **And the kings of the earth, who committed sexual immorality and lived in luxury with her, will weep and wail over her when they see the smoke of her burning.**

Here, John expounds on the powers of the world. They are fleeting and nearing their end. The key to this string of texts is found in verse seven, describing a lust for her own glory. At the core of Babylon's sin is the insatiable appetite for self-glory. Because God is a jealous God, He will not compromise when it comes to His glory. 2 Thessalonians 1:5-10 tells of the glory-story that comes to its peak at the second coming of Christ. All who lived for their own glory will be void of love and joy forever, while those who aimed to make their lives about the glory of Christ will experience the joy of His glory forever. This future reality has present implications that should sober us. We must take heed to Jesus' warning to the Pharisees in John 5:44, *"How can you believe, when you receive glory from one another*

---

[220] Leithart, *Revelation 12-22,* 218.
[221] Kelly, *Revelation, 336.*

and do not seek the glory that comes from the only God?" Do your day-to-day habits reveal your supreme desire is the glory of God? Are you driven by making a name for yourself? Are you a magnet for self-glory? The church is in the world, but the world should not be in the church. The church is a place that exists to glorify God, while the world seeks to glorify itself. At this point in the judgment, God is zooming in on the kings and authorities of the world and bringing their self-glory to a devastating end.

The next thing to be affected by the judgment of Babylon is the merchants. John writes,

> *"And the merchants of the earth weep and mourn for her, since no one buys their cargo anymore, cargo of gold, silver, jewels, pearls, fine linen, purple cloth, silk, scarlet cloth, all kinds of scented wood, all kinds of articles of ivory, all kinds of articles of costly wood, bronze, iron and marble, cinnamon, spice, incense, myrrh, frankincense, wine, oil, fine flour, wheat, cattle and sheep, horses and chariots, and slaves, that is, human souls.*
>
> *"The fruit for which your soul longed*
> *has gone from you,*
> *and all your delicacies and your splendors*
> *are lost to you,*
> *never to be found again!"*
>
> *The merchants of these wares, who gained wealth from her, will stand far off, in fear of her torment, weeping and mourning aloud,*
>
> *"Alas, alas, for the great city*
> *that was clothed in fine linen,*
> *in purple and scarlet,*
> *adorned with gold,*
> *with jewels, and with pearls!*
> *For in a single hour all this wealth has been laid waste."* (Rev. 18:11-17a)

God's judgment is, in a sense, reversing the cultural mandate (Gen. 1:26-28) and taking away all the things man has created and used for sustenance. When self-glory drives a people and culture, they exchange the truth for a lie and worship the creature/created rather than the Creator (cf. Rom. 1:23-25). What God made them for as fellow creators, they have used to glorify themselves, provoking God to execute justice in taking it all away. As James Hamilton writes,

> *"This list is a summary of the adornments, luxuries, and conveniences that compromise a life of worldliness. These items are all about having your best life now. The merchants used these items to provoke people to selfish indulgence. These items were not used to glorify God, and the people buying what these merchants were selling were not using these things to benefit others. Living for Babylon is all about living for yourself."*[222]

---

[222] Hamilton, *Revelation*, 340.

Perhaps it is clear by now that Revelation 18 and the fall of Babylon is the climax of judgment poured out in the seven bowls from Rev. 15-16?

Lastly in Revelation 18, God brings judgment upon the sea and all its workers and inhabitants. Read the devastation that follows:

"And all shipmasters and seafaring men, sailors and all whose trade are on the sea, stood far off [18] and cried out as they saw the smoke of her burning,

"What city was like the great city?"
And they threw dust on their heads as they wept and mourned, crying out,
"Alas, alas, for the great city
where all who had ships at sea
grew rich by her wealth!
For in a single hour she has been laid waste.

Rejoice over her, O heaven,
and you saints and apostles and prophets,
for God has given judgment for you against her!"

Then a mighty angel took up a stone like a great millstone and threw it into the sea, saying,

"So, will Babylon the great city be thrown down with violence,
and will be found no more;
and the sound of harpists and musicians, of flute players and trumpeters,
will be heard in you no more,
and a craftsman of any craft
will be found in you no more,
and the sound of the mill
will be heard in you no more,
and the light of a lamp
will shine in you no more,
and the voice of bridegroom and bride
will be heard in you no more,
for your merchants were the great ones of the earth,
and all nations were deceived by your sorcery.
And in her was found the blood of prophets and of saints,
and of all who have been slain on earth." (Rev. 18:17b-24)

The seafaring folk of Babylon have taken a final blow. Unlike the guessing game of Battleship, God knows where each and every wayward vessel is located. He strikes each one with precision showing His judgment is always personal. The people of God are commanded by the voice from heaven to rejoice over this judgment (cf. 18:20) because of all the unpaid injustices are now being paid in full. God is winsomely and decisively responding to the cry of 18:18 describing the greatness of the city of Babylon by responding in judgment by saying, *"Who is like you, O LORD, among the gods? Who is like you, majestic in holiness, awesome in glorious deeds, doing wonders? You stretched out your right hand; the earth swallowed them"* (Exodus 15:11-12). The millstone has been tossed into the sea with Babylon (cf. Jer. 51:60-64; Rev. 18:21) showing the permanence of this judgment. Babylon has gone down and will not come back up. Where we saw earlier in Revelation that those not marked by the beast were kept from trade and marketplace purchases, God has swept the rug out from all trade driven by self-glory and allegiance to Satan's Babylonian flag. It is done! God's people are free!

REVELATION 19:1-21

After the fall of Babylon, we enter a scene reminiscent of earlier portions of Revelation where the people of God rejoice and sing in victory. Revelation 19 is our entrance into the collective praise of Christians who witnessed God's righteous judgment. Their praise is predicated on the fall of those who were marked by the beast and oppressed those sealed by the blood of the Lamb. The celebration of praise flows from those who overcame by the blood of the Lamb. They rejoice that He has not let their cries for deliverance and justice fall on deaf ears. Likely, a different angle of the same multitude in Revelation seven, John sees the redeemed people of God rejoicing in heaven. He writes,

> **"After this I heard what seemed to be the loud voice of a great multitude in heaven, crying out, "Hallelujah! Salvation and glory and power belong to our God, for his judgments are true and just;**
> **for He has judged the great prostitute**
> **who corrupted the earth with her immorality,**
> **and has avenged on her the blood of his servants."**
>
> **Once more they cried out,**
> **"Hallelujah!**
> **The smoke from her goes up forever and ever."**
>
> **And the twenty-four elders and the four living creatures fell down and worshiped God who was seated on the throne, saying, "Amen. Hallelujah!" And from the throne came a voice saying,**
>
> **"Praise our God,**
> **all you his servants,**
> **you who fear Him,**
> **small and great"** (Rev. 19:1-5).

These worshippers are rejoicing in God's salvation, glory and power. God has come through on all of His promises. He has saved his people, powerfully rescuing them and judging evil. And all of this is to the glory of His wonderful name. The great prostitute of chapter 17 is gone, and all the followers of the beast have been dealt with. In verse three, John gives the imagery of smoke ascending to the sky. This is a pleasing aroma of justice to God and His people. John has Isaiah 34:10 in mind; *"Night and day it shall not be quenched; its smoke shall go up forever."* Isaiah was looking forward the day of vengeance where all would be made right. In Revelation, we see a throng of saints rejoicing that this day has come. Readers should both look forward to this future day and live in light of this reality now. Are we a people that need to wait until that day to rejoice in God's salvation, power, and glory? Throughout history there have been seasons of revival where local churches committed themselves to prayer. Their cities were drastically changed as fire of the Spirit fell upon their city, transforming grumblers to rejoicers, crooks to generous givers, and the outcasts to family. In that light, Leithart adds:

> *"The church's mission is to turn every city into a sacrifice of ascent. We no longer do this as Joshua did, with the sword and fire of flesh. Rather, the church carries on her harem war, her war of utter destruction, through the sword of the Word and the fire of the Spirit, the flaming sword that strips the flesh of the old city to transfigure its residents in the Spirit, so they can ascend to God. We offer up the city in the incense of our prayers and the smoke of our praise, so that God will send down his city, flashing with lightning and rumbling with thunder."[223]*

As the church, we are to be a people whose lives and present desires tell of the future reality. We are edging nearer towards our Savior every day! The twenty-four elders and the four living creatures (cf. Rev. 4:4, 6, 10; 5:14; 19:4) give their hearty "amen!" with a posture of praise, agreeing that the Lord has done all things well.

What John hears next whispers in our ears today as one of the most delightful truths: We will soon sup with the Lamb, face-to-face. Each of the four Gospels reveal Jesus and His disciples eating a meal just prior to His crucifixion and resurrection. It was a meal that initiated the Lord's Supper, which we still proclaim and celebrate today. But it also foretold of a meal that we will enjoy, no longer by faith, but by sight. A meal where the Lord's scarred hands will serve us food and drink. His once broken body will be with us in a state of glory, and so will ours. Instead of being terrified in the presence of the holy King who laid His life down for us, we anticipate this day. Indeed, He has loved us and freed us from our sins by His blood (cf. Rev. 1:5b; Rom. 8:1, 32). John gives us this comforting reminder that is told through the symbolism of the clothes we will be wearing,

> **"Let us rejoice and exult**
>   **and give Him the glory,**
> **for the marriage of the Lamb has come,**
>   **and his Bride has made herself ready;**
> **it was granted her to clothe herself**
>   **with fine linen, bright and pure"**—
> **for the fine linen is the righteous deeds of the saints.**
>
> **And the angel said to me, "Write this: Blessed are those who are invited to the marriage supper of the Lamb." And He said to me, "These are the true words of God."** (Rev. 19:7-9).

"The Marriage Supper of the Lamb" is full of joy and righteousness. No one may enter who has not washed their robes in the blood of the Lamb. Unlike weddings in America today, ancient weddings were quite a bit longer and more meaningful. The marriage was typically arranged, followed

---

[223] Leithart, *Revelation 12-22,* 250.

by a long betrothal where the groom would pay the bride-price to her father. A processional would happen as the bride was taken from her father's home to the groom's home. There, she would be beautifully adorned. A massive wedding feast would follow, often lasting a full week.

The key to this passage is seeing that the bride was once an unruly and sinful being but is now cleansed by the bridegroom Himself. William Hendrickson shows how the ancient wedding liturgy so applies to the people of God:

> "In Christ the bride was chosen from eternity. Throughout the entire Old Testament dispensation, the wedding was announced. Next, the Son of God assumed our flesh and blood: the betrothal took place. The price—the dowry—was paid on Calvary. And now, after an interval which in the eyes of God is but a little while, the Bridegroom returns and 'It has come, the wedding of the Lamb.' Then we shall be with Him forevermore. It will be a holy, blessed, everlasting fellowship: the fullest realization of all the promises of the gospel."[224]

This is the great and grand fulfillment of the whole divine purpose God had for us before the creation of the world: that we would be holy and blameless in Christ (Eph. 1:4)! The day we sit at the table with Christ our King, we will finally be fully human, fully free, and filled to the brim with inexpressible joy!

Joel Beeke reminds us,

> "Christ has paid the bride-price dowry for all the elect. Therefore, we who are true believers are legally and inseparably His. He is coming again for his bride, the church, to lead us home to His Father's house, where He will present us spotless before His Father in heaven. There will be a wedding procession and festivities that will last, not only for a week or two, but for all eternity. We will be with Christ and behold His glory. The story of salvation is a love story. The covenant of grace is not like a legal document from a solicitor's office; it is a marriage contract. Before the worlds were made, God the Father chose a bride for His Son and drew up a marriage contract between them. This wedding involves choice, not mutual attraction. It is a one-sided choice, for God chose us in eternity. Christ bought us at Calvary and took us to be His own through the preaching of the gospel. Soon He will come back for us. When He comes back, we will enjoy intimacy and fellowship with Him forever."[225]

This marriage should make our heart skip a beat, and increase our desires to be with our bridegroom. The anticipation of this day should cause praise to redound to the glory of our Father. The vast amount of words written about this future feast could never exhaust the joy meant to be gained from it now and forever. Hamilton attempts to help us long for this day with an extensive list of benefits found only in Christ:

> "We can scarcely imagine the glory of that wedding day. Never has there been a worthier bridegroom. Never has a man sacrificed more for his beloved. Never has a man gone to greater lengths, humbled Himself more, endured more, or accomplished more in the great task of winning his bride. Never has a Father more wealthy planned a bigger feast. Never has a more noble Son honored his Father in everything. Never has a man treated his bride-to-be more appropriately. Never has a more powerful

---

[224] Hendricksen, *More Than Conquerors*, 180.
[225] Beeke, *Revelation*, 476-77.

pledge, like an engagement ring, been given than the pledge of the Holy Spirit given to this bride. Never has a more glorious residence been prepared as a dwelling place once the bridegroom finally takes his bride. Never has a bridegroom done more to qualify his beloved to be his bride. Never has a bride needed her bridegroom more. Never has there been a wedding more significant than this one. Never has a prince with more authority taken a bride with less standing. Never has a bride had her prince die for her, rise from the dead for her, and give to her his own standing before the Father. Never has a bridegroom loved his bride more. Never has a bride waited as long for her bridegroom. Never has a bride sung more songs to her beloved. Never has there been a wedding with more guests than this one will have. Never has a wedding taken place on a more momentous occasion—the end of the overlapping ages and the ushering in of the kingdom. Never has there been a marriage like this one."[226]

Oh, what a day we await!

Next, in Revelation 19:11-21, John writes a vision that will be retold again in chapter 20:7-15. Until this point, Jesus has primarily been referred to as 'the Lamb who was slain.' But here, we get a picture of the second coming. Then, Jesus will be revealed as a Warrior. He will storm in on his warhorse to make all things right. Notice the vision is no longer just a door opened (cf. 4:1), but heaven itself is opened (cf. 19:1). Bringing imagery used from the great picture of the exalted Christ in chapter one, John writes,

"His eyes are like a flame of fire, and on his head are many diadems, and He has a name written that no one knows but Himself. [13] He is clothed in a robe dipped in blood, and the name by which He is called is The Word of God" (Rev. 19:12-13).

The all-seeing King of kings, who is above all, and ruler of all, is the focus of this passage. He has come to bring Psalm 2 to its superlative fulfillment. Here, He will break His enemies and the oppressors of His people with His rod of iron. This is the culmination. The King of Glory comes bearing a name no one knows but Himself. As Beeke urges,

"This reminds that whenever we talk about the Lord Jesus, we are talking about God. He may be Jesus of Nazareth, but He is also the unfathomable God. We cannot know everything there is to know about the Lord Jesus Christ. He is too great and too glorious for that. As much as we know about Him, there is still more that we don't know. In that sense, no one knows His name but He Himself."[227]

Not only is John seeing a vision to show Christ as the Supreme Ruler of the earth, but He is also the conqueror of Satan and the whole satanic parody. Notice what John does to show Christ's supremacy over the false trinity. In Revelation 12:3, Satan was described as wearing "seven diadems." In Revelation 13:1, the beast was wearing "ten diadems." But here in Revelation 19:12, Christ has on His head **"many diadems."** In this seemingly small detail, John is highlighting that "*the undefined*

---

[226] Hamilton, *Revelation,* 351.
[227] Beeke, *Revelation,* 497.

multiplicity of diadems shows Christ is the only true cosmic king, on a grander scale than the dragon and the beast, whose small number of crowns implies a kingship limited in time."[228]

As the vision continues, we are given a glimpse into a more vivid description and picture of Christ the King when John says, **"He is clothed in a robe dipped in blood, and the name by which He is called is The Word of God" (Rev. 19:13).** The blood-soaked garment has no connection to the cross on which this King once hung. Now, He is soaked in the blood of those who were crushed by the winepress of God's wrath (cf. 14:19-20). The Old Testament connection is from Isaiah 63, an oracle of the Lord's vengeance upon the unrighteous. Isaiah writes:

> *"Who is this who comes from Edom,*
> *in crimsoned garments from Bozrah,*
> *He who is splendid in his apparel,*
> *marching in the greatness of his strength?*
> *'It is I, speaking in righteousness,*
> *mighty to save.'*
> *² Why is your apparel red,*
> *and your garments like his who treads in the winepress?*
> *³ 'I have trodden the winepress alone,*
> *and from the peoples no one was with Me;*
> *I trod them in My anger*
> *and trampled them in My wrath;*
> *their lifeblood spattered on My garments,*
> *and stained all my apparel.'"* (Isa. 63:1-3)

As is seen throughout the whole narrative of the Bible, salvation and judgment typically come as a pair. As Beale writes,

> *"John thus affirms Isaiah's prophecy of God as a warrior and identifies Christ as that divine warrior. In Isaiah the warrior judges to achieve 'vengeance' and 'redemption' on behalf of his people (so Isa. 63:4), and the same goal is implicit in Revelation 19. Therefore, the stained garments symbolize God's attribute of justice, which He will exercise in the coming judgment."*[229]

We are getting a more detailed glimpse into the winepress vision of chapter 14. The angels of God come with Him as instruments of His wrath. Here, the picture is given a bit more color when John writes,

> **"And the armies of heaven, arrayed in fine linen, white and pure, were following Him on white horses. From His mouth comes a sharp sword with which to strike down the nations, and He will rule them with a rod of iron. He will tread the winepress of the fury of the wrath of God the Almighty. On His robe and on His thigh, He has a name written, King of kings and Lord of lords"** (Rev. 19:14-16).

---

[228] Beale, *Revelation*, 952.
[229] Ibid., 957.

This angel army comes riding on white horses just like the God-man, and a sword of judgment precedes from His mouth (Rev. 1:16). This imagery is meant to give a picture of the exact and cutting judgment from Jesus, the Word of God. This picture finds its roots in Isaiah 11:4, where the nations are struck down. We have already seen in previous visions how Christ's coming with a rod of iron (Psalm 2), and treading on the winepress of God's wrath (Isa. 63), are both outworking of the vengeance and justice of the King of Glory. Earlier, John said He has a name that no one knows but Himself. Here in 19:16 Jesus is marked on His robe and on His thigh with a kingship title of sovereignty and rulership as the King of kings and Lord of lords. Dennis Johnson writes, *"This title shows his supremacy over all other rulers, in earth or heaven (cf. Eph. 1:20-22, Phil. 2:9-11); and it signals that the final war predicted in Revelation 17:11-14 is about to occur."*[230]

The irony of this text is obvious. Where in Revelation 19:1-11, the people of God are *eating* with the Lamb, in Revelation 19:17-21 we read of a vicious and appalling picture of those opposed to the Lamb *being eaten*. Where the great harvest of Rev. 14:14-20 told of God's sharp sickle dividing the wheat from the chaff, Revelation 19 is like a fantasy movie for some and a horror movie for others. In no uncertain terms, God is declaring, "Eat or be eaten!"

More specifically, Revelation 19:17-21 is one angle in the drama of the second coming judgment. The second angle will take place again in 20:7-15. The roaring ministry of an angel shouting for the birds of the air to feast on the flesh of all those marked and associated with the satanic parody.

But God brings the final blow to the false trinity who have paraded around pretending to by the Triune God. John writes,

"And the beast was captured, and with it the false prophet who in its presence had done the signs by which he deceived those who had received the mark of the beast and those who worshiped its image. These two were thrown alive into the lake of fire that burns with sulfur" (Revelation 19:20).

The masquerade is over, and evil has had its day. There is only one true God and He alone is the victor. The beast and the false prophet have had their day. In C.S. Lewis' *The Last Battle,* there is an evil army led by a man named Tarkaan, who enlists a talking monkey named "Shift" as an image of the false prophet in Revelation 19. Narnia is being deceived by Tarkaan and this talking monkey, primarily because the monkey clothed a donkey in a lion's skin. He was imitating Aslan, the Christ-figure. This led to wide-scale deception. But, by the end of the book, Aslan stands victorious.[231] Lewis rightfully allegorized Revelation 19 in story-form. The masks have been taken off and the lasting and victorious King is Jesus, the King of kings and Lord of lords. The inescapable Old Testament allusion to this great day of wrath and justice was told just prior to the vision of the new heaven and new earth in Ezekiel 39. Ezekiel writes:

"As for you, son of man, thus says the Lord GOD: Speak to the birds of every sort and to all beasts of the field: 'Assemble and come, gather from all around to the sacrificial feast that I am preparing for you, a great sacrificial feast on the mountains of Israel, and you shall eat flesh and drink blood. [18] You shall eat the flesh of the mighty and drink the blood of the princes of the earth—of rams, of lambs,

[230] Johnson, *Triumph of the Lamb*, 274.
[231] C.S. Lewis, *The Chronicles of Narnia: The Last Battle* (New York, NY: Harper Collins, 2001), 757.

and of he-goats, of bulls, all of them fat beasts of Bashan. ¹⁹ *And you shall eat fat till you are filled, and drink blood till you are drunk, at the sacrificial feast that I am preparing for you.* ²⁰ *And you shall be filled at my table with horses and charioteers, with mighty men and all kinds of warriors,' declares the Lord GOD"* (Ezek. 39:17-20).

As the false prophet and the beast have met their demise, we will see that only Satan is left to be dealt with. He will be cast away into torment forever and ever in chapter 20. Until then, we must realize this: God is just, and nothing escapes His all-seeing eye. The first century believers would have read this as a comfort, and we should as well. If the Lord were not a Warrior, then sin could coexist with the holiness of God. This would damage His goodness. But as we have seen, the King has been given a kingdom and only those clothed in union with Christ will be granted access into His kingdom of light (cf. Col. 1:12-13). So, let our songs of praise exult in the justice and judgment of God. As the bars of Shai Linne so helpfully declare,

> *"Heaven's opened behold the white horse amazing to view,*
> *the one sitting on the horse called Faithful and True.*
> *He judges and makes war, the reign of Messiah,*
> *His eyes flames of fire, strange his attire.*
> *His robe dipped in blood, but his name is not Joseph,*
> *His aim is explosive, God's fame is demoted.*
> *Flashback long before this moment would end,*
> *He loved his opponents when He made atonement for sin.*
> *Resurrected at the Father's right hand He sat down,*
> *Well He's back now and found on his head mad crowns, smack down!*
> *The sights and sounds amazing,*
> *A sharp sword in his mouth to strike down the nations.*
> *Today is the day that He's welcoming the foreigners,*
> *Repent and believe that He hung up on the cross for ya.*
> *Otherwise you'll meet em' as a holy righteous slaughterer,*
> *Somebody call the coroner, the Lord is a Warrior!"* [232]

REVELATION 20:1-10

As the introduction to this study warned, we can get sucked up into the debates revolving how to interpret Revelation. As a result, some have shown a lack of love toward other brothers and sisters who hold a different view. No passage in Revelation has caused more speculation, more division, and a lack of love than Revelation 20:1-10.

It is the interpretation of this passage that drives people to identify themselves as either premillennial, amillennial, or postmillennial. And while there is importance to one's interpretation, we can easily "miss the forest for the trees." As I stated in the introduction, I hold the amillenial position. But I am mainly trying to lead us to a place of worship and awe as we seek to see Christ exalted.

---

[232] Matt Papa, feat. Shai Linne, *The Lord is a Warrior* (2 Cities Music, 2011).

With that said, these notes may bear marks of my theological position, but my conscience is far more driven to help us all see John's point in this passage; that is, *exalting Christ above all else*. We must learn from a prayer the Apostle Paul shared with the Thessalonians. The context of that letter was the return of Christ. Some of the members in the church were fearful because they were misled into thinking they missed the return of Christ. Paul prays, "*Now may our Lord Jesus Christ Himself, and God our Father, who loved us and gave us eternal comfort and good hope through grace, comfort your hearts and establish them in every good work and word.*" Paul's heartfelt devotion underlying his end-times theology was grounded in hope. He knew God's grace would comfort His people *by believing* His word *and working* it out in their lives. Isn't Revelation such a similar message? Let us cling to this as we trek through Revelation 20.

When John begins the next vision in chapter 20, the Greek wording is key. John begins with the Greek word "and" (*kai*). He is clearly connecting what he has to say in chapter 20 to what he was saying in chapter 19.[233] John wants us to see that Revelation 19 and 20 are an outworking of Ezekiel 38-39. Both books speak of Gog and Magog. Where Ezekiel 39 is a recapitulation of Ezekiel 38, so Revelation 20 is a recapitulation of Revelation 19.[234] Some of the similarities In Revelation 19 and 20 are as follows:

- Revelation 20:7-10 is retelling 19:17-21. Both texts involve the nations gathering for the same war (cf. Ezek 39:1-6; Rev. 20:8). Notice John's use of birds eating the flesh of unbelievers (cf. Ezek. 39:17-18; Rev. 19:17).

- Revelation 19:15 refers to "nations" being struck down. If the book of Revelation is chronological, how can the nations still exist in Revelation 20:3?

The amount of numbers used literally in Revelation are slim at most. Why start interpreting numbers literally with the "thousand years"?

With John's use of Ezekiel 38-39 as the backdrop to Revelation 19-20, look carefully at John's words in chapter 20:

> *"Then I saw an angel coming down from heaven, holding in his hand the key to the bottomless pit and a great chain. ²And he seized the dragon, that ancient serpent, who is the devil and Satan, and bound him for a thousand years, ³and threw him into the pit, and shut it and sealed it over him, so that he might not deceive the nations any longer, until the thousand years were ended. After that he must be released for a little while"* (Rev. 20:1-3).

Pause and realize what this would have meant to the original hearers and readers of John's Apocalypse. The evil one behind all of history's persecution and oppression of believers—from Abraham to John—Is being dealt with. God is subduing the serpent, whom He once promised to crush (cf. Gen. 3:15). The leader of all the evil kingdoms from Pharaoh, to Nebuchadnezzar, to Herod, and Domitian, is finally seeing their evil works come to an end. Just imagine!

---

[233] As you are probably aware of, the original Greek text has no chapter divisions. However, some of the chapter divine we have in our English translations are often driven by a change of thought or topic. I am proposing that John is still in the middle of the same thought.

[234] For an extensive, beautiful, and almost an unarguable view of this, see Beale's Revelation Commentary on pages 972-979.

Imagine you had lost a loved one at the hands of evil rulers. Then, imagine hearing and knowing that evil was being forever restrained. How extensive is the restraining of this evil and what are the thousand years that John mentions?

As expected up to this point, the thousand years is, more than likely, a symbolic representation of the time between Jesus' crucifixion and his second coming. What helps us come to that understanding is not just what the biblical narrative as a whole seems to suggest, but the extent of the binding of Satan.

The purpose of Satan's binding is made clear when John writes, **"so that he might not deceive the nations any longer, until the thousand years were ended."** A common mistake is to interpret Satan being bound as a conclusive binding to all of his deception and wickedness. But John makes the point that this binding is in effect to his inability to deceive the nations, which means that the heralding and believing of the gospel cannot be restrained. Sure, the serpent can still tempt and trick, but his ability to deceive the elect people of God has seen its final day.

After the crucifixion and resurrection of Christ, Satan was bound, and the good news has gone from Jerusalem, to Judea, to Samaria, to the ends of the earth (Acts 1:8) and cannot be silenced. It is true, SALVATION BELONGS TO THE LORD! A child walking through an alley may be frightened by the barking of an intimidating dog, but the leash that binds the dog restrains it and gives the child trust that he will make it home. Likewise, the people of God do not need to fear they will lose their salvation because Christ will finish what He has begun (cf. Phil. 1:6). Here is John's point: The Victory of Christ is sure. Even more convincing is the use of the Greek word for binding (*deo*) in both Revelation 20:2 as well as Matthew 12:29, which reads, "*Or how can someone enter a strong man's house and plunder his goods, unless he first binds the strong man? Then indeed he may plunder his house.*" Jesus' illustration in Matthew 12 has to do with "binding" Satan, which in that context, is about Jesus being the stronger man. He has come to bind Satan and ransack him, resulting in the salvation of souls. In short, John is picking up Jesus' teaching in Matthew 12 and applying it through a symbolic and apocalyptic lens in Revelation 20. All of the symbolism of the "the key" and the "bottomless pit" and so on are not limited to Revelation 20 but are also seen throughout Revelation as they are applied to the time between the cross and the second coming. Beale agrees: "*The 'key of the abyss' in 20:1 is similar to the keys in chs. 1, 3, 6, and 9, especially chs. 6 and 9, which all pertain to realities during the church age.*"[235]

John continues his vision with another usage of "and" (*kai*), expressing the continuance of the same vision. He writes,

"**Then I saw thrones and seated on them were those to whom the authority to judge was committed. Also, I saw the souls of those who had been beheaded for the testimony of Jesus and for the word of God, and those who had not worshiped the beast or its image and had not received its mark on their foreheads or their hands. They came to life and reigned with Christ for a thousand years. The rest of the dead did not come to life until the thousand years were ended. This is the first resurrection. Blessed and holy is the one who shares in the first resurrection! Over such the second death has no power, but they will be priests of God and of Christ, and they will reign with Him for a thousand years**" (Rev. 20:4-6).

---

[235] Beale, *Revelation*, 984.

When we remove presuppositions we have heard, or have been taught,[236] and ask basic interpretive questions like who, what, when, where, etc., I think we can actually see that Rev. 20 is far simpler than many have previously thought. A quick survey of Revelation 20:4-6 will set the scene. We first read that the thrones are occupied by martyrs and all who did not take the mark of the beast during the church age. I would propose that these are all who are united to Christ and reign with Him (cf. Rom. 8:15-17). This vision appears to take place in what some scholars would call the intermediate state. This is the heavenly place of worship as it is right now for souls that are with Christ in heaven, awaiting their redeemed bodies. What is John explaining here? In 4b-5 he repeats the phrase "came to life" two times. The repetition is a key to this text. The martyrs and saints of God came to life and reigned with Christ for a thousand years. Everyone else that is in Christ dies and will "come to life" at the end of the thousand years. John calls the latter, the "first resurrection." Ok, let's unpack this.

The whole Rev. 20:4-6 vision is a shift from the vision of the abyss and Satan, to what is happening in heaven *as a result* of the binding of Satan. Just as Satan was limited in his deception during the thousand years, likewise the saints of God in the intermediate state are awaiting final glory. All of those who are united to Christ have experienced the "first resurrection." Several passages may help us grasp this already-not-yet reality:

> "*Do not marvel at this, for an hour is coming when all who are in the tombs will hear his voice*[29] *and come out, those who have done good to the resurrection of life, and those who have done evil to the resurrection of judgment.*" (John 5:28-29)

> "*We were buried therefore with Him by baptism into death, in order that, just as Christ was raised from the dead by the glory of the Father, we too might walk in newness of life.*[5] *For if we have been united with Him in a death like his, we shall certainly be united with Him in a resurrection like his.*" (Romans 6:4-5)

> "*If then you have been raised with Christ, seek the things that are above, where Christ is, seated at the right hand   of God.*[2] *Set your minds on things that are above, not on things that are on earth.*[3] *For you have died, and your life is hidden with Christ in God.*[4] *When Christ who is your life appears, then you also will appear with Him in glory.*" (Colossians 3:1-4)

In my assessment of Revelation 20, and the whole counsel of God, the "first resurrection" is a spiritual one. However, some hold that these uses of "came to life" are in regard to two different resurrections; the first of believers and the second by unbelievers, separated by a literal 1,000 years. George Eldon Ladd agrees when writing about the use of "came to life": "*Natural inductive exegesis suggests that both words are to be taken in the same way, referring to literal resurrection.*[237] While this is a strong

---

[236] To this day I still often read the theology of the Left Behind series into the book of Revelation. When I was first made new by the Holy Spirit, those Left Behind books were the first I read. I read all of them in 3 months and loved them. After going to the Bible College that Tim Lahaye founded, the author of Left Behind, the foundation had been set. Yet, it was when a beloved professor and brother in the Lord helped ask questions that broke apart my presuppositions about this book that I was finally able to understand the general format and get a better understanding of chapter 20. I am still indebted to the gracious professors that were instrumental during my time in Bible College, as well as my seminary professors at Westminster Seminary California and Reformed Theological Seminary, both leading me to a more deep and worthwhile decade of studying this book. I say all of this to encourage you that the book needs to be read the way it was intended, but many of us are bound to the popular theology and interpretation found in the Left Behind books.

[237] George Eldon Ladd, "*Historic Premillennialism,*" in *The Meaning of the Millennium: Four Views,* ed. Robert G. Clouse (Downers Grove, IL: IVP Academic, 1977), 37.

argument for those who hold the premillennial position, I have a hard time agreeing due to what we have seen in Revelation so far, as well as the canon's portrayal as a whole of the church age.

First, the Scriptures never speak of a thousand-year interval between the physical resurrection of believers and unbelievers. Matthew 25:31-32; John 5:28-29; and 2 Thessalonians 1:5-10 are just a few of the passages that teach the simultaneous judgment of believers and unbelievers accompanying Christ's return.

Second, as I showed above with the passages in italics, "resurrection" in Scripture is often a spiritual resurrection. As Richard Phillips writes, *"Only the believer in Christ experiences two resurrections: the first a resurrection of the spirit to reign with Christ after death, and the second the bodily resurrection of all mankind for the final judgment in Christ's return."*[238]

Lastly, a simple reading of the text makes clear that when John uses "came to life," he is not making a positive comparison of the two groups of people. No, he is arguing:

> *"That by suffering death for their faith in Jesus, believers enter into a resurrection that the ungodly never enjoy, whereas in the return of Jesus the ungodly suffer a resurrection to death that believers will never know. One is a spiritual raising to heaven and the other a physical raising for the sake of hell."*[239]

What a comfort to all suffering believers throughout history! Not only will God judge the wicked who oppressed them, but the second death will *never* be in the cards for Christ's people; only eternal comfort and satisfaction in Christ!

As we move on to Revelation 20:7-10, it is vital to understand this passage is a retelling of what took place in Revelation 19:11-21. Where Revelation 19:11-21 was emphasizing the utter destruction and judgment of the beast and all those associated with him, Revelation 20:7-10 is zooming in on Satan and his followers. In short, the same host of unbelievers are experiencing the wrath of God, but the emphasis is on Satan rather than the beast. John's emphasis is placed on the last hoorah of Satan and his followers, as well as their final destruction. He begins with the last hoorah:

> **"And when the thousand years are ended, Satan will be released from his prison and will come out to deceive the nations that are at the four corners of the earth, Gog and Magog, to gather them for battle; their number is like the sand of the sea. And they marched up over the broad plain of the earth and surrounded the camp of the saints and the beloved city,"** (Revelation 20:7-9a).

John is given a vision that makes absolutely clear that at the end of the thousand years—the time between the cross and the second coming of Christ—that God will let Satan loose to deceive the nations, gathering them for battle. Within the structure and repetition of Revelation, we ought not be surprised. Over and over, we have seen Satan's deception rise throughout the church age and the unbelieving population fail to repent.[240] There is no question that a great rebellion rises with Satan's

---

238 Phillips, *Revelation*, 581.

239 Ibid., 582.

240 Both amillennial and postmillennial positions have much in common. Yet, it is the repetitive reality through Revelation (and the Gospels as well) that cut the feet from under those who believe that the millennium is a golden age of Christianity that continues to flourish. Yes, the Gospel will go forth because Satan was bound from deceiving the nations, but the idea that the world just gets better through a form of Christianization goes against the biblical narrative. Would a golden age be beautiful? Yes. Is it biblical? I don't think

last hoorah as a great multitude are gathered for battle. This is what Jesus had in mind in Matthew 24:21 when He said, *"For then there will be great tribulation, such as has not been from the beginning of the world until now, no, and never will be."* This ought not throw the people of God in a frenzy. For certain interpreters of this book, but the language of Revelation 20:7-9a makes clear that Satan is being dealt with by God. Yahweh is the one whom has "released" Satan and God will mop up the mess. As Douglas Kelly writes, *"He could never get loose from his bondage at his own will, until God in his sovereign timing takes off the chains from his hands and feet, opens the door and lets him out."*[241]

This battle is sad in the sense that those who are deceived are convinced they have a chance. Their minds are blinded to the realities of the gospel and the victory already secured at Calvary. This battle in Revelation 20:7-9a a retelling of the battle known as Armageddon in Revelation 16:16. The battle here is in the proximity of what John calls Gog and Magog, repeating what we discussed earlier as John's *application* of Ezekiel 38-39 to Revelation 19-20.

What John saw in Revelation 20:9b-10 was a vision of the "clean-up" of evil. The false trinity and all associated with them are judged:

"But fire came down from heaven and consumed them, ¹⁰ and the devil who had deceived them was thrown into the lake of fire and sulfur where the beast and the false prophet were, and they will be tormented day and night forever and ever."

The repetition of the imagery of "fire" ought to bring to mind many things to the Christian. Most prominently should be the theme of God's judgment. We should harken back to the flaming covenant torch (cf. Gen. 15:17), the burnt offering in the tabernacle (cf. Ex. 38:1-7), the fire reigning down on Nadab and Abihu (cf. Num. 26:61), the fire reigning down on the false prophets of Baal (cf. 1 Kings 18), etc. The biblical-theological theme of *fire* finds its ultimate fulfillment in the final and unquenchable lake of fire that Satan and those associated with him are thrown into forever. The reason Jesus talked about hell more than anything else is because it is the most severe of judgments, cloaked in finality. Christ warned so frequently of hell because He knows its torment. In fact, He suffered the eternal hell His people deserved. In six hours on the cross, Jesus endured God's eternal judgment for us. Revelation 20:7-10 is the devastating reality that a day is coming where gospel proclamation will cease and all those not united to Christ will forever remain in their sins, under God's wrath.

REVELATION 20:11-15

We love watching sports when an intense game comes to the final seconds. We call these "nail-biters." The intensity may even cause us to hold our breath in expectation. Revelation 20:11-15 has the most intense moment of all! As we come to the final scene of judgment, it precedes the ushering in of the new heaven and new earth. As intense as the scene is, we know the Alpha and Omega is in full control. He is *not even a bit* on edge. He is calm and collected, ready to Judge all of mankind. As Donald R. Johnson writes,

---

so. However, this ought not cause division because we are not saved by our views of the millennium and the onlooking world should come to know Jesus by our love for one another (John 13:34-35)...even when we might disagree.

[241] Kelly, *Revelation*, 387.

"The vision of the last and final judgment of mankind is consistent and complimentary to all the other visions of Christ's coming in Revelation. Compare, first, the sixth seal from 6:12-17, the seventh trumpet from 11:15-19, the earth's vineyard reaped from 14:14-20, and the seventh bowl from 16:17-21 (also see 19:17-21). We have already viewed this scene with different images and different symbols."[242]

Johnson is correct, and as we should expect by now, this is another angle of previous judgments. The unique part, however, is that this is the climax and final angle of the Second Coming. Therefore, we get a clear finality to God's plan for all creation. The beginning of the final judgment vision begins when John sees the following:

"Then I saw a great white throne and Him who was seated on it. From his presence earth and sky fled away, and no place was found for them. [12] And I saw the dead, great and small, standing before the throne, and books were opened. Then another book was opened, which is the book of life. And the dead were judged by what was written in the books, according to what they had done" (Rev. 20:11-12).

This great white throne is the same throne we were introduced to in detail in Revelation 4. This throne is occupied by the all-glorious One, and it is the source of all things. Notice that "the books" are the key to John's vision in this passage. As all of humanity stands before the throne of God, *the books* are opened. Only one of these books is designated as "***the book of life.***" The other book may be a book of judgment, but we can conclude that if a person's name is not written in the book of life, they are not associated with Christ nor sealed by the Spirit. Leithart writes,

"Anyone whose name is missing is 'thrown into the lake of fire' (v. 15) to spend eternity in torment with the beasts and the dragon. Having one's name recorded in the book of life is what saves one from the second death in the lake of fire. The two books perhaps signify the relation go grace and works: The saints are judged according to works (22:12) but produce works only because they have received the gift of life and are recorded, by the sheer grace of God, in the book of life."[243]

The Author and Giver of life has opened up His books, and for the last time the wheat and chaff, the sheep and the goats, those in Him and not in Him, are being judged.

There is a real and sobering finality to this. When we picture our loved ones, who do not know Jesus, this is the curtain call. Repentance is no longer an option, gospel proclamation has ceased, and eternal torment has been initiated. But the glorious goodness for those in Christ could not be sweeter to the taste. Imagine being a first century believer who had lost a spouse, child, or fellow believer at the mouths of lions or gladiatorial conquest. Now imagine hearing John's Apocalypse read aloud as you hear this:

---

[242] Donald R. Johnson, *Victory in Jesus* (Conway, AR: Free Grace Press, 2018), 305.
[243] Leithart, *Revelation 12-22*, 332.

"And the sea gave up the dead who were in it, Death and Hades gave up the dead who were in them, and they were judged, each one of them, according to what they had done. ¹⁴ Then Death and Hades were thrown into the lake of fire. This is the second death, the lake of fire. ¹⁵ And if anyone's name was not found written in the book of life, he was thrown into the lake of fire" (Revelation 20:13-15).

The great and final news that is part of this judgment is that death has been dealt with and is punted into the lake of fire. Can you imagine? Knowing that death no longer exists? It's gone! The great sting we all suppress and act like it isn't coming for us will cease to be a reality! What comes true that day is found in John Owen's famous book titled, *The Death of Death in the Death of Christ*. The victory of Christ was once something that was already true for believers, but not-yet fully experienced. Here at the throne of the Victor, the Lamb puts death to death once and for all!! No wonder why the book of Revelation is filled with so many songs of victory! This is where we stand up, yes you, and shout with Paul and all the redeemed saints of God,

> *"Death is swallowed up in victory."*
> *"O death, where is your victory?*
> *O death, where is your sting?"* (1 Cor. 15:54c-55)

The people of God throughout Revelation have been called to persevere and overcome. We overcome by Christ's victory at Calvary and the empty tomb. Upon conversion, we are given a new will that longs to obey Jesus and make much of Him. In one sense, Christ *alone* is the overcomer. But He also seals us with the Spirit to guarantee we will overcome. The Great White Throne Judgment is where the Son judges us as righteous in His sight and stamps in the book of life, "Overcomer!" The race of grace is done, and we are ushered into our new bodies and new home forever. The great Old Testament promise when God says, *"I shall be your God, and you shall be My people"* will be fully realized. All of this is because we are those who have overcome the wicked one and his plots through our union with Christ. 1 John 5:4-5 says, *"For everyone who has been born of God overcomes the world. And this is the victory that has overcome the world—our faith. ⁵ Who is it that overcomes the world except the one who believes that Jesus is the Son of God?"*

Maybe you are unsure of whether or not you will be accepted on that final Day? Notice the Apostle John places all of our assurance in the person of Christ. John assures us that if we believe in Him, we *will* overcome. For it is not the strength of our faith that saves us, but the object of our faith. We are saved by Christ and Christ alone. And on that Day, the well-known lyrics to the last verse in *How Great Thou Art* shall roll off our lips, no longer by faith, but by sight.

> *"When Christ shall come, with shout of acclamation,*
> *And take me home, what joy shall fill my heart.*
> *Then I shall bow, in humble adoration,*
> *And then proclaim: 'My God, how great Thou art!'"*[244]

---

[244] Carl Boberg, *How Great Thou Art*, 1885.

TELEIOS

ACADEMY

WEEK 11
STUDY

REVELATION 21:1-27

Enjoying the Eternal Glory of God by Sight

MEDITATION: As you embark into Revelation 21:4, ask God for help to behold and worship Him.

1. From the text, list all the broken things God is making new. What covenant picture does God give as a description of His people? Where has John mentioned this before?

2. When you think of heaven, does it typically include the earth? Why or why not? Read verse two and explain where heaven will be located forever.

3. Does Revelation 21:1-4 reveal that we will behold God by faith or by sight?

4. How is Revelation 21:1-4 a contrast to Genesis chapter three? What does this tell us about the character of God?

APPLICATION: Do you think the world pictured in Rev. 21:1-4 is a world everyone would desire? Take a moment to jot some notes in preparation to explain this vision of heaven to an unbelieving friend.

MEDITATION: As you meditate on Revelation 21:5-8 realize you are meeting with the Alpha and Omega.

1. In Revelation 21:5, what is the connection between God's promise to make all things new and the command to write these things down?

2. Throughout Revelation, God has referred to Himself as the "the Alpha and the Omega." With the whole book in mind, how is this meant to comfort the first century hearers and readers?

3. In verse six when the thirsty are satisfied, what biblical images do you think John has in mind? Why are these so important?

4. Read Revelation 21:7-8 and write down the different kinds of people John has in mind. What separates these people?

APPLICATION: Your soul longs to be satisfied. This week, where have you run *other than* the spring of soul-quenching water offered in Christ? Confessing this to the Lord *and* to a trusted member in your community will help you forsake these "broken cisterns" (cf. Jeremiah 2:11-13). Right now, drink deeply from the Source of Life.

MEDITATION: Pray for eyes to see Christ's bride *as He sees her* as you study Revelation 21:9-14.

1. Describe some of the physical characteristics of the New Jerusalem.

2. Who is present in the New Jerusalem?

3. What is the significance of all the descriptions of the gates in verses 12-14?

APPLICATION: When you think of the glory of God what comes to mind? What do you think it will be like to behold the radiance and glory of God in person? Write out a prayer asking God to fix your focus on His glory.

MEDITATION: Ask God to stun you with the beauty of Christ as you meditate on Revelation 21:15-21.

1. What is the purpose of measuring the New Jerusalem in Revelation 21:15-16? What is the significance of the measurements listed?

2. Verses 18-20 list a host of precious jewels. What Old Testament allusion helps us understand the significance of these jewels?

3. Revelation 21:21 gives imagery of heaven that even *lost* people would use to describe heaven. How does a *biblical* understanding of this imagery give us a better grasp of John's intent?

APPLICATION: If you could choose your own job in the new heaven and new earth, what would it be and why? Write out a verse to memorize on page 305.

MEDITATION: Ask God to enlighten your eyes and heart as you walk with Him in Revelation 21:15-21.

1. What/who is the temple of God in the new heaven and new earth? How does this correspond with Jesus' teaching about the temple in the Gospel of John (cf. John 2:19-21)?

2. Read Revelation 21:23-25. What are some of the *results* of being in the presence of Christ and the glory of God? Is God the only one who possesses glory in the text? If not, who else? What might all this mean?

3. According to Revelation 21:26-27, who are the citizens of this new earth? Who is prohibited from entering the new earth? Why?

APPLICATION: As you read and meditate on a new earth, with no evil or sin, list some specific aspects of that glorious state that excite you most.

WEEK 11
COMMENTARY

REVELATION 21:1-27
Enjoying the Eternal Glory of God by Sight

REVELATION 21:1-27

ENJOYING THE ETERNAL GLORY OF GOD BY SIGHT

REVELATION 21:1-4

The world has not always been the way it currently is. It once was perfect. Even now, there are traces of God's good fingerprint everywhere around us, but we all know things are broken. The calamity of natural disasters, the gut-wrenching pain of losing a loved one, or the relational factions woven throughout humanity, have left scars in all of us. Everyone longs for a better world. In the beginning, the world was free from brokenness and pain. The first two chapters of Genesis reveals the way things once were. Everything was the way God intended it to be. Revelation 21-22 is, in one sense, a return to the Garden. It shows a world flourishing with the presence of God among His people. In another sense, Revelation 21-22 is far superior to the original Garden. As we make our way through these final two chapters of John's Apocalypse, we encounter the world to come. The future world is not grounded in speculation. This vision was given to John from the Lord Jesus Christ Himself. As John wrote in his Gospel, this Jesus is preparing a room for us.

> *"Let not your hearts be troubled. Believe in God; believe also in Me. In my Father's house are many rooms. If it were not so, would I have told you that I go to prepare a place for you? And if I go and prepare a place for you, I will come again and will take you to Myself, that where I am you may be also."*

In Revelation 21, as John looked up, he saw things both familiar and unfamiliar:

"Then I saw a new heaven and a new earth, for the first heaven and the first earth had passed away, and the sea was no more. And I saw the holy city, new Jerusalem, coming down out of heaven from God, prepared as a bride adorned for her husband." (Rev. 21:1-2).

John once wrote of God coming down in the flesh to save His people (cf. John 1:1-18). That is the familiar part of John's vision in Revelation 21. But less familiar to John in this vision is that God will bring a new heaven and new earth down with Him. The first earth and all its curse-ridden brokenness has passed away in this vision and has to make way for the new. The beauty of this new creation comes *down* towards the congregation of God, the same way a bride comes down the aisle towards the wedding attendants. This is reminding the people of God that we are the bride and are approaching that great marriage supper of the Lamb (Rev. 19:1-6).

This passage also helps us see that God does not favor spiritual things above the physical but will unite all thing in heaven and on earth to His Son (cf. Eph. 1:10). Graeme Goldsworthy beautifully explains:

> "The fact that Jesus Christ is now at the right hand of the Father in heaven, and that He has gone to prepare a place for us in the Father's house, does not mean that our final destiny is to be separated from the physical universe. Jesus has taken His own body to heaven. In that is bound up the redemption and renewal of the physical universe. It is keeping with the scriptural perspective that John sees the new heaven and new earth, and that the new Jerusalem comes down out of heaven from God. We need not suppose that this is meant to convey a literal descent of the city out of the sky. It is the final touch to the regenerating work of God. It establishes the kingdom which is not from this world. The heavenly country which Abraham longed for (Heb. 11:16) is not a land in the sky, but a tangible dwelling for redeemed mankind and one in which people of God will relate truly to God, mankind and the world. It is a dwelling from God, a city from heaven. But when it is set up in the centre of the regenerated earth, it will mean that the dwelling place of God is with men. This is how the story began in the paradise of Eden, and this is how it will end in the regained paradise of God's kingdom."[245]

This has many implications involving the physical realm in which we now live. From our bodies, to nature, to business, etc., we are not awaiting a spiritual realm where the physical things of this world will exist. Rather, we are waiting for the physical and spiritual to unite in the world to come. Heaven will be a physical place where we work, but without toil. It will be a place where we are with God by sight. A place where we truly eat and drink to the glory of God (cf. 1 Cor. 10:31). Even more so, our earthly relationships will be void of all sin. There will be no envy or pride. In his incredibly helpful book on how to rightly enjoy the physical things of earth, Joe Rigney writes,

> "Why did God make this world? Why did he make a world for his own glory in Christ and then fill it to the brim with pleasures—physical pleasures, sensible pleasures, emotional pleasures, and relational pleasures? Why did God make a world full of good friends, sizzling bacon, the laughter of children, West Texas sunsets, Dr. Pepper, college football, marital love, and the warmth of wool socks?"[246]

Rigney answers:

> "The pages of Scripture overflow with creational analogies and metaphors to help us understand the glorious and ineffable mystery of the triune God. God is a Father, and so he gives us earthly fathers so that we'd know what he's like. God is a shield and fortress. He is a roaring lion who devours his enemies."[247]

---

[245] Goldsworthy, 304-305.
[246] Joe Rigney, *The Things of Earth: Treasuring God by Enjoying His Gifts* (Wheaton, IL: Crossway, 2015), 25.
[247] Ibid., 65.

We are meant to view the physical world as bearing the marks of our Creator. All good things are meant to be indicators of the goodness of the Giver. Revelation 21:1-2 moves our eyes to a future day where our affections will never elevate the gifts above the Giver. Because of that, we will rightly enjoy the good gifts as well. C.S. Lewis said it best when he wrote, *"Aim at Heaven and you will get earth 'thrown in': aim at earth and you will get neither."*[248]

As John's ink spreads across the scroll, his next passage really sums up the whole drama of Scripture, and the entire story of humanity in one verse.

> **"And I heard a loud voice from the throne saying, 'Behold, the dwelling place**[1] **of God is with man. He will dwell with them, and they will be His people, and God Himself will be with them as their God'"** (Revelation 21:3).

Throughout the Old Testament, the covenant people of God longed for the day where the covenant stipulations of the law would not be *primarily* outward but inward. In Jeremiah 31, God gave a glimpse into the day where the New Covenant would be ushered in and God would finally dwell with man permanently: *"For this is the covenant that I will make with the house of Israel after those days, declares the LORD: I will put my law within them, and I will write it on their hearts. And I will be their God, and they shall be My people"* (Jer. 31:33). Christ came to earth, died on the cross, rose from the dead, and has ascended to the place of glory, and He has sent the Spirit to dwell within believers. The Apostle John brings the uppermost longing of God's people into view as God comes down to dwell with man. We will no longer look to Christ by faith, but by sight! What a great comfort for these suffering saints who see the brokenness of the world. John wants them to know that the earth will soon be inhabited by God Himself, void of all sickness, death, and sin. Beale adds,

> *"Since a physical temple was a particularistic, nationalistic institution, a sign of God's and Israel's separation from the unclean nations, it had no room in John's new Jerusalem, not only because believing Jew and Gentile are united in Christ in the new Jerusalem but also because they have all gained the status of priests serving before God's presence (20:6; 22:3-4). Therefore, this is the first hint that there is no literal temple in the new Jerusalem, which will be explicitly stated in 21:22, where the ultimate redemptive-historical reason for the absence of a physical temple is that God and Christ are the final, enduring form of the temple, to which the physical OT temple always pointed."*[249]

The deepest longing of the heart and soul will be met for Christians when finally and forever we are with their God. This moment will also produce a new order of life absent of every effect of the Fall in Genesis three. Let us carefully consider the Spirit's description of this future reality. At first it could seem unrealistic. Some may suppose it is too good to be true. Meditate verse by verse. Believe the pains and sorrows of this life, as heavy as they might seem, are a mist (cf. James 4:14). What John shares in Revelation 21:4 will be our *eternal reality*. Let this sink in: **"He will wipe away every tear from their eyes, and death shall be no more, neither shall there be mourning, nor crying, not pain anymore, for the former things have passed away"** (Rev. 21:4). Maybe you have endured repeated injustices. Maybe you have walked through the pain of a miscarriage, or other losses of loved ones. Maybe you look at your life as one filled with regret and sorrow. Whatever tears you have cried,

---

[248] C.S. Lewis, *Mere Christianity* (New York, NY: HarperCollins, 2005), 134,
[249] Beale, *Revelation*, 1047-48.

whatever loss has scarred you, God promises that He will *personally* wipe away *every* tear from our eyes. I can't imagine any act more intimately personal than this: The Creator Himself, the One who endured deathly blows due to my own sin, gently approaching me to mercifully wipe away all my tears. We often, and rightfully, see God as transcendent and utterly different than us. But here, John is telling of the day that distance will be replaced by God's proximity and immanence, sadness by joy, and sin by holiness and purity. Beeke encourages, *"Have you been hurt by some form of impurity? Who hasn't, right? Look at 21:1, 2 and be encouraged. Trust Christ and hope for the glory of the purity of the cleanness of the new heaven and new earth and the holy city."*[250] John is stringing together a host of Old Testament passages from Isaiah that God's people have longed for throughout history. Through John, the Spirit is promising they will one day be our eternal reality. Consider some of these promises:

> *"Awake, awake, put on your strength, O Zion; put on your beautiful garments, O Jerusalem, the holy city; for there shall no more come into you the uncircumcised and the unclean."* (Isa. 52:1)

> *"I will greatly rejoice in the LORD; my soul shall exult in my God, for He has clothed me with the garments of salvation; He has covered me with the robe of righteousness, as a bridegroom decks Himself like a priest with a beautiful headdress, and as a bride adorns herself with her jewels."* (Isa. 61:10)

> *"He will swallow up death forever; and the Lord GOD will wipe away tears from all faces, and the reproach of His people He will take away from all the earth, for the LORD has spoken."* (Isa. 25:8)

> *"Remember not the former things, nor consider the things of old. ¹⁹ Behold, I am doing a new thing; now it springs forth, do you not perceive it? I will make a way in the wilderness and rivers in the desert."* (Isa. 43:18-19)

John presses home the fact that God has redeemed the world from its brokenness. The groaning of creation (cf. Romans 8:20-23) will be quieted, and forever creation will only know the goodness of God. All the overcomers who have been washed by the blood of the Lamb are now gladly breathing Narnian air:[251] a true and visible world where the spiritual and physical are purified and equally unite under the kingship of Christ. Herman Bavinck writes,

> *"This renewal of the visible world highlights the one-sidedness of the spiritualism that limits future blessedness to heaven. While the kingdom of God is first planted spiritually in human hearts, the future blessedness of biblical hope, rooted in incarnation and resurrection, is creational, this-worldly, visible, physical, bodily hope."*[252]

The former things of this world will soon pass away, and we will be walking in the cool of the day with our Lord and with one another. Food will taste the way it was supposed to; our bodies will be glorified for eternity; and the sorrows of this world will be left to the former world we once lived in. Until then, let us fix our eyes on Christ and consider Him daily (cf. Heb. 12:2-3).

---

[250] Beeke, *Revelation*, 383.
[251] I stole "Narnian air" from Joe Rigney and his book *Live Like A Narnian*.
[252] Herman Bavinck ed. John Bolt, *Reformed Dogmatics: Abridged in One Volume* (Grand Rapids, MI: Baker Academic, 2011), 767.

REVELATION 21:5-8

As all sadness and sorrow departed in Revelation 21:1-4, the King speaks with victorious shouts of blessing to His people. Where I live in San Diego, the beach is often overshadowed by grey clouds blocking the sun. But as the day progresses, the sun burns away the clouds, shimmering its reflection off the ocean. Likewise, Christ's words in Revelation 21:5-8 are meant to burn away any remaining sorrow and doubt. The first statement Jesus declares is, **"Behold, I am making all things new" (Rev. 21:5b).** This is really a summary statement to 21:1-4 and all that our trinitarian God has accomplished in redeeming the creation. In the last chapter, we saw Isaiah foretold of God doing "a new thing." John expands on that promises, applying it to the entire cosmos. Jesus makes *all things* new. The citizens of the future newness are those who are presently new creatures, trophies of grace, redeemed by the Spirit of God (cf. 2 Cor. 5:17).

The next statement Jesus heralds is a command to **"Write this down, for these words are trustworthy and true" (Rev. 21:5c).** This statement transports us back to our Lord's words at the beginning of the book when He commanded John, *"Blessed is the one who reads aloud the words of this prophecy, and blessed are those who hear, and who keep what is written in it, for the time is near"* (Rev. 1:3). Not only does this stress the importance of having access to God's Word, but it also makes clear that the message of Revelation applies to everyone between Christ's first and second coming. Even if you have neglected Revelation until now, God promises to bless you for walking through it now (cf. Rev. 1:3) These words are trustworthy and true (cf. 21:5). God's Word, from beginning to end, is where we hear the voice of God, producing continual transformation in our lives. The London Baptist Confession of Faith describes the Bible this way:

> *"We may be moved and induced by the testimony of the church of God to a high and reverent esteem of the Holy Scriptures; and the heavenliness of the matter, the efficacy of the doctrine, and the majesty of the style, the consent of all the parts, the scope of the whole (which is to give all glory to God), the full discovery it makes of the only way of man's salvation, and many other incomparable excellencies, and entire perfections thereof, are arguments whereby it doth abundantly evidence itself to be the Word of God; yet notwithstanding, our full persuasion and assurance of the infallible truth, and divine authority thereof, is from the inward work of the Holy Spirit bearing witness by and with the Word in our hearts."*[253]

Revelation is God's Word, declaring the comforting victory of His Son and the joys of the world to come. Let us pay attention, hear, read, and be blessed.

Jesus then declares, **"It is done! I am the Alpha and the Omega, the beginning and the end" (Rev. 21:6a).** This phrase bookends the message of Revelation (cf. 1:8; 21:6). Bigger, this is the bookend of creation. Christ is the beginning of all things and the end of all things. Geerhardus Vos once wrote, *"Ours is a religion whose centre of gravity lies beyond the grave in the world to come."*[254] The self-declaration that He is the Alpha and Omega draws us into Christ's eternality. I would argue the fruit of the Spirit, which begins when we are made new, is also the daily posture of all people in the new heaven and new earth, As Paul describes it, *"But the fruit of the Spirit is love, joy, peace, patience, kindness, goodness, faithfulness, [23] gentleness, self-control; against such things there is no law"* (Galatians 5:22-23). These

---

[253] The London Baptist Confession of Faith: 1689 (Carlisle, PA: Reformed Baptist Publications, 2014) ,1.5.
[254] Geerhardus Vos, *Grace and Glory* (1922; repr., Edinburgh: Banner of Truth Trust, 1994), 165.

fruits are to break forth in Christ's people now. But will one day they will be the only way of the people of God.

Next, Jesus declares our deep soul-satisfaction. He says to John, **"To the thirsty I will give from the spring of the water of life without payment" (Rev. 21:6b).** This summarizes the posture of the people of God in the new creation. They will forever drink deeply from the well of God's goodness. Though we come with empty hands, we will leave full of God's steadfast love. In John 4, the woman who comes to the well with her water jar leaves that jar behind (cf. John 4:28) because she has found the One who satisfies her soul with living water (4:14). Again, John seven tells of a week-long celebration for The Feast of Booths. At the end of the week when everyone would have full bellies, Jesus knew their souls were not satisfied. Therefore, He stood up and cried out, *"If anyone thirsts, let Him come to Me and drink"* (John 7:37). All of these have echoes of Isaiah 55:1-2 which beckons the thirsty,

> *"Come, everyone who thirsts, come to the waters; and he who has no money, come, buy and eat! Come, buy wine and milk without money and without price. ² Why do you spend your money for that which is not bread, and your labor for that which does not satisfy? Listen diligently to Me, and eat what is good, and delight yourselves in rich food."*

In the Christ's new creation, our souls will not cease to thirst. Instead our great longings will be continuously met and satisfied in Christ. As Young identifies in his wonderful commentary on Isaiah, *"The language is evidently designed to point out that the water, wine, and milk are obtained not by human purchase but by divine grace, the free gifts of God."*[255] I am glad that our desires will continue in the new creation. This means all the longings and desires of this present evil age will finally be satisfied and celebrated in Christ. We will finally be content. All our satisfaction will be found where David told us so long ago: *"Delight yourself in the LORD, and He will give you the desires of your heart"* (Psalm 37:4).

Jesus finishes speaking in our current section by reminding:

> **"The one who conquers will have this heritage, and I will be his God and he will be my son. But as for the cowardly, the faithless, the detestable, as for the murderers, the sexually immoral, sorcerers, idolaters, and the liars, their portion will be in the lake that burns with fire and sulfur, which is the second death"**
> **(Rev. 21:7-8).**

This clear statement echoes earlier words of the Lord of Harvest. He will separate those who believe and those who do not. First, those who believe are not simply welcomed as a guest but given the familial designation of *son*. There is no greater status in this world than to be an adopted child of the living God. These family roots go deep. J.I. Packer writes,

> *"The thought of our Maker becoming our perfect parent—faithful in love and care, generous and thoughtful, interested in all we do, respecting our individuality, skillful in training us, wise in guidance, always available, helping us to find ourselves in maturity, integrity and uprightness—is a thought which can have meaning for everybody, whether we come to it by saying, 'I had a wonderful father, and I see that God is like that, only more so,' or by saying, 'My father disappointed me here, and here,*

---

[255] Edward J. Young, *The Book of Isaiah: Volume 3 Chapters 40-66* (Grand Rapids, MI: Eerdmans Publishing Co., 1972), 375.

and here, but God, praise his name, will be very different,' or even by saying, 'I have never known what it is to have a father on earth, but thank God I now have one in heaven,' The truth is that all of us have a positive ideal of fatherhood by which we judge our own and others' fathers, and it can safely be said that the person for whom the thoughts of God's perfect fatherhood is meaningless or repellant does not exist."[256]

The sons of God will receive the entire inheritance Christ earned through His life, death and resurrection. The Father will look upon His people and delight in them just as He delights in His Son. In truth, the new heaven and new earth will be one big happy family sharing the same Father. We will be under the eternal shepherding of our Elder Brother, who is not ashamed of us (cf. Heb. 2:11).

John reminds all who do not believe of their set-in-stone reality…or should I say fire? These people would not repent. They held on to ungodly characteristics and spurned the Lord of glory. The new heaven and new earth strictly prohibits all who are not holy and blameless in Christ (cf. Eph. 1:4). The inhabitants and citizens of heaven (Phil. 3:20) are characterized by joy that unbelievers have rejected for temporary pleasures. God will supply them with dissatisfaction forever. Living water has satisfied His people (cf. 21:6), but the wretched and unregenerate will thirst forever, parched lips and souls. David's soul was satisfied in a dry and weary land where there was no water (cf. Ps. 63:1). But these parched souls will be cast into the lake of fire. There, an eternal rat-race of searching for rest and satisfaction will never end. We may read and think, "Praise God that I am bound for the new heaven and new earth." We certainly ought to rejoice that God will finish the work He began in us (cf. Phil. 1:6). Remember, though, this was a letter to be read *inside* the church. The Scriptures repeatedly speak of those who appear to be God's children outwardly but eventually deny Him. As Dennis Johnson writes,

"The list of sinners may describe those who, under pressure of persecution, denied the faith, murderously betrayed their fellow Christians to the persecuting authorities and practiced sexual immorality and magic that went along with idolatry. Their inheritance is not in the pain-free new earth, but their part is in the lake of fire and brimstone."[257]

This is a sober warning that fits in the whole message of Revelation. Through John, the Spirit is calling His people to overcome. Those identified with the Son of God will be welcomed home. Those identified with the harlot and the false trinity will find their home in the fiery lake.

REVELATION 21:9-14

I had the honor of serving in the United States Army immediately after the atrocities of the September 11th attacks on the World Trade Center, the Pentagon, etc. One of the things I learned from serving during wartime is the enjoyment freedom brings after service. So is the case with the angel that places John's eyes on the post-spiritual war between the cross and second coming of Jesus. The same angel that was commissioned to pour out one of the seven bowls of wrath, is now rewarded with the sight of the Lamb for whom he fought. John writes, ***"Then came one of the seven angels who had the seven bowls full of the seven last plagues and spoke to me, saying, 'Come, I will***

---

[256] J.I. Packer, *Knowing God* (Downers Grove, IL: InterVarsity Press, 1993), 205.
[257] Dennis Johnson, *Triumph of the Lamb*, 308.

show you the Bride, the wife of the Lamb.'" (Rev. 21:9). As we have discussed, judgment and salvation always come together. This angel is an instrument of heralding God's judgment and salvation. He administered judgment and has now been rewarded the honor of showing John the redeemed, for whom the Lamb shed His blood, what G.B. Caird says, *"Perhaps John believed that the demolition squad had also an interest in the reconstruction for which they had cleared the ground."*[258] The picture John gives us is stunning to say the least. This is a word of warning to those who distort the doctrines of grace, primarily seeing other believers as depraved. While this is true apart from Christ, in Christ the people of God are given new hearts and new wills that are no longer depraved in God's eyes. By grace, we are His treasured possession. John's picture is as follows:

> **"And He carried me away in the Spirit to a great, high mountain, and showed me the holy city Jerusalem coming down out of heaven from God, having the glory of God, its radiance like a most rare jewel, like a jasper, clear as crystal. It had a great, high wall, with twelve gates, and at the gates twelve angels, and on the gates the names of the twelve tribes of the sons of Israel were inscribed—on the east three gates, on the north three gates, on the south three gates, and on the west three gates. And the wall of the city had twelve foundations, and on them were the twelve names of the twelve apostles of the Lamb"** (Rev. 21:10-14).

John describes Christians as a beautified and renewed city, decked out from head to toe in the grace of God. John is taken *"in the Spirit"* to the top of a mountain to view this city, which symbolizes the saints. Upon a mountain with a panoramic view, John wants us to think of the many biblical connections to mountaintops. Typically, this position represents the presence of God. As Richard Phillips writes,

> *"Three times in the Gospels we read that Jesus retreated to mountaintops to pray during time of difficulty (Matt. 14:23; Luke 6:12; 9:28). From mount Sinai onward, mountains are associated with God's presence, so it was natural for Jesus to meet here with His Father, anticipating His future dwelling as well in eternal communion with His people on the high mount of God."*[259]

To be specific, in New Jerusalem, redeemed saints are the place where God dwells. That is what makes heaven so heavenly. This glorious city is wrapped in the glory of God. John said it is **"coming down out of heaven from God, having the glory of God, its radiance like a most rare jewel, like a jasper, clear as crystal."** This is the holy city where only holy people dwell and thrive. This is the culmination of what God is currently doing in us, as Paul writes, *"And we all, with unveiled face, beholding the glory of the Lord, are being transformed into the same image from one degree of glory to another. For this comes from the Lord who is the Spirit"* (2 Cor. 3:18). The glory reconstruction process has been accomplished, and only the holy are allowed to be citizens in this glorious city. This glory is pictured in the likeness of a **"most rare jewel, like a jasper, clear as crystal."** Why does John using the imagery of jewels and stones? Like the glory that comes down to earth with this holy people, so the stones represent the glorious high priest who is the King of this city. Leithart adds,

---

[258] G.B. Caird, *The Revelation of St. John the Divine* (San Francisco, CA: Harper, 1966), 269.
[259] Phillips, Revelation, 634.

"Already in the midst of history, when she is still surrounded by kings and nations, the bride is adorned, cosmetized, celebrating the eternal marriage feast. She wears precious stones as her foundation stones, which overlap with the stones of the high priest's breastplate. Like the harlot, this is a priestly city, a priestess people who serves the throne of God, though also a temple city that contains the throne of God."[260]

He also helps us identify these stones by writing,

"Jasper is the stone of Judah (4:3), the replacement firstborn and the royal tribe. The identification is supported by the fact that the list of stones in chapter 21 begins with jasper (21:19). Jerusalem is not only a city glorious with the glory of the Enthroned One, but, because she is a Judahite city, a Davidic city, is glorious with the royal glory of the Sitting on the throne."[261]

The key point John wants us to see regarding the holy people of God is that they are holy as He is holy (1 Peter. 1:16). They are not holy be their own earning, but they have been made holy by the blood of the Lamb. Or as Dennis Johnson writes, *"The Lord of glory indwells His people and floods His new community with the beauty of His holiness."*[262]

As we read above, this city is also surrounded by a wall. John writes,

"It had a great, high wall, with twelve gates, and at the gates twelve angels, and on the gates the names of the twelve tribes of the sons of Israel were inscribed— on the east three gates, on the north three gates, on the south three gates, and on the west three gates. And the wall of the city had twelve foundations, and on them were the twelve names of the twelve apostles of the Lamb."

It appears to be a square or rectangular city bearing the names of the twelve tribes of Israel we saw earlier in Revelation 7:4-8. These walls are described as being built on the foundation of the twelve apostles, with the cornerstone being the Lamb. As Paul said in Ephesians 2:19-20, *"So then you are no longer strangers and aliens, but you are fellow citizens with the saints and members of the household of God, 20 built on the foundation of the apostles and prophets, Christ Jesus Himself being the cornerstone."* John is describing all the saints from the Old and New Covenants united into this beautiful city. Jesus is the Rock and Glory of this city. His radiance shines so brightly that it reflects off the faces of His people. This is the joy of the new heaven and new earth.

REVELATION 21:15-21

The heavenly city has been described so far as the place where God and His glory dwell together with His people. In John's eschatological and final vision of the city of God, he retells a

---

[260] Leithart, *Revelation 12-22*, 372.
[261] Ibid., 371.
[262] Johnson, *Triumph of the Lamb*, 635.

familiar Old Testament image. In the introduction to the final vision in the book of Ezekiel, the prophet tells us,

> *"In visions of God He brought me to the land of Israel, and set me down on a very high mountain, on which was a structure like a city to the south.* ³ *When He brought me there, behold, there was a man whose appearance was like bronze, with a linen cord and a measuring reed in His hand. And he was standing in the gateway"* (Ezek. 40:2-3).

Ezekiel 40-48 was a thrilling vision to an exiled people longing for a new temple for God to dwell with His people. The measurements of the temple are a perfect square, reminiscing the grandiose days of the tabernacle where God dwelled with His people. Likewise, John's vision picks up this square temple idea and writes,

> **"And the one who spoke with me had a measuring rod of gold to measure the city and its gates and walls.** ¹⁶ **The city lies foursquare, its length the same as its width. And he measured the city with his rod, 12,000 stadia. Its length and width and height are equal.** ¹⁷ **He also measured its wall, 144 cubits by human measurement, which is also an angel's measurement"** (Rev. 21:15-17).

John is enticing his readers—who are in a sort of exile themselves—with a picture of the final city of God, the place that the tabernacle and the temple were mere types and shadows. This is the final resting place for God and His people. Beale argues that the square shape is not just reminiscent of the tabernacle, but also the square shape of the of the breast piece (cf. Ex. 28:16), the altar and the mercy seat in the tabernacle, etc. In short, Beale believes that the square shape is often used to represent completeness and wholeness.[263] This would make sense when we realize this is the final revelation of the final dwelling place of God where we are finally made complete and whole in Christ.

The vastness of this city, revealed in cube size, reaches high and wide. When the angel measures the city, we are told that it is 12,00 stadia. This is the size of the entire *Mediterranean world from Jerusalem to Spain.*[264] Not only is it that vast in length, but also in height. This brilliant architectural anomaly, whether symbolic or not, is meant to awe the reader that our God has prepared a home for us unlike any other. It is also so vast that all the redeemed and resurrected from all nations can coincide in the presence of God together forever. This is of great significance to saints from all ages because our God is the Divine Creator who will give His people a grand dwelling place, full of work, technology, music, and friendships that all bear His creative fingerprint. C.S. Lewis once wrote,

> *"I was standing today in the dark toolshed. The sun was shining outside and through the crack at the top of the door there came a sunbeam. From where I stood that beam of light, with the specks of dust floating in it, was the most striking thing in the place. Everything else was almost pitch-black. I was seeing the beam, not seeing things by it. Then I moved, so that the beam fell on my eyes. Instantly the whole previous picture vanished. I saw no toolshed, and (above all) no beam. Instead I saw, framed in the irregular cranny at the top of the door, green leaves moving on the branches of a tree outside and*

---

263 Beale, *Revelation*, 1075.
264 Phillips, *Revelation*, 644.

beyond that, 90 odd million miles away, the sun. Looking along the beam and looking at the beam are very different experiences.[265]

Can you imagine the day where you never again abuse the gifts of God? A place where every gift will be used properly to exalt the Giver? The city of God will no longer be a place where people worship the created instead of the Creator (cf. Rom. 1:26). It will be a landscape full of those who have been renewed, and who are driven to glorify God with every second, every breath, and every good gift from the Father of Lights (cf. James 1:17).

John zooms in on the wall and returns to the imagery of precious jewels and the gates when writing,

"The wall was built of jasper, while the city was pure gold, like clear glass. The foundations of the wall of the city were adorned with every kind of jewel. The first was jasper, the second sapphire, the third agate, the fourth emerald, the fifth onyx, the sixth carnelian, the seventh chrysolite, the eighth beryl, the ninth topaz, the tenth chrysoprase, the eleventh jacinth, the twelfth amethyst. And the twelve gates were twelve pearls, each of the gates made of a single pearl, and the street of the city was pure gold, like transparent glass" (Rev. 21:18-21).

Our culture uses common phrases found in this passage regarding the material prosperity found in heaven, such as "the pearly gates" or the "streets of gold," John is emphasizing the glory of God beaming forth throughout this heavenly city. The rainbow-like array of stones and crystals brings to mind the priestly garments to those familiar with the Old Testament. Moses writes,

"You shall set in it four rows of stones. A row of sardius, topaz, and carbuncle shall be the first row; [18] and the second row an emerald, a sapphire, and a diamond; [19] and the third row a jacinth, an agate, and an amethyst; [20] and the fourth row a beryl, an onyx, and a jasper. They shall be set in gold filigree. [21] There shall be twelve stones with their names according to the names of the sons of Israel. They shall be like signets, each engraved with its name, for the twelve tribes" (Ex. 28:17-21).

These stones and crystals were fastened to the chest of the priestly garments and the priest before he would go into the holy of holies and offer sacrifices. While we could spend some time on the meaning of each stone and crystal, what is most significant is what their collective colors represent. The rainbow-beautified wall was a reflection of the rainbow that surrounds the throne of God in all His splendor and glory (cf. Rev. 4:3). Those in the presence of God will constantly be reminded that the glory of God truly does cover the entire earth (cf. Habakkuk 2:14). And it is because of our great High Priest, Jesus, that His people will be wrapped and enveloped in the glory of God forever. While God may have given a rainbow to Noah as a covenant to never again flood the earth, the New City is flooded with a rainbow symbolizing the inescapable glory of God. What a joy!

Notice in our passage that safety seems to be a concern at first glance. There is a wall and it begs the question, is there something God wants to keep out? Growing up, my parents often talked of their childhood years and how doors didn't need to be locked at night but were primarily decorative. Likewise, here, the enemies of God have been evicted to the lake of fire. Where the Garden of Eden

---

[265] C.S. Lewis, *Meditation in a Toolshed*, http://www.pacificaoc.org/wp-content/uploads/Meditation-in-a-Toolshed.pdf, 1.

was penetrable, the new heaven and new earth is not. The wall tells the saints that no serpent shall ever enter the dwelling place of God and His people. We can then sing with David,

> *"We have thought on your steadfast love, O God,*
> *in the midst of your temple.*
> *As your name, O God,*
> *so, your praise reaches to the ends of the earth.*
> *Your right hand is filled with righteousness.*
> *Let Mount Zion be glad!*
> *Let the daughters of Judah rejoice*
> *because of your judgments!*
> *Walk about Zion, go around her,*
> *number her towers,*
> *consider well her ramparts,*
> *go through her citadels,*
> *that you may tell the next generation*
> *that this is God,*
> *our God forever and ever.*
> *He will guide us forever."*
> (Psalm 48:10-14)

REVELATION 21:22-27

In the Gospel of John, the religious leaders had many disagreements with Jesus. A recurring theme in many of these disagreements related to Jesus' claim to be the temple of God (cf. John 2:19-21). He came and "tabernacled" among them (1:14) and made clear, *"Destroy this temple, and in three days I will raise it up."* This was a form of blasphemy to the religious leaders because who could knock down the dwelling place of God, let alone, build such a glorious architectural structure in three days? But, Jesus was referring to Himself. He was making it clear that He was the temple of God and was putting an end to the era of the physical temple. In Revelation 21:22, John gives us the future reality that began at Christ's resurrection when he writes, **"And I saw no temple in the city, for its temple is the Lord God Almighty and the Lamb."** Peter Leithart adds, *"When John tells us there is no temple, he is announcing the end of the postlapsarian world, the end of exclusion from Eden, the end of temples with their curtains and walls and buffer spaces. In the holy city, everyone who enters is in the throne room."*[266] Jesus takes all dividing walls, all obstacles, anything that could separate us from the unadulterated glory of God and clears it away. In addition to removing hindrances, He welcomes us into the presence of God forever. Although the tabernacle and the temple had separate structures where God would dwell, now all peoples from all nations who are sealed with the blood of the Lamb walk continuously in the presence of God. The curtains have dropped, and this new cube-shaped city is all the holy of holies, and we walk free and liberated in His presence. As Beale explains, *"The Old Testament tabernacle and temples were symbolically designed to point to the cosmic eschatological reality that God's tabernacling presence, formerly limited to the*

---

[266] Leithart, *Revelation 12-22*, 388.

holy of holies, was to be extended throughout the whole earth."[267] This scene in Revelation 21 is the home for which we have truly longed. This is where the redeemed exist for eternity. *God* is the temple.

Not only is the physical temple obsolete in the new City of God, but John also tells his readers,

> **"And the city has no need of sun or moon to shine on it, for the glory of God gives it light, and its lamp is the Lamb. By its light will the nations walk, and the kings of the earth will bring their glory into it, and its gates will never be shut by day—and there will be no night there"** (Rev. 21:23-26).

To understand all these beautiful images in Revelation 21-22, we are reminded constantly that the images represent reality. Will there be streets of gold? Maybe. Will there literally be no sun? Maybe. Wherever we land, the reality is that God is present with His people and His glory is the superlative experience. This is because the great and glorious shekinah glory fills the entire city of God and no physical light sources, even the sun, could be seen with God's glory as the radiating back drop. As Beale writes, *"The light-giving sources of sun and moon were essential for the life and prosperity of the old Jerusalem when God's presence was limited to the temple. But now in the new cosmos God's complete presence among His people is what beautifies them and satisfies their every need."*[268] This is breathtaking because we do not walk in the radiance of such glory as foreigners but find our home and existence in it. That is what John says, **"By its light will the nations walk, and the kings of the earth will bring their glory into it,"** it is the eternal life source that holds all things together (Col. 1:15-17; Heb. 1:3). John may have in mind Micah 4:1-2, which says,

> *"It shall come to pass in the latter days that the mountain of the house of the LORD shall be established as the highest of the mountains, and it shall be lifted up above the hills; and peoples shall flow to it, ² and many nations shall come, and say: 'Come, let us go up to the mountain of the LORD, to the house of the God of Jacob, that He may teach us His ways and that we may walk in His paths.' For out of Zion shall go forth the law, and the word of the LORD from Jerusalem."*

Not only will the people of God from every tribe, nation, and tongue (Rev. 5:9) walk by the light of the glory of God, but kings bring their glory into this city. John seems to be making a point that some of the things we do here on earth by the grace of God, will also be found to have their place in the city of God. I think this also tells us that some of God's gracious economy here and now regarding leadership will also be part of the economy of the new heaven and new earth. Imagine leaders and bosses who only have the glory of God in mind and rule with love and consider the interests of others as supreme. Imagine kings and politicians who never lead for self-glory or for the sake of power, but only to magnify the Lord of glory. This is not just a city without sin and tears and death, it is a city where life is continuously bursting forth through every seam. Everyone is loved, and the gates never shut on the saints who are continuously welcome.

Yet, writing in the first century, John wants to drive home the point that evil will not dwell in this future home when he writes, **"They will bring into it the glory and the honor of the nations. ²⁷ But nothing unclean will ever enter it, nor anyone who does what is detestable or false, but**

---

[267] G.K. Beale, *The Temple and the Church's Mission: A Biblical Theology of the Dwelling Place of God* (Downers Grove, IL: Intervarsity Press, 2004), 25.

[268] Beale, *Revelation*, 1094.

only those who are written in the Lamb's book of life" (Rev. 21:26-27). This is not supposed to invoke pictures of zombie-like folks swarming the walls but is a picture of the purity of the dwelling place of God and His people. It is a place where the redeemed that were counted holy and blameless in Christ (Eph. 1:4) will dwell. Those not "in Christ" cannot dwell here because they are not citizens of this place (Phil. 3:20). They are the impure, those that are hostile to God (Rom. 8:7). Those who are citizens are those foretold of in many Old Testament passages:

> *"And a highway shall be there, and it shall be called the Way of Holiness; the unclean shall not pass over it. It shall belong to those who walk on the way; even if they are fools, they shall not go astray."* (Isa. 35:8)

> *"Awake, awake, put on your strength, O Zion; put on your beautiful garments, O Jerusalem, the holy city; for there shall no more come into you the uncircumcised and the unclean."* (Isa. 52:1)

> *"And every pot in Jerusalem and Judah shall be holy to the LORD of hosts, so that all who sacrifice may come and take of them and boil the meat of the sacrifice in them. And there shall no longer be a trader in the house of the LORD of hosts on that day."* (Zech. 14:21)

This is the home of the redeemed and the Redeemer. It is a place of joy and purity. As Derek Thomas encourages,

> *"God intends to create a people who will respond to Him in worship and adoration. This has been God's intention from the beginning. In the new heaven and new earth, the worship of God will be pure. There will be no source of evil left. It will be international. The 'nations' will walk there (21:24, 26). There is no temple, because everything will be temple!"*[269]

---

[269] Thomas, *Let's Study Revelation*, 177.

TELEIOS

ACADEMY

WEEK 12
STUDY

REVELATION 22:1-21
Access Granted: The New Eden

MEDITATION: Ask God that you would flourish from His life-giving fruit as you look at Christ in Revelation 22:1-5.

1. Read Ezekiel 47:1-12 along with Revelation 22:1-3. What are some similarities? What is John expressing to his readers regarding this river?

2. What are some ways that the new heaven and the new earth are *better* than the garden of Eden? Look through Genesis 1-2 and Revelation 21-22, listing similarities and differences.

3. What imagery from Revelation 21:23-24 does John reuse in Revelation 22:5? Why?

APPLICATION: What can you apply to life today in light of what is promised to come in the new city?

MEDITATION: Ask God for faith as He reveals His truth in Revelation 22:6-9.

1. Read Revelation 22:6-9, then list some of the characteristics of John's conclusion. With a suffering people in mind, what did God declaring to them? How would this message encourage them?

2. Revelation 1:3 began with a promise of blessing for those who read this book. How is Revelation 22:7 *similar* and *different* from Revelation 1:3? How do these two blessings function as bookends?

3. Why do you think the book of Revelation has such an emphasis on hearing and keeping the word of God? What are the dangers of only hearing?

APPLICATION: Write out a prayer for the Lord to return soon. Do your longings and affections for heaven rise as you pray?

MEDITATION: While reading Revelation 22:10-16 today, trust God to faithfully work in your life.

1. Is the book of Revelation sealed in 22:10-11? What effect does this have? Why does Jesus command John and the churches to let both types of people keep doing what they are doing?

2. In verses 12-13, what recompense will Jesus bring with Him at His return? Who will this effect?

3. What is the entrance ceremony to the New City in Revelation 22:14? What present day implications does this have for us?

APPLICATION: How will you specifically love those who John expects to do evil and be filthy (22:11)? Share this plan with someone in your group.

MEDITATION: Whole-heartedly accept the invitation of Revelation 22:17-19, come to the Lord.

1. When you consider the role of the Holy Spirit, does He glorify Himself or Christ? How do we see this in Revelation 22:17?

2. Read Isaiah 55:1-2 along with Revelation 22:17. What is the *call* in these passages, and what is the *cost?*

3. Read Deuteronomy 4:2 and Revelation 22:18-19. What is at stake for those who add to God's Word? Why? What does this say about the overall message of Revelation?

APPLICATION: What are some ways the Holy Spirit has glorified Christ in your time of reading and prayerful meditation upon the Word today? Write out a verse to memorize on page 305.

MEDITATION: May the grace of the Lord Jesus be with you as press into Him through Revelation 22:20-21.

1. What are some conclusions from your study in Revelation–knowing it is the last inspired words from God in the Bible? Consider the original audience and what would comfort them and also spur them on to overcome in the midst of their current circumstances.

2. What promise does Jesus make in Revelation 22:20? How does this promise increase affections for Jesus, while simultaneously spurring readers on to present faithfulness?

APPLICATION: Do you tend to pray, "Come, Lord Jesus!" only when you are suffering? Have you ever prayed this in the midst of plenty? Why or why not?

WEEK 12
COMMENTARY

REVELATION 22:1-21
Access Granted: The New Eden

REVELATION 22:1-21

ACCESS GRANTED:
THE NEW EDEN

REVELATION 22:1-5

The book of Ezekiel was shocking in its day. God's people were in exile when they received Ezekiel's message. Though shocking, it was also a word of rich comfort declaring that God's glory was going with them into exile. For those who understood God's presence *primarily* reserved for the temple in Jerusalem, this all-access opening to fellowship with God would have been joyfully received. In the final vision of Ezekiel in chapters 40-48, he tells of the new heaven and new earth.[270] Ezekiel 47 is a stunning vision of a river of life flowing from the temple, lined with trees, in many ways reminiscent of the garden of Eden. John picks up this imagery,

> ***"Then the angel showed me the river of the water of life, bright as crystal, flowing from the throne of God and of the Lamb through the middle of the street of the city; also, on either side of the river, the tree of life with its twelve kinds of fruit, yielding its fruit each month. The leaves of the tree were for the healing of the nations. No longer will there be anything accursed, but the throne of God and of the Lamb will be in it, and His servants will worship Him"*** (Revelation 22:1-3).

The key to understanding John's point in this water imagery lies in what he says about its Source. The water flows from the throne of God and the Lamb. In the same way the water flows from the temple in Ezekiel 40-48, we now see that the resurrected temple, the Lord Jesus Christ, is the Source of all life. *Jesus* is the nourishment for everything in the new City of God! This has echoes of Genesis 2:10 and the river that flowed through the garden of Eden. In John 7:37, Jesus offered the same water at the end of the feast of booths. He held out the endless grace of the Spirit of God to whoever was thirsty. Likewise, the new heaven and new earth will be a place where all her citizens will no longer look beyond Christ for satisfaction. Everything we will ever need will be found in Christ.

---

[270] Dispensationalists would disagree here and see Ezekiel 40-48 as a literal prophecy of a literal temple in literal Jerusalem. However, if you take the measurements that Ezekiel is given, you will quickly notice that Jerusalem cannot hold such a sizable temple without moving it at least 60 miles north. The imagery Ezekiel uses and the way Revelation picks it up in ch. 21-22, makes it a simple and beautiful fulfillment of the temple in the New heaven and new earth.

Psalm 46:4 says, *"There is a river whose streams make glad the city of God, the holy habitation of the Most High."* Jonathan Edwards once preached,

> *"The beauty of trees, plants, and flowers, with which God has bespangled the face of the earth, is delightful; ... the beauty of the highest heavens is transcendent; the excellency of angels and the saints in light is very glorious: but it is all deformity and darkness in comparison of the brighter glories and beauties of the Creator of all."*[271]

The Lord of glory is the beauty we all long to see. In the New City, we will forever behold Him face-to-face!

The City of God will be filled with beauty and joy *because* our Trinitarian God will be present with us. In fact, this is exactly what Ezekiel promised at the close of his book: *"And the name of the city from that time on shall be, 'The LORD Is There.'"* (Ezek. 48:35b). Notice on both sides of this river is a tree of life. John was given a superlative vision of our future home. This home will infinitely exceed the qualities and characteristics of the Garden of Eden. The Garden of Eden had the tree of life and the tree of the knowledge of good and evil (Gen. 2:9). But here, in the city of the redeemed, there are only life-giving trees.

My family lives in San Diego. The climate is beautiful most of the year, but we especially look forward to Spring. That's because we anticipate enjoying the fruit from our neighbor's property. Thinking about it now brings delight. I'm thankful they generously share with us. Visually, the orchards are beautiful. Physically, my children love to pick and peel it. We all delight to smell the citrus and taste the sweetness. There's also delight in the abundance of it all. Because they are so generous and have such an abundance, we also delight to know we can go pick more anytime we desire.

Look at the New City in Revelation. The trees are ripe with twelve types of fruit which bring sustenance and healing to the nations (Rev. 5:9). Hamilton says this,

> *"The last phrase of 22:2 tells us that when the redeemed enjoy the new and better Eden, old hurts will be healed. The nationalism, the racism, the acrimony, the bitterness, and the long history of warfare will be healed. The nations will be healed by the leaves of the tree of life. The redeemed of every tribe will enjoy the crystal-clear water of life, the twelve fruits of the 'tree of life,' and 'healing.'"*[272]

Hamilton also provides the following comparison and contrast between Genesis and Revelation[273]:

GENESIS	REVELATION	WAYS THE NEW GARDEN IS BETTER
Genesis 2:10: "A river flowed out of Eden to water the garden"	Revelation 22:1: "the river of the water of life, bright as crystal,	• Living Water • "Bright as crystal"

[271] Jonathan Edwards, *The Works of Jonathan Edwards,* ed. Perry Miller, John E. Smith, and Harry S. Stout (New Haven, CT: Yale University Press, 1957-2008), 10:421.

[272] Hamilton, *Revelation*, 404.

[273] Ibid.

GENESIS	REVELATION	WAYS THE NEW GARDEN IS BETTER
	flowing from the throne of God and of the Lamb"	• "Flowing from the throne of God and of the Lamb"
Genesis 2:9: "The tree of life was in the midst of the garden"	Revelation 22:2: "on either side of the river, the tree of life with its twelve kinds of fruit, yielding its fruit each month. The leaves of the tree were for the healing of the nations"	• The tree is on both sides of the river • "Twelve kinds of fruit" (Ezekiel 47:12) • Continual production • "Healing"

The astonishing reality of all of this is made clear when John shows what is *not* present in the city. He says, **"No longer will there be anything accursed"** (Rev. 22:3). In Galatians 3:13, we are told that Jesus became a curse by hanging on the cross so that we could be free. The City of God is the climax, and eternal fruit, of the cross and resurrection of Jesus. Because Jesus absorbed the curse for us, no curse if left. None. No pains or sorrows have a home in God's Eternal City. Sickness will be no more. Death will be tossed into the lake of fire. Even the Holy Spirit will cease His ministry of groaning with us, because our prayers will be entirely pure (Rom. 8:26).

These benefits and the curse-free culture are for those sealed by the Lamb of God. Those that are associated with the Lamb now by faith will get the greatest reward in their new home, as John says, **"They will see His face, and His name will be on their foreheads"** (Rev. 22:4). Let that sink in. You will see His face! All the trust, all the prayers, all the good works done by faith will become sight. There is no greater reward and no greater motivation to our present trust than this promise. Michael Reeves writes, *"Heaven is heavenly precisely because it is the place of communion with Christ, where His glory is enjoyed."*[274] John's original readers would have delighted and longed for this day, and so should we. As Richard Bauckham writes, *"The face expresses who a person is. To see God's face will be to know who God is in his personal being. This will be the heart of humanity's eternal joy in their eternal worship of God."*[275] John recapitulates what he already told his readers in 21:23-25 when he says, **"And night will be no more. They will need no light of lamp or sun, for the Lord God will be their light, and they will reign forever and ever"** (Rev. 22:5). Again, we will reign with Christ in perfect unity and purity forever and ever. The glory of God in the face of Christ will be the eternal lamp that guides every citizen of the City. This is something we will experience by sight, but for now we gaze at Christ by faith. As Paul encouraged the Corinthians,

> *"Since we have such a hope, we are very bold, not like Moses, who would put a veil over his face so that the Israelites might not gaze at the outcome of what was being brought to an end. But their minds were hardened. For to this day, when they read the old covenant, that same veil remains unlifted, because only through Christ is it taken away. Yes, to this day whenever Moses is read a veil lies over*

---

[274] Michael Reeves, *Spurgeon on the Christian Life: Alive to Christ* (Wheaton, IL: Crossway, 2018), 177.
[275] Richard Bauckham, *The Book of Revelation*, 233.

their hearts. But when one turns to the Lord, the veil is removed. Now the Lord is the Spirit, and where the Spirit of the Lord is, there is freedom. And we all, with unveiled face, beholding the glory of the Lord, are being transformed into the same image from one degree of glory to another. For this comes from the Lord who is the Spirit." (2 Cor. 3:12-18)

REVELATION 22:6-9

One of the greatest sorrows many of us have endured has resulted from broken promises. We should be able to trust our friends and loved ones. Unfortunately, everyone is eventually let down. The original audience of Revelation was counting the cost of following Jesus. One of the temptations revealed about the churches in Revelation 2-3 is our propensity to doubt Christ's promises. As John concludes his apocalypse, he emphasizes Jesus' words of promise to him and the seven churches:

"And He said to me, 'These words are trustworthy and true. And the Lord, the God of the spirits of the prophets, has sent His angel to show His servants what must soon take place.' And behold, I am coming soon. Blessed is the one who keeps the words of the prophecy of this book'" (Rev. 22:6-7).

Jesus declared the words of this book are "trustworthy and true." If readers took stock of Revelation 21-22 as true and trustworthy, it would put a sparkle of hope in each eye. Knowing our God cannot lie (cf. Heb. 6:18) compels us to take Revelation—especially the victory of the Lamb—and hold onto it with full assurance. The Lord's encouragement to John is not just that these things are true, but that God has given His people a book including all he had shown him. We are not just called to hear and believe, but to **"keep the words of the prophecy of this book."** This statement reminds us of a lot of language from 1 John. There, John shows that "hearing" and "doing" are two sides of the same coin. Leithart explains:

"Throughout the final section of Revelation, John emphasizes the need for active obedience. He pronounces a blessing on those who keep (tereo) the words of the prophecy of the book (22:7), and another on those who regularly wash their clothing (22:14). Jesus did not unveil Himself in His bride to satisfy our curiosity about the first century or the distant future. Revelation demands not merely assent and curiosity but obedience. Revelation ends on the same note as John's first epistle: 'Little children, keep yourselves from idols.'"[276]

Those who have been washed by the Lamb are consistentenly called to conquer and overcome. This is *not* a call to earn salvation, but a fruit of those who are in Christ. God is not opposed to our effort. He's opposed to our earning. This is what Paul had in mind in Philippians three. After unfolding that justification and righteousness is owing to Christ alone (cf. Phil. 3:3-11), Paul explains the fruit as follows: *"Not that I have already obtained this or am already perfect, but I press on to make it my own, because Christ Jesus has made me His own"* (Phil. 3:12). Jesus' instruction to John and his audience could not lead to antinomianism. To put it practically, Jesus does not want us to sit on the couch waiting for His return. Rather, we are given the Spirit in order to be a light to the nations. The

---

[276] Leithart, *Revelation 12-22*, 422.

motivation for good works is bound up in the promise Jesus heralded: ***"And behold, I am coming soon."*** Similarly, Jesus taught in Matthew 24:45-46, "*Who then is the faithful and wise servant, whom his master has set over his household, to give them their food at the proper time? Blessed is that servant whom his master will find so doing when He comes.*" If the Master were to return today, would He find you ready? Would He find you invested in the affairs of His kingdom, or would He find you building your own little kingdom for your own pleasure and glory? The citizens of the New City are a people who invest in that city now. The promise that Jesus is coming soon, and the blessings that come with hearing and obeying Him, are the means of keeping our eyes fixed on the finish line. As Richard Phillips urges, "*We are to resist evil, knowing that it is soon to be judged and that Christ will not allow His people to be defeated. Knowing the certainty of our victory in Christ, we are to do the will of God and bear testimony to Christ's blood.*"[277] The new regenerate heart that replaced our former heart of stone comes with new affections and new abilities to obey. Christians are called out of darkness, and enlisted as representatives of Christ. We are to glorify Him through hearing His Word, trusting Him, *and* obeying Him.

As John hears the voice of the Lion and the Lamb, he included his readers in the words of his response:

> ***"I, John, am the one who heard and saw these things. And when I heard and saw them, I fell down to worship at the feet of the angel who showed them to me, but he said to me, 'You must not do that! I am a fellow servant with you and your brothers the prophets, and with those who keep the words of this book. Worship God'"*** (Rev. 22:8-9).

The same angel that served as John's heavenly tour guide became the object of his worship. He was so overwhelmed by the entire apocalypse that he fell down with the *correct response* aimed at the *wrong person*. The angel was merely a messeger of the Revelation. Christ is the Source. John's mistake actually serves to highlight the holiness of God above the angels, and all created things. Beale writes,

> "*John may have mistaken the angel for the divine, heavenly Christ of 1:13ff. and 10:1ff., who does deserve worship. Whatever the motive, the angel's prohibition is intended as a warning to Christians, not merely against worship of angels in particular, but against any form of idolatry, which was a problem in the churches of Asia Minor (e.g., see on 2:14-15, 20-21; 9:20).*"[278]

The ultimate blessing of hearing and obeying the "trustworthy and true words" of Revelation, is the worship of God. The angel concured in his rebuke, ***"Worship God."***

REVELATION 22:10-16

Christians in all ages have lived among the wicked. From Genesis to Revelation, God's people lived among pagans who denied God and were hostile toward the saints. Those who mocked Noah, were enemies of Elijah, and the self-righteous Pharisees of Jesus' day, are each examples of the challenge Christians face in every age. Instead of removing us from these challenges, it brings glory to God as we declare the gospel among His enemies.

---

[277] Phillips, *Revelation*, 680.
[278] Beale, *Revelation*, 1128.

In Daniel 12, God sent His messenger angels to answer Daniel's question in regard to the nature of the kingdom of God prior to the return Christ. The conversation is recorded in Daniel 12:8-10:

"I heard, but I did not understand. Then I said, "O my lord, what shall be the outcome of these things?" He said, "Go your way, Daniel, for the words are shut up and sealed until the time of the end. Many shall purify themselves and make themselves white and be refined, but the wicked shall act wickedly. And none of the wicked shall understand, but those who are wise shall understand."

Daniel was called to shut up and seal the revelation from God, and continue living in holiness in the midst of a wicked world. John picks up Daniel's language, applying it to readers. We read in Revelation 22:10-11,

"And he said to me, "Do not seal up the words of the prophecy of this book, for the time is near. Let the evildoer still do evil, and the filthy still be filthy, and the righteous still do right, and the holy still be holy."

Dwelling among the wicked is a reality for all generations, but notice the difference between the time of Daniel and Revelation. Daniel was told to seal up the scroll, John is told to leave it unrolled. Why the change? Dennis Johnson helps by showing,

"The sealing of Daniel's prophecy signaled that the time of its fulfillment was remote, standing in a different epoch of God's redemptive plan from the prophet (cf. Dan. 9:26). What John has seen, however, concerns the redemptive-historical epoch in which he is living—the span between the resurrection of Christ and his return, the 1,260 days between the enthronement of the woman's child and his return as the captain of heaven's calvary. Because John stands with his hearers in the time in which the conflict of the ages has reached its critical pitch in the sacrifice of the Lamb and the expulsion of the dragon accuser from heaven, every individual needs to face immediately the sort of person he or she is today, without assuming a perpetual string of tomorrows in which change might occur."[279]

In short, Daniel beheld future realities, but John saw them in one present panorama.

Living among the wicked is often costly for the righteous. In fact, Revelation is filled with believers losing their lives for following Jesus. Jesus reminds John and His people, **"Behold, I am coming soon, bringing my recompense with me, to repay each one for what he has done. I am the Alpha and the Omega, the first and the last, the beginning and the end"** (Rev. 22:12-13). Throughout the Old Testament there is a theological tension that results from people *not* getting what they deserve. This includes God's people who sinned over and over, but did not receive final judgment. At the coming of Christ, this tension is finally dealt with. Answering this delimma, Paul wrote of Jesus:

"whom God put forward as a propitiation by His blood, to be received by faith. This was to show God's righteousness, because in His divine forbearance He had passed over former sins. [26] It was to

---

[279] Johnson, *Triumph of the Lamb*, 325.

show His righteousness at the present time, so that He might be just and the justifier of the one who has faith in Jesus" (Rom. 3:25-26).

It was in view of the coming cross of Christ that God could Passover sins of former generations. He reserved for Jesus upon the cross the wrath they deserved, that they might be justified and prove Himself Just. But, for those who do not trust in Jesus alone for pardon, He is coming soon, bringing recompense. Every moment a person spent loving self instead of God will be repaid. Every lie, every impure thought, He will repay. The "smallest" of sins will be repaid in lake of fire forever. As sober as this is, it is meant to *comfort* the people of God. This teaches us about the character of God. On one hand we should long for the salvation of our enemies, but on the other hand it is perfect and just to pray for God to make things right. Joel Beeke says,

> "*The words indicate the fixed state in which both the righteous and the wicked find themselves at Christ's return. The truth is that when our Lord returns, there will be no second chance. There will be no further opportunities for repentance. John is making the point that when a person dies, his eternal destiny is fixed.*"[280]

Let us rejoice greatly in our salvation, plead with the wicked as if Christ were coming back today, and know that at His coming all things will be made right. This same idea is repeated with different imagery when John writes,

> **"Blessed are those who wash their robes, so that they may have the right to the tree of life and that they may enter the city by the gates. Outside are the dogs and sorcerers and the sexually immoral and murderers and idolaters, and everyone who loves and practices falsehood"** (Rev. 22:14-15).

Whereas Revelation 22:10-11 described the righteous and the wicked *during the millennium*, 22:14-15 describes them *in eternity*. The imagery shows the eternal blessings enjoyed by the redeemed, and the wicked left forever outside the gates, stuck in their sin forever.

The entrance into this exclusive community requires being washed in the blood of the Lamb. These have no righteousness of their own. Their trust is entirely in Jesus Christ. Their robes are the robes of Christ's righteousness.[281] In regard to these robes, Beeke says,

> "*Every one of us wears a robe. All our thoughts, words, and deeds go into the making of this robe. This robe is splattered, dirty, and full of holes, the Bible tells us. Even our righteousness is as filthy rags in God's sight. The only hope we have of entering the New Jerusalem is somehow to clean and mend our robes. Nothing on planet earth can cleanse a sinner's filthy rags except the blood of Jesus Christ. Blessed are they who wash their robes in that blood. All who plunge beneath that stream lose their guilty stains.*"[282]

---

[280] Beeke, *Revelation*, 589.

[281] Some of the greek manuscripts replace "wash their robes" with "do his commandments." Either way, the idea of trusting in Christ undergirds the main idea in the passage.

[282] Beeke., *Revelation*, 590-91.

Those who are robed in Christ's righteousness, united to Him by faith, have access to the tree of life. This would be especially profound to the original hearers. Many had been cast out the city gates due to their association with Christ. J.V. Fesko, explaining the nature of Christ on earth, says, *"He is the elect, the chosen of the Lord, and the head of His holy bride, the church; He is the object of election. He has suffered outside the gates on behalf of His elect (Heb. 13:12); those who reject Christ must themselves suffer outside the gates as Revelation makes abundantly clear."*[283] Imagine the joy and wonder knowing that one day you will be inside the gates with Christ, cleansed, and given full access to the tree of life! All who mistreated you and never repented will have no place there.

Jesus signs His name to John's letter. ***"I, Jesus, have sent my angel to testify to you about these things for the churches. I am the root and the descendant of David, the bright morning star"*** (Rev. 1:16). Jesus draws upon a phrase He used earlier in Revelation 2:28 and 5:5 to identify Himself as the true King of kings and the Light of the world. As Dennis Johnson writes,

> *"Thus these two titles pose the mystery of his person in a way complimentary to the dilemma that Psalm 110 posed for Jesus' theological opponents: Is Messiah David's son, or David's Lord (Matt. 22:41-46)? In that Holy Week dispute, and now in this triumphant self-disclosure at the close of Revelation, Jesus answers, 'Both! I am David's son, the offspring in whom God's promise of endless righteous rule is finally fulfilled.' Jesus is the bright Morning Star foreseen by Balaam, the royal champion who would arise from Israel to conquer God's enemies, including Balaam's employer, Moab (Num. 24:17; Rev. 2:28)."*[284]

This King and Victor is not a distant ruler, fixated on Himself at the expense of His citizens. No, He has sent an angel to testify to the churches that He will make good on all of His promises. In His eternal kingdom, His people are loved and receive His care. He built the New Jerusalem and brought it down to earth to give us eternal access to Him and to one another. The city teems with living water, and is nourished by the tree of life. This is what we were created for. We were made to dance and sing with joy in God's manifest presence. James Hamilton writes,

> *"He is God, and He is man, lion and lamb, slain and risen, conqueror and peacemaker, reigning and returning, servant and king, creator and consummator. He is Lord. How do you react to that proclamation? Do you resent it? Do you feel a certain disdain for all this? Or does your heart sing?"*[285]

REVELATION 22:17-19

As the grand conclusion to Revelation unfolds we are drawn into a loud declaration rising from God's Spirit-filled people. The unified voices are those sealed with the Spirit, expressing their deepest longings. John writes, ***"The Spirit and the Bride say, 'Come.' And let the one who hears say, 'Come.' And let the one who is thirsty come; let the one who desires take the water of life without price"*** (Rev. 22:17). Not only does this text reveal the greatest longing of Christians, it also reminds us of the Holy Spirit's primary ministry—to glorify Christ. When Jesus ate His last meal with

---

[283] J.V. Fesko, *The Trinity and the Covenant of Redemption,* (Great Britain, Mentor Imprint, 2016), 223.

[284] Johnson, *Triumph of the Lamb,* 328.

[285] Hamilton, *Revelation,* 417.

the disciples, He taught them about the Spirit's ministry. He said, *"He will glorify Me, for He will take what is Mine and declare it to you"* (John 16:14). The Spirit longs to shine the spotlight on the person and work of Jesus Christ. He is not concerned with His own glory, nor drawing attention to Himself. The third Person of the Trinity is sovereign and possesses an unwavering passion for the supremacy of Christ. He illumines each passage Scripture, revealing Jesus and His glory. In Revelation 22:17, John explains the Spirit in within those who have been made alive to Christ. The saints are enabled to glorify Jesus by the Spirit's Christ-exalting ministry. The ongoing plea of the redeemed is for Christ to *"**Come**."*

Notice, all seven visions in Revelation conclude with the second coming of Christ. Saints *do not* long for His coming because it is the end, but rather, it is the real beginning. The return of Jesus will be the Day where our faith becomes sight. It will be the Day that justice is fully satisfied. It will be the Day our sin and sorrows depart. It will be the Day when only joy remains. It will be the Day when the full benefits of our salvation are fully enjoyed in our new and eternal home under the immediate presence and reign of our Lord. Therefore, the plea of the redeemed ever remains, "Come, Lord Jesus."

In Revelation 22:17, John has a beautiful Old Testament passage in mind. For our eternal satisfaction, John draws from the deep well of Isaiah 55:1-2. Isaiah writes to a ragged and sinful people,

> *"Come, everyone who thirsts, come to the waters; and he who has no money, come, buy and eat! Come, buy wine and milk without money and without price. Why do you spend your money for that which is not bread, and your labor for that which does not satisfy? Listen diligently to me, and eat what is good, and delight yourselves in rich food."*

In Isaiah 55, God calls those who cannot save themselves to come and eat and be satisfied. He is calls the people who have royally messed up their lives to come and enjoy the all-satisfying God of grace. He calls all who tried to find satisfaction in success, sexual intimacy, reputation, etc., to come to the Lord of satisfaction and find what you have been searching for.

John picks up Isaiah's imagery in the cry from heaven for saints to "Come!" Until now, John has made clear divisions between believers and unbelievers throughout the book. But here, Christ seems to be summoning all unbelievers to realize their plight before Him. In mercy, He also calls them to "Come." Take note, reader. The final book of the Bible concludes with Christ's call for all people to see His worth and all-satisfying goodness. The only right response is to obey, and simply, "Come!"

You may be thinking of a friend, family member, or co-worker who has heard the gospel over and over but is still hostile towards Christ. The great news is that Christ has not yet returned and is still inviting them to come and feast at the marriage supper of the Lamb (cf. Rev. 19:6-10). Don't give up on God's ability to save! Be lovingly persistent as you pray and share Jesus with them. Let them see how satisfying Christ is to you. Do not hide your worship. For God's glory, let others know that you contributed nothing to your redemption, and He gave you everything. Don't sell a cheap Christianity. Offer the true gospel, which yields lasting satisfaction in God. Pray that the Spirit will allow you to take the hand of your loved ones, and guide them to the Source of life, *Christ Himself.*

Paul Miller calls us to imagine ourselves before Jesus when he writes,

> *"Imagine that your prayer is a poorly dressed beggar reeking of alcohol and body odor, stumbling toward the palace of the great king. You have become your prayer. As you shuffle toward the barred gate, the guards stiffen. Your smell has preceded you. You stammer out a message for the great king: 'I*

want to see the king.' Your words are barely intelligible, but you whisper one final word, 'Jesus. I come in the name of Jesus.' At the name of Jesus, as if by magic, the palace comes alive. The guards snap to attention, bowing low in front of you. Lights come on, and the door flies open. You are ushered into the palace and down a long hallway into the throne room of the great king, who comes running to you and wraps you in His arms."[286]

We never outgrow our need for God. John was thoroughly aware of his inability in himself as he urged all to fly to Jesus to find lasting satisfaction. John Calvin explained how this view of Christ's second coming creates *present* hope. He wrote,

"This is the crowning and choice consolation of the pious, that when the Son of God will be manifested in the glory of His kingdom, He will gather them into the same fellowship with Himself. For to what purpose does He make mention of His coming in power, but in order that they may in hope leap forward to that blessed resurrection which is as yet hid."[287]

Calvin's words that we may *"in hope leap forward"* is a way of simply believing by faith that Jesus will return for His people. Like John's original audience, we too should pray for Jesus to come. In times of trial and in times of plenty, we should long for Jesus more than anything else. We were created for God and redeemed by Jesus' blood to be with Him forever. Thus, we look forward to that Day. Then, we will be fully ourselves. Who we were made to be. Let us long for that glorious Day! As D. Martyn Lloyd-Jones urged his congregation,

"The most vital question to ask about all who claim to be Christian is this: Have they a soul thirst for God? Do they long for this? Is there something about them that tells you that they are always waiting for His next manifestation of Himself? Is their life centered on Him? Can they say with Paul that they forget everything in the past? Do they press forward more and more that they might know Him, and that the knowledge might increase, until eventually beyond death and the grave they may bask eternally in the 'sunshine of His face'?"[288]

After the cry for Jesus to "Come," and His invitation for all to "come" to Him, we hear an important warning. John writes,

"I warn everyone who hears the words of the prophecy of this book: if anyone adds to them, God will add to him the plagues described in this book, [19] and if anyone takes away from the words of the book of this prophecy, God will take away his share in the tree of life and in the holy city, which are described in this book" (Rev. 22:18-19).

John knew the apocalyptic nature of his book may lead some to the danger of adding to or taking away from it. For modern readers who are 2,000 years removed from this type of literature, we ought to carefully heed this caution. Perhaps John Calvin and Martin Luther never wrote commentaries on Revelation for this reason? On the other hand, the devotional nature of Revelation,

---

[286] Paul E. Miller, *A Praying Life: Connecting with God in a Distracting World* (Colorado Springs, CO: NavPress, 2009), 135.

[287] John Calvin, *Commentary on 2 Thessalonians* (Grand Rapids, MI: Baker Books, 2009), 318-19.

[288] D. Martyn Lloyd-Jones, *God's Ultimate Purpose: An Exposition of Ephesians 1,* (Grand Rapids, MI: Baker, 1978), 349.

and the clear themes of Christ's victory and comfort for His people ought to relieve any fears of delving into John's writing.

John picks up on the warning Moses issued in Deuteronomy 4:2. It reads, *"You shall not add to the word that I command you, nor take from it, that you may keep the commandments of the LORD your God that I command you."* While Moses was commanding not to add to the revealed commandments of God, John is commanding that no one add to the Revelation of God. The warning is severe, and rightfully so. Disregard for this warning will cost everything. John warns that anyone who adds or takes away from God's holy revelation will not share in the tree of life and the coming City of God.

There are many views of what John had in mind in this warning. In the context of the whole message, he seems to be calling his hearers to simply follow and obey Jesus. Otherwise, people will violate the Divine Author by adding their own laws or applications. The Pharisees of Jesus' day were well-known for their man-made additions to God's Word. We, too, are in danger of adding to or taking away from God's Word. Dennis Johnson writes, *"The divine Witness is not to be toyed with! He jealously guards the integrity of his word, for it is through this word that He jealously guards his beloved bride from the devil's lies."*[289] We need to embrace this warning, but not be crippled by it. Instead of hesitation, we are free to drink deeply from the Word of God by faith, knowing it reveals exactly what God intends for us. Wise people devote themselves to "the sacred writings," for they are "able to make us wise unto salvation" (2 Tim. 3:15-17).

REVELATION 22:20-21

When I was in the Army, handwritten letters were more common, and I cherished them. When I was overseas I was thoroughly discouraged at my circumstances numerous times. When feeling down and out, a letter would often lift my spirits. I remember receiving a letter from a close friend on a particularly difficult day. He had been counting down the days until my return. He concluded his letter with a call for me to finish strong, keep my eyes on my surroundings, and to come home in one piece. I needed that message more than he knew!

Similarly, Jesus closes this letter with a call to overcome, and with a promise to His people. John writes, **"He who testifies to these things says, 'Surely I am coming soon.' Amen. Come, Lord Jesus!"** (Rev. 22:20). Here, Jesus is emphasizing the absolute surety that He will come again. His words are intended to dissolve all doubt. He uses the word "surely" (*nai*)—a small Greek word packed with powerful assurance. This word *"denotes affirmation, agreement, or emphasis."*[290] In a word, Jesus emphasizes the reality and affirms the certainty of His second coming. Hendricksen encourages us to respond to Christ's promise by calling out, "Come!" He writes,

> *"It means 'carry out thy plan in history with a view to thy coming.' That divine plan includes the principles of moral government revealed under the symbolism of lamp stands, seals, trumpets, conflict with the dragon and his allies, bowls of wrath, the wedding of the Lamb, etc. In and through all these means and agencies cause Thy purpose to be realized and speed Thy coming! Whoever hears this*

---

[289] Johnson, *Triumph of the Lamb*, 330.

[290] Arndt, W., Danker, F. W., Bauer, W., & Gingrich, F. W., A Greek-English Lexicon of the New Testament and Other Early Christian Literature (Chicago, IL: University of Chicago Press, 3rd ed.), 665.

prophecy when it is read in the Church—and whoever reads it—let him add his individual voice to the grand chorus of voices; let him say, 'Be coming.'[291]

Maybe you are single and have been praying much for a spouse, but little for the Lord's return? Maybe you have shifted your hope to politics, while losing your first love for Jesus? Maybe you are an elder at your church and have shifted your time and affections toward building the church while forgetting the Head of the church who alone can eternally satisfy her? Whatever the distraction, the Lord Jesus can reorient you to Himself. He can refocus all our misdirected longings if we will repent and pray heartily and joyfully, *"Come, Lord Jesus!"*

Revelation is a book of lofty visions. Sometimes they are difficult to interpret. As a result, some leave Revelation to the "professionals." But this letter was written to churches just like yours. The closing line of the book is a short and sweet benediction, reminding us the Spirit wants us to read and understand. This letter is for people like you and I, in churches like ours. We are those for whom Jesus died and was raised. This is His message *to us*. To convey this beautiful point, John writes, **"The grace of the Lord Jesus be with all. Amen"** (Rev. 22:21). To help us grasp the practical implications of *this grace* between the two comings of Christ, Derek Thomas tells a story about John Wesley. He writes, *"When John Wesley was asked what he might do if he knew Jesus was to return on a certain date, he apparently looked at his diary for the day, read out his engagements, and said, 'That is what I would do.'"*[292] The same grace that purchased people from the dead and made them alive is the same grace that will get those people home.

The Father, the Son, and the Holy Spirit are with us by grace now and forevermore. The practical *application* of the book of Revelation in its entirety is primarily, *"Look to Jesus!"* But the benediction delivers exactly what we need between Christ's resurrection and second coming: *Grace*! James Hamilton closes his commentary with some grand realities for the Christian. Let us worship the Lamb as we close with Hamilton's insights:

* *From death came life.*
* *From defeat came victory.*
* *From darkness came light.*
* *From despair came hope.*
* *From judgment came salvation.*
* *From shame came glory.*
* *Through Satan's machinations God's purpose was fulfilled.*
* *By the wicked deeds of men God accomplished His ordained plan.*
* *From the breaking came healing.*
* *From the defiling of the Holy One comes cleansing.*
* *Because He was forsaken of God, Jesus Christ can promise His own that He will never leave them.*
* *Because He rose, we know that He will come again.*[293]

"To Him who loves us and has freed us from our sins by His blood." (Rev. 1:5b)

---

[291] Hendricksen, *More Than Conquerors,* 209-10.
[292] Derek Thomas, *Let's Study Revelation,* 184.
[293] James Hamilton, *Revelation,* 420.

APPENDIX

APPENDIX A

PRIESTLY SINGING IN REVELATION[294]

Music has a unique way of moving people's affections outside of themselves towards something greater. Throughout history, music has been a means of moving people from depression towards joy. In fact, Martin Luther once wrote, *"Next to the Word of God, music deserves the highest praise.... The gift of language combined with the gift of song was only given to man to let him know that he should praise God with both word and music, namely, by proclaiming [the Word of God] through music."*[295] Most of us would speak with great endearments of music in general, but what if music has a greater role than just a delightful noise for our ears?

If you are a Christian or have ever visited a church, you have likely noticed that singing has an important role in the liturgy. In Paul's letter to the Colossians, one of the most visual expressions of those who have been loved by God is singing to Him and one another. Paul writes in Colossians 3:16, "Let the word of Christ dwell in you richly, teaching and admonishing one another in all wisdom, singing psalms and hymns and spiritual songs, with thankfulness in your hearts to God." In one sense, to love is to sing.

THE BELIEVER'S PRIESTLY ROLE OF SINGING

Yet, singing has a more authoritative and weighty role than we might acknowledge. In 1 Chronicles 15, King David delivered the ark of God back to its proper place among God's people in Jerusalem. In fact, it is a star-studded event full of all the glitz and glamour properly due to God. The host of musicians present at this event were meant to demonstrate the weighty reality that God dwells with His people. In 1 Chronicles 15:16-24, we find a list of singers and instrument players—all part of the drama of the returning ark of the covenant. But nestled in this list of singers and musicians is an often-overlooked verse. 1 Chronicles 15:22 says, "Chenaniah, leader of the Levites in music, should direct the music, for he understood it." Why is this little verse so important? Throughout the Bible, we learn that the Levites were the priestly figures God called and set aside to function as mediators between God and men. We often focus on the priestly work of atonement and sacrifice (e.g. Lev. 16), and rightfully so. But have you ever noticed that the priestly role of *singing* is in some sense a mediator

---

[294] This is an article I originally wrote for *The Beautiful Christian Life* but adapted for the Teleios Academy study of Revelation. The original can be found here: https://www.beautifulchristianlife.com/blog/your-priestly-role-of-singing?rq=Singing

[295] Martin Luther, *Luther's Works, Vol. 53: Liturgy and Hymns* (Fortress Press, 1965), 323.

between man and God? There appears to be a weight here that necessitates us honoring the role of song as a priestly function, as well as recognizing that what it accomplishes is pleasing to God.

JESUS, OUR SINGING HIGH PRIEST, LEADS US TO SING

As mentioned earlier, we often make much of the priestly role in atonement, especially regarding our great high priest, the Lord Jesus Christ. The great news is that we don't have to divorce the priestly role of atonement from the priestly joy of singing. After the Last Supper with His disciples, Jesus prepared to enter into His priestly work of sacrificing Himself on behalf of His beloved people. Knowing that He would soon be arrested, falsely accused, and crucified, the High Priest *led the disciples in a song of preparation for His work of atonement.* In a short but vitally important verse, Matthew 26:30 says, "And when they had sung a hymn, they went to the Mount of Olives."

After Jesus completed His priestly work of atonement, Hebrews 10:20 assures us that the veil that once separated God and man has been torn, allowing access for all of God's people into the presence of our God. The Mediator *sang His way to the cross* and opened a place for all of our prayers and songs to go. This means that in the present time we are to be a singing people, joyfully making the affections of our hearts burst forth towards our singing Savior.

Not only that, He has made us a kingdom of priests who now and forevermore will sing to Him. The book of Revelation is filled with song after song of a suffering people delighting in the God who sent His Son to die and be raised so that we might have victory in Him. Revelation 5:9-10 gives us a picture of our future singing as the apostle John writes,

> "*And they sang a new song, saying,*
> "*Worthy are you to take the scroll*
> *and to open its seals,*
> *for you were slain, and by your blood you ransomed people for God*
> *from every tribe and language and people and nation,*
> *and you have made them a kingdom and priests to our God,*
> *and they shall reign on the earth.*"

Let us resolve to be a people who—In the good and the bad—*sing*, knowing that we have a God who sings over us in delight (cf. Zeph. 3:14-17).

APPENDIX B

SEVEN BEATITUDES IN REVELATION

Throughout the journey of Revelation, we saw John's purposeful use of allusions to the Old Testament. Grasping John's connections to the Old Covenant should shape the way we hear and see the entire message. In Revelation 1:3 he wrote, *"Blessed is the one who reads aloud the words of this prophecy, and blessed are those who hear, and who keep what is written in it, for the time is near."*

Throughout the book, it is also impossible to escape John's intentional use of the number *seven*. The book is divided into seven sections, it is written to seven churches (1:4), and the letter is a byproduct of the seven spirits who are before the throne (1:4). Although I did an introduction on the way John uses Old Testament allusions, I thought it would also be helpful to highlight a structural observation that may help you better grasp the layout of Revelation.

Most Christians are familiar with the Beatitudes from Jesus' Sermon on the Mount (cf. Matthew 5:2-12). But how many of us are familiar with the seven Beatitudes in the book of Revelation? Where the Beatitudes in the Sermon on the Mount can be seen as a way of kingdom living for those already converted by God, the Beatitudes in Revelation are from God's perspective. They are given as an encouragement to persevere in the midst of suffering. The vision John gives the seven churches, and us today, is a glimpse into God's vantage point of us from Heaven and His promise to bless His people who trust in Him. Here they are:

1. *"Blessed is the one who reads aloud the words of this prophecy, and blessed are those who hear, and who keep what is written in it, for the time is near."* (Rev. 1:3).

2. *"And I heard a voice from heaven saying, 'Write this: Blessed are the dead who die in the Lord from now on.' 'Blessed indeed,' says the Spirit, 'that they may rest from their labors, for their deeds follow them!'"* (Rev. 14:13).

3. *"Behold, I am coming like a thief! Blessed is the one who stays awake, keeping his garments on, that he may not go about naked and be seen exposed!"* (Rev. 16:15).

4. *"And the angel said to me, 'Write this: Blessed are those who are invited to the marriage supper of the Lamb.' And he said to me, 'These are the true words of God.'"* (Rev. 19:9).

5. *"Blessed and holy is the one who shares in the first resurrection! Over such the second death has no power, but they will be priests of God and of Christ, and they will reign with Him for a thousand years."* (Rev. 20:6).

6. *"And behold, I am coming soon. Blessed is the one who keeps the words of the prophecy of this book."* (Rev. 22:7).

7. *"Blessed are those who wash their robes, so that they may have the right to the tree of life and that they may enter the city by the gates."* (Rev. 22:14).

It is clear God intends to bless His people. Reading these seven blessings in the wider context of the book serves to emphasize this point. Whether it is the blessing of hearing His voice in Scripture, resting from the violent onslaught of the world, or the blessing of forgiveness and access to the tree of life forever, we can be sure of God's heart toward His people.

Yes, this life can be hard at times, often at most times. But we have a God whose heart beats for us and longs to shower us with His endless grace and mercy. For the first-century believer, or those being persecuted in Syria today, these Beatitudes are meant to bolster our faith. These beatitudes provide a glimpse into the love God longs to lavish on us.

ADDITIONAL "SEVENS" IN REVELATION

In addition to these beatitudes, there are many other "sevens" in Revelation.

- *Seven times the word "Christ" is used.*
- *Seven times Christ announces His coming.*
- *Seven times the form "the Lord God Almighty" appears.*
- *Seven "amens."*
- *The "prophets" are referred to seven times.*
- *"The one who sits on the throne" is used seven times.*
- *The Spirit is referred to fourteen times (two sevens)*
- *The name of Jesus occurs fourteen times (two sevens).*
- *The "Lamb" is mentioned twenty-eight times (four sevens).*[296]

---

[296] Richard Bauckham, *The Climax of Prophecy* (New York, NY: T&T Clark Ltd., 1993), 174-198.

BIBLIOGRAPHY

Barnhouse, Donald Grey. *Revelation: An Expositional Commentary*. Grand Rapids: Zondervan, 1971.

Bauckham, Richard. *The Climax of Prophecy*. New York, NY: T&T Clark Ltd., 1993.

——*New Testament Theology: The Theology of the Book of Revelation*. New York: Cambridge University Press, 2013.

Bavinck Herman. *Reformed Dogmatics: Abridged in One Volume* ed. John Bolt, Grand Rapids: Baker Academic, 2011.

Beale G.K. and Gladd, Benjamin L. *Hidden But Now Revealed: A Biblical Theology of Mystery*. Downers Grove: InterVarsity Press, 2014.

Beale, G.K. *The New International Greek Testament Commentary: The Book of Revelation*. Grand Rapids: Wm. B. Eerdmans Publishing Co., 1999.

—— *The Temple and the Church's Mission: A Biblical Theology of the Dwelling Place of God*. Downers Grove: Intervarsity Press, 2004.

Beeke, Joel R. *Lectio Continua: Revelation*. Grand Rapids: Reformation Heritage Books, 2016.

Bennett, Arthur. *Valley of Vision*. Carlisle: The Banner of Truth Trust, 2013.

Caird, G.B. *The Revelation of St. John the Divine*. San Francisco: Harper, 1966.

Calvin, John. *Commentary on 2 Thessalonians*. Grand Rapids: Baker Books, 2009.

——*Institutes of the Christian Religion*. ed. Henry Beveridge. Peabody: Hendrickson Publishing, 2008.

Carson, D.A. "This Present Evil Age," in *These Last Days: A Christian View of History,* ed. Richard D. Phillips and Gabriel Fluhrer. Phillipsburg: P&R Publishing, 2011.

Chesterton G.K., https://www.goodreads.com/quotes/403140-fairy-tales-do-not-give-the-child-his-first-idea.

DC Talk and the Voice of the Martyrs, *Jesus Freaks vol. 1*. Tulsa: Alsbury Publishing, 1999.

Duguid, Iain. *Reformed Expository Commentary: Daniel*. Phillipsburg: P&R Publishing, 2008.

Edwards, Jonathan. *Heaven*. Carlisle: The Banner of Truth Trust, 2008.

——*The Excellency of Christ*. https://www.monergism.com/blog/jonathan-edwards-excellency-christ.

——*The Works of Jonathan Edwards,* ed. Perry Miller, John E. Smith, and Harry S. Stout. New Haven: Yale University Press, 1957-2008.

Fesko, J.V. *The Trinity and the Covenant of Redemption*. Great Britain, Mentor Imprint, 2016.

Goodwin, Thomas. *The Heart of Christ in Heaven Towards Sinners on Earth*. Carlisle: The Banner of Truth Trust, Year not printed.

Goldsworthy, Graeme. *The Goldsworthy Trilogy: The Gospel in Revelation*. Colorado Springs: Paternoster, 2012.

Hamilton, James, Jr. *Preaching the Word: Revelation*. Wheaton: Crossway, 2012.

Hendriksen, William. *More Than Conquerors*. Grand Rapids: Baker Books, 1998.

Horton, Michael. *Introducing Covenant Theology*. Grand Rapids: Baker Books, 2006.

Johnson, Dennis. *Triumph of the Lamb*. Phillipsburg: P&R Publishing, 2001.

Johnson, Donald R. *Victory in Jesus*. Conway: Free Grace Press, 2018.

Jones, Mark. *Knowing Christ*. East Peoria: The Banner of Truth Trust, 2016.

Kelly, Douglas F. *Mentor Expository Commentary: Revelation*. Ross-shire, Scotland: Mentor, 2012.

Kuyper, Abraham. https://www.goodreads.com/quotes/99035-there-is-not-a-square-inch-in-the-whole-domain.

Ladd, George Eldon. *"Historic Premillennialism,"* in *The Meaning of the Millennium: Four Views,* ed. Robert G. Clouse. Downers Grove: IVP Academic, 1977.

Leithart, Peter J. *International Theological Commentary: Revelation 1-11*. New York: T&T Clark, 2018.

—— *International Theological Commentary: Revelation 12-22*. New York: T&T Clark, 2018.

Lewis, C.S. *Chronicles of Narnia: The Last Battle*. New York: HarperCollins Publishers, 1998.

—— *Meditation in a Toolshed*, http://www.pacificaoc.org/wp-content/uploads/Meditation-in-a-Toolshed.pdf

—— *Mere Christianity*. New York: HarperCollins, 2005.

—— *The Problem of Pain*. New York: HarperCollins, 2002.

Lloyd-Jones, D. Martyn. *God's Ultimate Purpose: An Exposition of Ephesians 1*. Grand Rapids: Baker, 1978.

Luther, Martin. *Luther's Works, Vol. 53: Liturgy and Hymns*. Fortress Press, 1965.

Maclaren, Andrew. *Expositions of Holy Scripture,* 17 vols. Grand Rapids: Baker Books, 1982.

Miller, Paul E. *A Praying Life: Connecting with God in a Distracting World*. Colorado Springs: NavPress, 2009.

Morris, Leon. *Tyndale New Testament Commentaries: The Revelation of St. John*. Grand Rapids: Eerdmans, 1969.

Newbell, Trillia J. *United: Captured by God's Vision for Diversity*. Chicago: Moody Publishers, 2014.

Ortlund, Dane C. *Edwards on the Christian Life: Alive to the Beauty of God*. Wheaton: Crossway, 2014.

Packer, J.I. *Knowing God*. Downers Grove: InterVarsity Press, 1993.

Phillips, Richard. *Reformed Expository Commentary: Revelation*. Phillipsburg: P&R Publishing, 2017.

——*Reformed Expository Commentary: Zechariah*. Phillipsburg: P&R Publishing, 2007.

Poythress, Vern S. *Theophany: A Biblical Theology of God's Appearing*. Wheaton, IL: Crossway, 2018.

——*The Returning King: A Guide to the Book of Revelation*. Phillipsburg: P&R Publishing, 2000.

Reeves, Michael. *Spurgeon on the Christian Life: Alive to Christ*. Wheaton: Crossway, 2018.

Rigney, Joe. *The Things of Earth: Treasuring God by Enjoying His Gifts*. Wheaton, IL: Crossway, 2015.

Rutherford, Samuel. *Letters*. Carlisle: The Banner of Truth Trust, 2012.

Smith, James K.A. *You Are What You Love*. Grand Rapids: Brazos Press, 2016.

Storms, Sam. *Kingdom Come: The Amillennial Alternative*. Ross-shire, Scotland: Mentor, 2013.

Stott, John R. W. *What Christ Thinks of the Church: An Exposition of Revelation 1-3*. Grand Rapids: Baker Books, 2003.

Swete, Henry Barclay. *Commentary on Revelation,* 2 vols. 1911; reps., Grand Rapids: Kregel, 1977.

Thomas, Derek. *Let's Study Revelation*. East Peoria: The Banner of Truth Trust, 2011.

Vincent, Milton. *A Gospel Primer for Christians: Learning to See the Glories of God's Love*. Self-published, 2008.

Vos, Geerhardus. *Grace and Glory*. 1922; repr., Edinburgh: Banner of Truth Trust, 1994.

Wallace, Daniel B. *Greek Grammar: Beyond the Basics*. Grand Rapids: Zondervan, 1996.

Walvoord, John F. *The Revelation of Jesus Christ*. Chicago: Moody Press, 1973.

Young, Edward J. *The Book of Isaiah: Volume 3 Chapters 40-66*. Grand Rapids: Eerdmans Publishing Co., 1972.

VERSES TO MEMORIZE WITH MY SMALL GROUP

1.

2.

3.

4.

5.

6.

7.

8.

9.

10.

11.

12.

TELEIOS ACADEMY BIBLE STUDIES

The following volumes are available *in pilot form* for purchase:

- ❖ Genesis 1-11 – "Let there be Light"

- ❖ Genesis 12-50 – "GOD of our Fathers"

- ❖ Exodus – "Salvation Belongs to the LORD"

- ❖ Isaiah – "He saw Christ's Glory"

- ❖ Matthew – "It is Fulfilled"

- ❖ Luke – "God in the Flesh"

- ❖ John – "That You May Believe"

- ❖ Acts 1-15 – "You Will Be My Witnesses"

- ❖ Acts 16-28 – "To the Ends of the Earth"

- ❖ Johannine Epistles – "God is Light"

- ❖ Revelation – "Worthy is the Lamb"

For more information about Teleios Academy visit: www.gracechurchmemphis.com

ABOUT KALEO CHURCH

Kaleo Church exists to be a Christ-treasuring community formed by the Gospel and sent into the world through the power of the Holy Spirit and for the glory of God.

For more information visit: kaleochurch.com

ABOUT GRACE CHURCH

Grace Church exists to glorify GOD by treasuring Jesus Christ and spreading His eternal joy.

For more information visit: gracechurchmemphis.com

ABOUT TREASURING CHRIST TOGETHER

Our mission is to spread a passion for the supremacy of God in all things for the joy of all peoples through Jesus Christ by nurturing healthy pastors and healthy churches to plant healthy churches.

Kaleo Church and Grace Church are both part of the *Treasuring Christ Together Network* of churches.

For more information visit: tctnetwork.org